Persuasion in Parallel

CHICAGO STUDIES IN AMERICAN POLITICS

A series edited by Susan Herbst, Lawrence R. Jacobs, Adam J. Berinsky, and Frances Lee; Benjamin I. Page, editor emeritus

Also in the series:

Additional series titles follow index

Persuasion in Parallel

How Information Changes Minds about Politics

ALEXANDER COPPOCK

THE UNIVERSITY OF CHICAGO PRESS   CHICAGO AND LONDON

The University of Chicago Press, Chicago 60637
The University of Chicago Press, Ltd., London
© 2022 by The University of Chicago
All rights reserved. No part of this book may be used or reproduced in any manner
whatsoever without written permission, except in the case of brief quotations in critical articles and reviews. For more information, contact the University of Chicago Press,
1427 E. 60th St., Chicago, IL 60637.
Published 2022
Printed in the United States of America

31 30 29 28 27 26 25 24 23 22   1 2 3 4 5

ISBN-13: 978-0-226-82182-5 (cloth)
ISBN-13: 978-0-226-82184-9 (paper)
ISBN-13: 978-0-226-82183-2 (e-book)
DOI: https://doi.org/10.7208/chicago/9780226821832.001.0001

Library of Congress Cataloging-in-Publication Data

Names: Coppock, Alexander, author.
Title: Persuasion in parallel : how information changes minds about politics /
    Alexander Coppock.
Other titles: Chicago studies in American politics.
Description: Chicago ; London : The University of Chicago Press, 2022. | Series: Chicago
    studies in American politics | Includes bibliographical references and index.
Identifiers: LCCN 2022015068 | ISBN 9780226821825 (cloth) | ISBN 9780226821849
    (paperback) | ISBN 9780226821832 (ebook)
Subjects: LCSH: Persuasion (Psychology)—Political aspects.
Classification: LCC JA85.5 .C66 2022 | DDC 320.072—dc23/eng/20220419
LC record available at https://lccn.loc.gov/2022015068

Contents

CHAPTER ONE

Persuasion in Polarized America

In dismay over the deep disagreements that divide Americans by party, by race, by class, by generation, by geography, we sometimes give in to the idea that at least the other side is stupid. At least the other side is full of irrational idiots who fail to see reason. They never learn from new information, never change their minds, never admit when they're wrong. If anything, trying to convince them on the basis of evidence and logic makes things worse and we become even more polarized. Each successive day seems to widen the gulf between Democrats and Republicans, between progressives and conservatives, between the haves and have-nots, between the white supremacists and the rest of us, between we who are reasonable and they who are unreasonable.

It's a tempting feeling. When we see the unbelievable political positions some people support, the notion comes naturally that their ability to reason must be broken. When others come to different conclusions from ours, despite having access to the same information we do, we think there must be something wrong with their information processing, or how they learn from the world to inform their policy attitudes.

In the academic literature, this idea goes by the name "motivated reasoning." A number of variants of the theory exist, but most posit that individuals are motivated by both accuracy goals (wanting to get it right) and directional goals (wanting to arrive at a particular conclusion). In this view, directional goals are the problem. When directional goals dominate, people distort their interpretation of new information, always learning they were more right than they knew, regardless of what the new information shows. When people are motivated to reason to arrive at preferred conclusions, the effect of evidence on attitudes is "heads I'm righter, tails you're wronger," because no matter how the evidentiary coin comes up, it is twisted toward directional goals. Under this theory, our political opponents' capacities for reason are broken, since everyone's are.

A key prediction of motivated reasoning theory is backlash: exposure to counter-attitudinal evidence will cause people to hold more strongly to their preexisting positions. Festinger, Riecken, and Schachter (1956) give a forceful articulation of this idea in the introduction to *When Prophecy Fails*, their study of cultists after a predicted doomsday fails to materialize:

> Suppose an individual believes something with his whole heart; suppose further that he has a commitment to this belief, that he has taken irrevocable actions because of it; finally, suppose that he is presented with evidence, unequivocal and undeniable evidence, that his belief is wrong: what will happen? The individual will frequently emerge, not only unshaken, but even more convinced of the truth of his beliefs than ever before. (1956, 3)

Two decades later, Lord, Ross, and Lepper (1979) claim to have demonstrated this sort of "attitude polarization" in the laboratory. They conclude:

> If our study demonstrates anything, it surely demonstrates that social scientists can not expect rationality, enlightenment, and consensus about policy to emerge from their attempts to furnish "objective" data about burning social issues. If people of opposing views can each find support for those views in the same body of evidence, it is small wonder that social science research, dealing with complex and emotional social issues and forced to rely upon inconclusive designs, measures, and modes of analysis, will frequently fuel rather than calm the fires of debate. (1979, 2108)

Motivated reasoning theory was introduced into political science by Taber and Lodge (2006), who also purport to show that people respond to information by updating their views in opposite directions. They write:

Our studies show people are often unable to escape the pull of their prior attitudes and beliefs, which guide the processing of new information in predictable and sometimes insidious ways. (2006, 767)

With this book, I hope to convince you that this idea from motivated reasoning theory simply does not describe how people respond when presented with persuasive information. On the contrary, people update in the direction of information, by a small amount. I will show how the evidence in favor of the most dire prediction of motivated reasoning—backlash—rests on weak research designs. When these designs are strengthened, the conclusions flip. The idea that trying to persuade the other side is counterproductive may *feel right*, but the goal of this book is to demonstrate that it *is wrong*.

The Persuasion in Parallel Hypothesis

This book makes a single argument, over and over: persuasion occurs in parallel. Using evidence gleaned from many randomized experiments, I will show that when people encounter new information, they don't distort it to further entrench their preexisting views—instead, they are persuaded in the direction of that information. If persuasion occurs in parallel, people from different groups respond to persuasive information in the same direction and by about the same amount. While baseline political views are very different from group to group, responses to information are quite similar. For example, when people encounter pro-immigration arguments, regardless of whether they are immigration opponents or proponents, they increase their support for immigration a little bit. The converse is also true. Anti-immigration arguments will decrease support among both proponents and opponents of immigration just the same. We see this common pattern across dozens of policy issues and across many different subdivisions of Americans.

Throughout the book, I'll rely on the visual metaphor of parallel lines to describe this idea. Parallel lines have the same slope (changes with respect to the horizontal axis) but may have different intercepts (positions on the vertical axis). Figure 1.1 is a schematic representation of the persuasion in parallel hypothesis. The figure shows two parallel lines, one for the circles group and one for the triangles group. The separa-

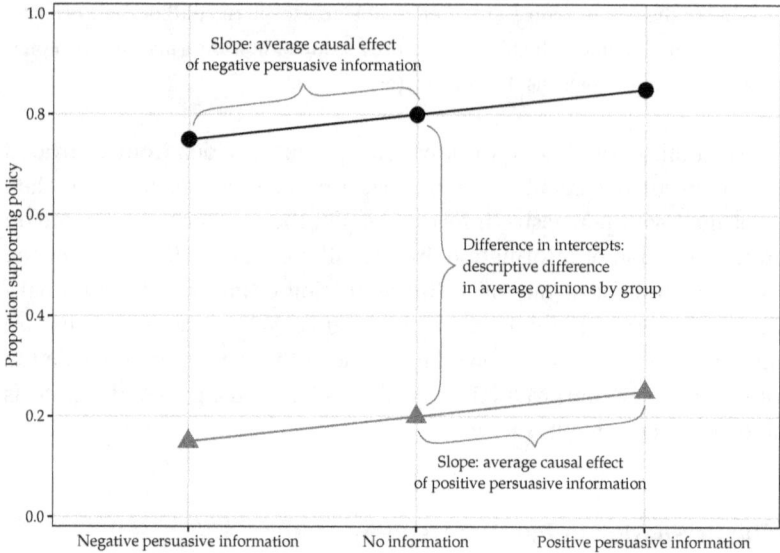

FIGURE I.I. The persuasion in parallel hypothesis
Note: This figure is a schematic representation of the persuasion in parallel hypothesis. The vertical axis represents support for a hypothetical policy and the horizontal axis represents exposure to different levels of a hypothetical treatment. The triangles and circles stand in for any politically salient subdivision of Americans into groups that disagree over a public policy. The descriptive difference between the groups is large, but the average causal effects of information are the same for both groups.

tion of people into circle and triangle groups stands in for any division of Americans into opposing subgroups: proponents and opponents of a policy, Republicans and Democrats, or young and old, to name a few. The difference in intercepts reflects the descriptive difference in the average opinions of the circle and triangle groups. This difference can be large, because groups in our polarized society can be bitterly divided over political issues.[1] When I say that the circle and triangle groups are persuaded in parallel, I mean that the average causal effects of persuasive information are the same for both groups, *even though* the groups still disagree when exposed to positive or negative information.

The claim that persuasion always occurs in parallel for everyone, regardless of the content or provenance of the persuasive information, is obviously far too broad. I promise that important caveats and conditions are coming for readers who forge on. In the meantime, I want to emphasize that although there may be exceptions, persuasion in parallel is the norm. It happens many millions of times a day as people scroll through social media feeds and talk with friends and coworkers about the news. Politicians, journalists, pundits, academics, and advertisers are constantly barraging people with persuasive attempts to vote for a candidate, to believe a fact, to behave a certain way, or to buy a product. These attempts are probably a little bit effective for most everyone who hears them.

Persuasive information encompasses a wide set of political communications. It refers to facts and arguments designed to move target attitudes in a particular direction. Claims about why we need particular policies, what they would do, and how much they would cost are all persuasive information. The persuasion in parallel hypothesis is about persuasive information only, not other kinds of communication that lack a target or a direction.

Probably the largest class of political communication that does not count as persuasive information is group cues. Group cues are messages about which groups support which positions. Party cues—information that indicates where a political party stands on the issues—are prominent examples of group cues. Group cues can exert powerful influence over policy attitudes, and whether the effect is positive or negative can depend on group membership. For example, learning that Republicans in Congress support a particular bill usually increases support among Republican survey respondents but decreases support among Democratic respondents. The distinction between group cues and persuasive information can sometimes be blurry because messages contain elements of both, but we will nevertheless keep these two kinds of communication theoretically distinct.

The amount of opinion change in response to persuasive information is usually small. Small means something like five percentage points or a tenth of a standard deviation in response to a treatment like an op-ed, a video advertisement, or a précis of a scientific finding. Small changes make sense. If persuasive effects were much bigger, wild swings in attitudes would be commonplace and people would be continually changing their minds depending on the latest advertisement they saw.

Persuasive effects decay. Ten days after people encounter persuasive information, average effects are about one-third to one-half their original magnitude. After ten days, we have only limited evidence about whether they persist or fade. In one study only, I measured persistence after thirty days, finding a "hockey stick" pattern in which treatment effects had decayed somewhat by day ten but no further by day thirty.

The strongest evidence for the claim that people are persuaded in parallel derives from randomized experiments in which some people are exposed to information (the treatment group) while others are not (the control group). These experiments show over and over that the average treatment effects of information are positive. By positive, I mean that they are in the direction of information. These average causal effects also hold for subgroups: young and old, better- and less-well-educated, Republican and Democrat, Black and White, women and men, we all respond in the direction of information by about the same amount.

The strong form of the persuasion in parallel hypothesis is that information has the exact same effect for everyone. Falsifying this hypothesis is trivially easy. All we would need is one statistical test that shows that effects are stronger for one group than another. The experiments described in this book offer occasional examples of such tests. When the average effect for Democrats is 3 percentage points and the average effect for Republicans is 5 percentage points, a sufficiently large experiment would declare these two average effects "statistically significantly different." But these sometimes statistically significant differences are rarely politically significant.[2] Qualitatively speaking, the effects of treatment on policy attitudes are quite similar even across wildly diverse groups of people.

The weak form of the hypothesis is that *backlash* doesn't occur. Backlash (or backfire—I don't draw any distinction between the two terms) would occur if information had positive effects for some but negative effects for others. Falsifying this weaker hypothesis would also be easy. All we would need is one statistical test that finds evidence of a positive effect for one group but a negative effect for a different group. None of the many experiments reported in this book measure any instances of backlash, but other authors have claimed to find them (e.g., Lazarsfeld, Berelson, and Gaudet 1944; Nyhan and Reifler 2010; Schaffner and Roche 2016; Zhou 2016). Backlash has probably occurred, but it is definitely not the norm (Wood and Porter 2019; Nyhan et al. 2019; Swire-Thompson, DeGutis, and Lazer 2020). In their book *False Alarm*, Porter and Wood (2020) randomize more than fifty factual corrections of misinformation and uncover exactly zero instances of backlash.

Even so, many theories accommodate and predict backlash, including the Receive-Accept-Sample model (Zaller 1992), the John Q. Public model (Lodge and Taber 2013), and the Cultural Cognition model (Kahan 2012). The Receive-Accept-Sample model allows backlash through "countervalent resistance" to uncongenial communication flows (Zaller 1992, 122). The John Q. Public model includes the "affect transfer" and "affect contagion" postulates through which the negative affective evaluation of a communication will cause backlash effects on the attitudes the persuasive attempt was meant to change (Lodge and Taber 2013, 56–58). Under the Cultural Cognition model, people engage in "protective cognition" to defend their variously individualistic or communitarian cultural values against challenges from scientific information, thereby "reinforc[ing] their predispositions" (Kahan 2010, 296). These models may be useful for explaining other phenomena, but at a minimum their predictions of backlash are (in my view) incorrect. My critique of these theories will be mostly empirical—the predicted backlash doesn't materialize across many dozens of tests for it—but I will draw out a theoretical critique as well. In brief, my view is that these theories mistake affective evaluations of messages and messengers for the persuasive effects of those messages. Since many people don't *like* counter-attitudinal messages, we might mistakenly think they "reject" them. But as we will see, people update their policy attitudes in the direction of information they like and information they don't like just the same.

Example: Flat Tax Op-Ed Experiment

The evidence in favor of the persuasion in parallel hypothesis will come much later in the book, in chapter 5. The reasons to trust in that evidence—the experimental designs—will be described in chapter 4. And the details of the theoretical structure those designs depend on will be laid out in chapter 3. Since that's a lot to work through before getting to the punch line, this section will describe one example of persuasion in parallel to tide us over.

Emily Ekins, David Kirby, and I ran an experiment to measure how much, if at all, an opinion piece in the *Wall Street Journal* changes minds on tax policy. The randomly assigned treatment group read an op-ed by Senator (and, at the time of the experiment, presidential hopeful) Rand Paul of Kentucky. In "Blow Up the Tax Code and Start Over" (Paul 2015), Senator Paul proposed a 14.5 percent flat tax that he predicted would cause the economy to "roar." Paul primarily argues for his flat tax proposal on fairness grounds. He anticipated objections that the proposal is a giveaway to the rich (he'd close loopholes) and that the proposal would induce massive deficits (he'd balance the budget). He called the IRS a "rogue agency" and blamed Washington corruption for the convolutions of the tax code. The op-ed is a thousand words long, makes a complicated argument, and demonizes relatively obscure bureaucrats most Americans wouldn't have heard of. It's insidery, a little punchy, and lacks strong evidence for its claims, which is to say, it's a good example of contemporary political communication.

Post-treatment, we asked both the treatment group and a control group that did not read any op-ed "Would you favor or oppose changing the federal tax system to a flat tax, where everyone making more than $50,000 a year pays the same percentage of his or her income in taxes?" While the op-ed does identify the author as a "Republican from Kentucky," and so includes a partisan cue, I argue that the bulk of the treatment operates via persuasive information, largely because the goal Senator Paul's op-ed was to contrast his tax policy with those of his opponents in the Republican presidential primary.

We ran this experiment twice. We conducted the first version once with a convenience sample obtained via Amazon's Mechanical Turk (MTurk) service. The people on Mechanical Turk aren't representative of all Americans, but they are nevertheless Americans.[3] We also ran the experiment on a sample of policy professionals. These people are also not representative of all Americans—they are DC staffers, journalists, lawyers, and other professionals with some degree of connection to policy-making. For the moment, please don't let the samples' lack of representativeness bother you. We'll return to questions of generalizability and external validity in chapter 4.

Figure 1.2 shows the results of both versions of the experiment. The MTurk experiment is on the left and the policy professionals experiment is on the right. I've overlaid the group averages by sample (MTurk or Elite), partisanship (Republican or Democrat), and treatment condition (treatment or control) on top of the raw data. Democrats and Republicans clearly differ with respect to the flat tax. On MTurk, partisans in the control group differ on average by over a full point on the 1 to 7 scale. Among the policy professionals, the gap is closer to 2.5 points. Despite these baseline differences, both Republicans and Democrats on MTurk change their minds in response to the op-ed by similar amounts: 1.13 (robust standard error: 0.20) for Republicans and 0.54 points (0.15) for Democrats. A similar pattern holds for the policy professionals: 0.52 (0.25) for Republicans and 0.29 (0.20) for Democrats. These data offer

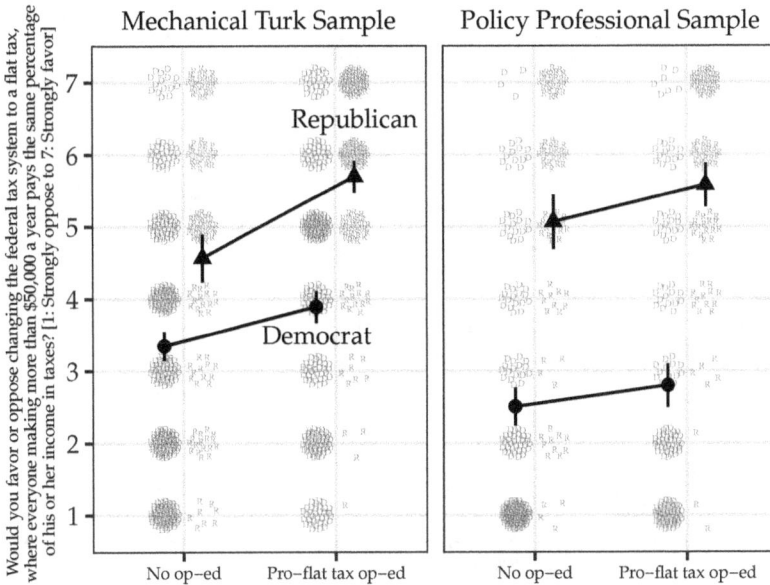

FIGURE I.2. Flat tax experimental results
Note: Survey experimental data from 860 MTurk respondents and 518 policy profession-als who provided immediate and 10-day follow-up responses (Coppock, Ekins, and Kirby 2018). Democratic responses are shown in circles and Republican responses in triangles. The slopes of the lines connecting the average outcomes by condition represent average causal effects. On MTurk, the average effects are 1.13 (robust standard error: 0.20) for Re-publicans and 0.54 points (0.15) for Democrats. Among policy professionals, these values were 0.52 (0.25) for Republicans and 0.29 (0.20) for Democrats.

clear evidence of persuasion in parallel. Despite some mild differences in the magnitudes, the effect estimates are qualitatively similar and are plainly all in the same direction. If there were backlash along par-tisan lines, the slopes for Democrats and Republicans would be oppo-sitely signed. Instead of parallel motion, we would have contrary motion. That's not what we find here—nor is it what we find in any of the persua-sive information experiments to come.

We also recontacted our experimental subjects ten days after they did or did not read Senator Paul's opinion piece, and again asked their opin-ions about the flat tax. Figure 1.3 shows the results. Among the elite sam-ple, the effects are less than half as large after ten days as they were im-mediately post-treatment. Among the MTurk subjects, effects persist at 80 percent of the original magnitude for Republicans and 58 percent for Democrats. While it's clear that the effects of persuasive information do

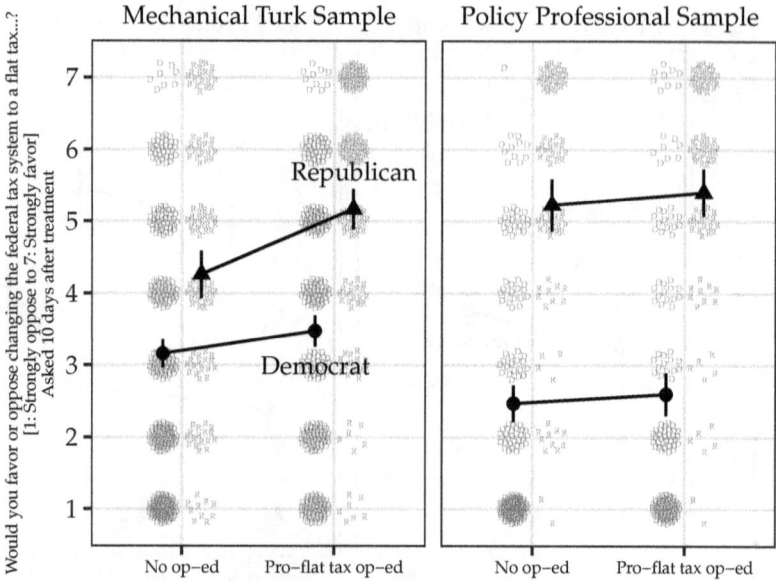

FIGURE 1.3. Flat tax experimental results: 10-day follow-up
Note: Survey experimental data from 860 MTurk respondents and 518 policy professionals who provided immediate and 10-day follow-up responses (Coppock, Ekins, and Kirby
2018). On MTurk, the average effects after 10 days were 0.908 (robust standard error: 0.22)
for Republicans and 0.32 points (0.15) for Democrats. Among policy professionals, these
values were 0.18 (0.25) for Republicans and 0.13 (0.20) for Democrats.

dissipate over time, we nevertheless observe persistent treatment versus
control differences even after ten days.

The rest of the book contains many figures that look just like figures 1.2 and 1.3, with various elements swapped in or out. I will report experiments that I've conducted myself with collaborators, experiments by
others that I have replicated on new samples, and experiments by others
that I have reanalyzed using my preferred set of tools. While the specifics
of the randomly assigned persuasive information, the survey items used
to measure policy opinions, and the subgroup divisions will vary, the pictures tell very similar stories: small effects in the direction of information.

Parallel Publics

The idea that public opinions move together in parallel has a long history
in American politics scholarship. In *The Rational Public*, Page and Sha-

piro (1992) used surveys that ask the same questions over many years to repeated cross-sections of the US population to argue for the existence of "parallel publics." They found that for most issues, opinion changes trend in the same direction for many segments of society. According to Page and Shapiro, opinion doesn't tend to polarize in the sense that as Democrats become more supportive of an issue, Republicans become less supportive of it. On the contrary, if Democrats warm to an issue, so too do Republicans.

Since *The Rational Public*, political scientists have amassed evidence in favor of the parallel publics thesis in a huge number of domains: defense spending, redistribution, presidential approval, crime, even healthcare. (To name a few of the dozens of articles and books that echo this finding, see Huxster, Carmichael, and Brulle 2015 on climate change; Eichenberg and Stoll 2012 on defense spending; Enns 2007 on welfare spending; Kellstedt 2003 on busing; or Porter 2020 on government waste.) Green, Palmquist, and Schickler (2002, 135) and Hochschild and Einstein (2015, 54) both document clearly parallel trends on attitudes about the Lewinsky scandal by partisan group. In April 1998, 32 percent of Democrats and 70 percent of Republicans believed Clinton had the affair; those figures increased by 14 points among both groups to 46 percent among Democrats and 84 percent among Republicans by the end of July.

To see some evidence of persuasion in parallel from the sort of nonexperimental data used in *The Rational Public*, consider figure 1.4, which shows how attitudes toward same-sex marriage have evolved over time. The data come from repeated cross-sectional polls of Americans conducted by the Pew Research Center between 2001 and 2019 (Pew Forum 2019). Pew researchers estimated support for same-sex marriage in twenty-five separate demographic subgroups based on partisanship, ideology, religion, religious attendance, race, generation, and gender. In all twenty-five, the proportion favoring gay marriage was higher in 2019 than it was in 2001, the beginning of data collection. Fitting straight lines to each series, we can estimate the average amount each group changed its position over time. Overall, the average change (or slope with respect to time) is about 1.7 percentage points per year. The slopes for some groups are slightly larger (Democrats 2.1 points per year, White mainline Protestants 2.1 points per year) than for others (Republicans 1.2 points per year, White evangelical Protestants 1.2 points per year), but the overall pattern is very similar from one subgroup to the next.

As we'll delve into in chapter 4, comparing magnitudes of change is not straightforward because the comparisons are sensitive to scaling. Whereas Democrats saw a greater percentage *point* change (28 points) than Republicans (16 points), Republicans experienced a larger *percent* change (76 percent increase) than Democrats (65 percent increase). It is not at all obvious which increase is "bigger." Suffice it to say that the magnitudes of change are similar but not the same, and they are difficult to rank.

The parallel publics pattern is quite widespread; there are, however, some clear-cut exceptions. For example, figure 1.5 shows how the last thirty years have seen a dramatic partisan *divergence* in abortion attitudes. Given the sharp contemporary divisions by party, it may be surprising to learn that Republicans and Democrats in the 1970s and 1980s held almost identical average opinions about the circumstances under which abortion should be allowed. The parties have moved in opposite directions on this issue ever since. Here we have obvious evidence of contrary rather than parallel motion. In passing, I will note that the parties appear to mostly agree on the ranking of the "reasons," and very large majorities of both parties support legal abortion in at least one case.

The evidence from repeated cross-sectional polls like those shown in figures 1.4 and 1.5 can only take us so far. The descriptive patterns of how the average opinions of various subgroups of society do or do not move together are interesting, but important methodological issues arise when we want to use these data to draw causal inferences. These issues fall into three main categories.

First, we *want* to think of over-time change in opinion as the result of a causal process—but what treatment are these changes in response to? The variable on the horizontal axes of all these graphs is time, not some particular set of persuasive messages. It is difficult to conceptualize what the treatment is, since the media transmit a complex mix of persuasive messages on the one hand and group cues on the other. One "easy" explanation for the discrepancy between figures 1.4 and 1.5 is that the media environment may have included more positive persuasive messages for gay marriage over time but more polarizing group cues on abortion over time. Second, even if we could reasonably claim that the treatment is something like the balance of persuasive messages transmitted via mass media, we can't be sure that different segments of the population are exposed to the same set of messages. Differential exposure to pro- and counter-attitudinal messages, even if mild, could seriously confound

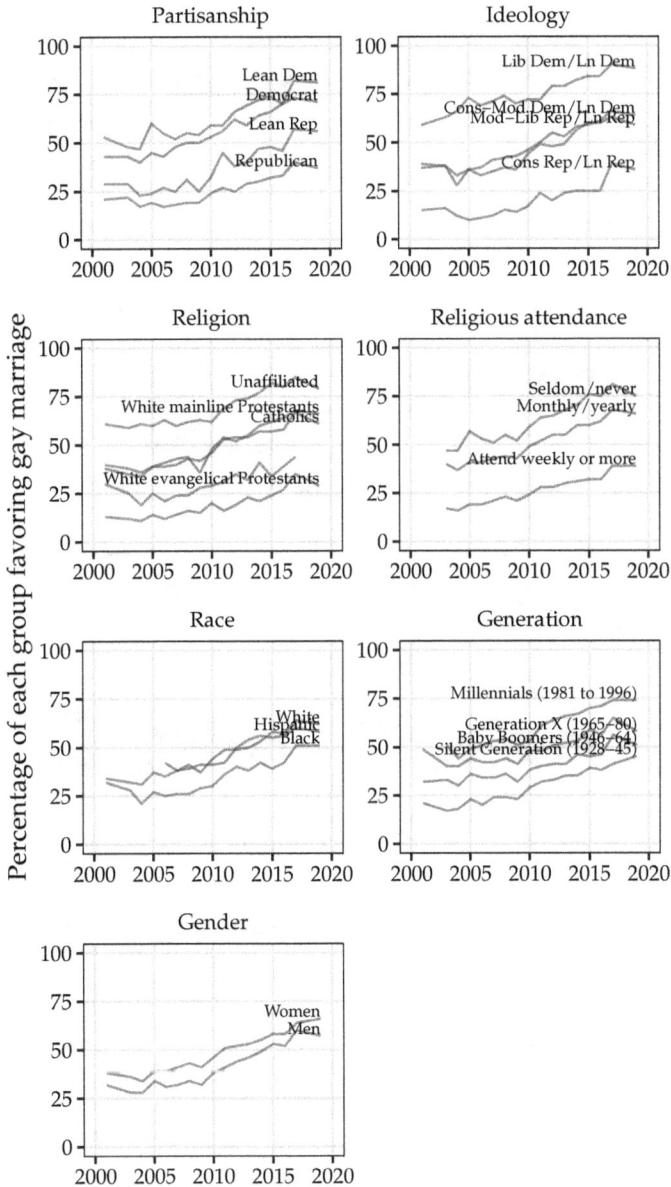

FIGURE I.4. American attitudes toward gay marriage, 2001–2019
Note: Data from the Pew Research Center (Pew Forum 2019). Despite clear differences in intercepts (position on the vertical axis), the slopes (change with respect to the horizontal axis) are all similar, with an average slope of a 1.7-percentage-point increase in support for gay marriage per year.

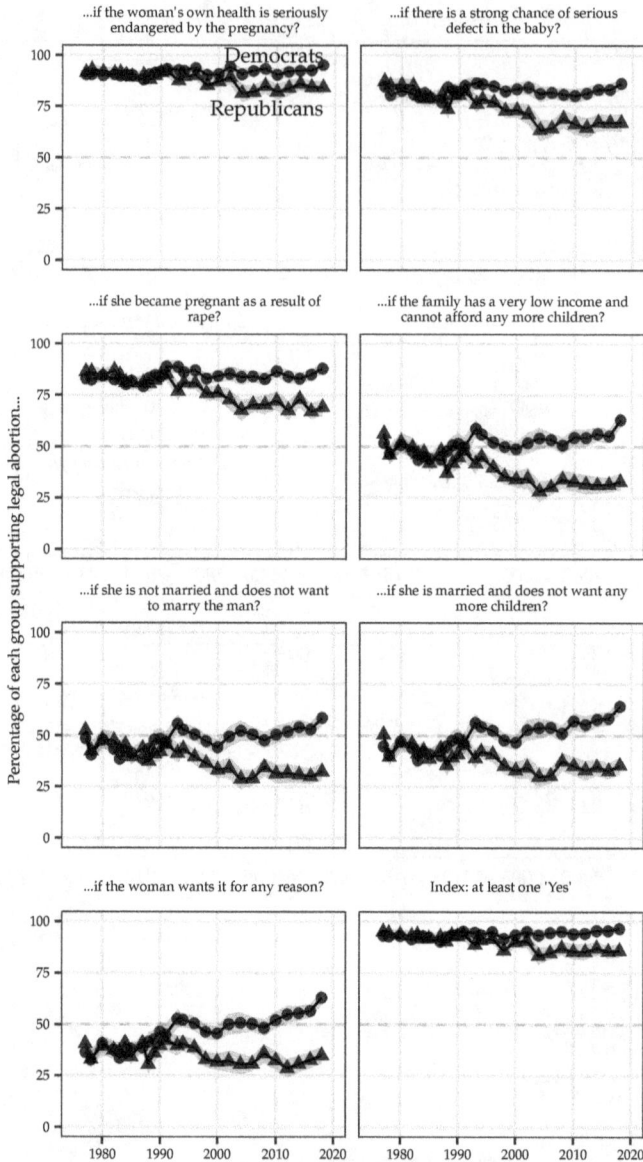

...if the woman's own health is seriously endangered by the pregnancy?

...if there is a strong chance of serious defect in the baby?

...if she became pregnant as a result of rape?

...if the family has a very low income and cannot afford any more children?

...if she is not married and does not want to marry the man?

...if she is married and does not want any more children?

...if the woman wants it for any reason?

Index: at least one 'Yes'

Percentage of each group supporting legal abortion...

FIGURE 1.5. American attitudes toward legal abortion by circumstance, 1977–2018
Note: Data from the General Social Survey (1977–2018). The question asked, "Please tell me whether or not you think it should be possible for a pregnant woman to obtain a legal abortion . . ." in each of these seven circumstances. Despite clear partisan agreement on abortion through 1990, the gap between Republicans and Democrats has grown ever since, with more Democrats but fewer Republicans supporting legal abortion in each circumstance.

our inferences. Third, these repeated cross-sectional polls aren't panel studies. In a panel study the same people are reinterviewed at multiple points in time, but in a repeated cross-sectional design the people who respond to the survey are different each year. Crucially, the cross-sectional design means that the composition of the groups could change over time. The kinds of people who call themselves Republicans in 1980 may be different from the kinds who call themselves Republicans today. Stated differently, the partisan divergence in abortion attitudes might not be the result of Republicans and Democrats being persuaded in opposite directions, but rather the result of pro- and anti-choice people sorting themselves into the parties differently over time (Killian and Wilcox 2008; Levendusky 2009; Mason 2018).

Because of the inferential difficulties associated with repeated cross-sectional data, the main source of evidence in this book will come from randomized experiments. These studies have their own weaknesses and infirmities too, and I'll try to be as clear and forthcoming about those as possible throughout. But the main reason to turn to experiments to study persuasion is that we can be in control of the main causal agent we want to study. We're studying persuasive information, so that's what we'll randomize.

What's at Stake

By the end of the book, I hope to have convinced you that the persuasion in parallel hypothesis is at least approximately correct. This single finding—approximately parallel changes in attitudes in response to persuasive information—has major implications for how we think about people who hold different views from ours and their capacity for change.

First and foremost: *the other side is persuadable.* Even though polarization may have taken hold in many quarters, it is nevertheless worth our time to make arguments in favor of our preferred policies because we end up changing minds, even if just a little. That said, having conversations about politics is often painful. It's painful at family gatherings, it's painful on social media, it's painful among friends and coworkers. We pay a social cost when we disagree with others, but that doesn't mean the attempt has no effect at all on others' attitudes.

Second, political misinformation is dangerous, because people are persuaded by false information and true information alike. We have to

hold those who control media platforms of every stripe—print, broadcast, or social—accountable for the spread of lies, conspiracy theories,
and propaganda. Corrections to misinformation are effective since they
too are a kind of persuasive information, but we would obviously be far
better off if misinformation were not spread in the first place.[4]

Third, we must recognize that we ourselves are persuadable as well.
Being open to arguments from our opponents doesn't make us hypo-
crites—it just means we are like everyone else: a little bit persuadable.

Where We're Headed

This book is aimed at chapter 5, which will lay out the evidence from a
large number of survey experiments that persuasion occurs in parallel.
To get there, we're first going to correct the record on perhaps the most
widely cited and influential study that claimed the opposite. Lord, Ross,
and Lepper (1979) purport to demonstrate that information causes "attitude polarization," which is equivalent to backlash as we've defined it.
Chapter 2 will show that that claim is not correct, and unpacking the
study's research design will explain why. In chapter 3 I will provide definitions and distinctions, and in chapter 4 I will explain how my research
design (the panel survey experiment) allows us to evaluate the persuasion in parallel hypothesis. Chapter 5 presents the evidence from those
experiments. Chapter 6 demonstrates the over-time durability of these
persuasive effects. The first six chapters of this book will be light on
theory, but chapter 7 will show what the evidence from these persuasion experiments does and does not mean for two of the most important
theories of information processing, Bayesian learning and motivated
reasoning. Chapter 8 will conclude by offering an explanation for why
it *feels* like backlash is common even though it is not and why we should
nevertheless persist in trying to persuade the other side.

Reinterpreting a Social Psychology Classic

"Biased Assimilation and Attitude Polarization: The Effects of Prior Theories on Subsequently Considered Evidence," by Charles G. Lord, Lee Ross, and Mark R. Lepper, was published in the *Journal of Personality and Social Psychology*, the flagship social psychology journal, in 1979. The study claims to demonstrate that information can polarize opinion in the sense that it has positive effects for some but negative effects for others. While the design of the study was somewhat complicated (and will be described in full detail below), the crux of it was this: undergraduate subjects, half of whom supported capital punishment and half of whom opposed it, were shown a mix of evidence on the question of whether capital punishment is successful in deterring crime. In response to the same information, capital punishment proponents reported becoming more pro-capital punishment while opponents reported becoming less pro-capital punishment. The authors summarize their finding like this: "The net effect of exposing proponents and opponents of capital punishment to identical evidence—studies ostensibly offering equivalent levels of support and disconfirmation—was to increase further the gap between their views" (Lord, Ross, and Lepper 1979, 2105).

Lord, Ross, and Lepper's study has been hugely influential. It has been cited thousands of times, usually quite breezily, to support the idea that counter-attitudinal information causes backlash. Petty and Cacioppo (2012) summarize the result as "Importantly, the net effect of reading both studies was to polarize subjects' beliefs: initially anti-punishment subjects became even more opposed to capital punishment and initially pro-punishment subjects became even more favorable to capital punishment." Haidt (2001) cites the study when claiming that backlash is to be expected when people have strongly held views: "However, if both parties began with strongly felt opposing intuitions (as in a debate over abortion), then reasoned persuasion would be likely to have little effect, except that the post hoc reasoning triggered in the other person could lead to even greater disagreement, a process labeled 'attitude polarization' by Lord, Ross, and Lepper (1979)." Nisbett et al. (2001) gloss the study as having found that "when people read about two different studies, one supporting their view on capital punishment and one opposing it, they were more convinced of their initial position than if they had not read about any studies." Lord, Ross, and Lepper (1979) has become the go-to reference for evidence for backlash.

When my collaborator Andy Guess and I read the study in graduate school, we had a hunch that the conclusions were exactly backward. We identified two weaknesses in the research design: the attitude change measurement was biased and the assignment to treatment was not randomized. In a replication of the original study conducted on a much larger and more diverse sample, we addressed both weaknesses and came to the opposite conclusion. Whereas Lord, Ross, and Lepper concluded that capital punishment proponents and opponents moved further apart in response to the same information, we found that they moved in parallel.

Very importantly, our study was not a "failed replication" of the sort highlighted by the recent large-scale efforts to estimate the reproducibility of results in a number of social scientific fields (e.g., Open Science Collaboration 2015). In those cases, replicators followed the original study's design and analysis procedures as faithfully as possible but were often unable to reproduce the results. Empirical findings that were once part of the accepted canon are drawing scrutiny for "questionable research practices" (John, Loewenstein, and Prelec 2012). These include "p-hacking," the shady practice of settling on model specifications that just barely achieve statistical significance (Simmons, Nelson, and Simonsohn 2011), and "HARKing" (hypothesizing after results are known), the conscious or unconscious process by which scholars retrofit their theories to match their empirical results (Kerr 1998). The case of Lord, Ross, and Lepper (1979) is different. It's not that we can't replicate their results—indeed, when we analyze our study the same way they did theirs, we obtain very similar answers. Instead, our complaint is with the original design itself, which in our view was not strong enough to reliably estimate the effects of capital punishment information on attitudes. In the remainder of this chapter, I'll walk through the original design and results, explain how our replication extended and amended the original design, and present the revised findings.

The Original Lord, Ross, and Lepper (1979) Study

In the late 1970s, Lord, Ross, and Lepper brought together a group of forty-eight undergraduates at Stanford University to study what happens when people encounter information with which they disagree. As measured by a pre-survey, half of the students were capital punishment proponents and the other half were capital punishment opponents.

The subjects were exposed to a set of information treatments that consisted of fabricated studies that purported to show that capital punishment either did or did not deter crime. Capital punishment was a hotly debated topic at the time, with arguments for and against the practice touching on deep questions of morality and legitimate uses of state violence. Underlying this debate, however, was the empirical question of whether capital punishment even does what it is supposed to do, which is deter would-be criminals from committing crimes that carry the death penalty.[1] All subjects saw two studies: one in favor of capital punishment, the other opposed. The order of the studies was randomly assigned, but everyone saw both a pro-capital punishment study and an anti-capital punishment study. After each study, subjects were asked two questions:

1. How, if at all, has your attitude toward the death penalty changed based on the results and subsequent description and critiques of the study? [Response scale from −8 to 8]
2. How, if at all, has your belief changed about the efficacy of the death penalty in deterring crime? [Response scale from −8 to 8]

Table 2.1 reproduces table 3 from the original article. The table shows that on both outcome variables, proponents reported becoming more supportive of capital punishment and opponents reported the reverse. In the top half of the table, we see that proponents reported that their attitudes increased by 0.8 points after they read the pro-capital punishment

TABLE 2.1 **Reproduction of Lord, Ross, and Lepper (1979), table 3**

	Proponents	Opponents
Change in attitudes toward the death penalty		
After pro-capital punishment study	0.8	−0.9
After anti-capital punishment study	0.7	−0.8
Combined	1.5	−1.7
Change in beliefs in deterrent efficacy		
After pro-capital punishment study	0.7	−1.0
After anti-capital punishment study	0.7	−0.8
Combined	1.4	−1.8

study and that they *also* increased when they read the anti-capital punishment study, this time by about 0.7 points. The opposite pattern held among the opponents, who reported average changes of −0.9 and −0.8 points for the pro- and anti-capital punishment studies, respectively.[2] The responses to the belief in deterrent efficacy question in the bottom half of the table followed the same pattern. Proponents said their beliefs in deterrence increased by an average of 0.7 points after reading both studies; opponents said their beliefs decreased by an average of 1.0 points after the anti-capital punishment study and 0.8 points after the pro-capital punishment study. The "Combined" rows sum the responses that subjects gave after each study. If taken literally, these figures mean that (for example) proponents moved 0.8 points after the pro-capital punishment study and 0.7 points after the anti-capital punishment study, for a total of 1.5 points worth of movement.

It was on the basis of these data that Lord, Ross, and Lepper concluded that counter-attitudinal information can polarize attitudes. Let's pause here to reflect on the deep societal dysfunction that result would imply. The conclusion of the study is that regardless of the evidence— regardless of whether the report says capital punishment is effective or counterproductive in deterring crime—proponents become more pro and opponents become more con. If this were the way information actually worked, then any persuasive attempt would cause people to hold stronger and more extreme versions of the attitudes they previously held.

What Went Wrong?

This study has two main flaws, each of which is sufficient to change the conclusions when corrected. The first problem is biased outcome measurement and the second is the lack of random assignment.

The outcome measurement is biased because of how subjects are asked to self-assess the causal effect of the treatment on their attitudes. Causal effects are about *counterfactuals*. What would my attitude have been if I hadn't seen the counter-attitudinal information, and how does that compare to my attitude now that I have been exposed such information? Assessing the difference between counterfactual states of the world is *very hard*, and indeed is probably the most central problem that social scientists grapple with on a daily basis.

My collaborator Matthew Graham and I show that people are quite bad at reporting how much their attitudes have changed (Graham and Coppock 2021). They tend to overestimate the amount of change and frequently get the sign wrong. Our best guess at the explanation for this poor performance is something called "response substitution" (Gal and Rucker 2011), wherein people answer the question they want to answer, rather than the question that was asked. Lord, Ross, and Lepper asked subjects to report how much the treatment information changed their minds. If subjects engaged in response substitution, instead of answering the actual question asked, they expressed something like their level of support for capital punishment—not the change in their support. This form of measurement error would explain why proponents use higher values on the scale and opponents use lower values. Under the response substitution theory, they do so not because they are accurately reporting their best guess of their *change* in attitudes, but because they are reporting their existing *level* of support or opposition.

Andy Guess and I were not the only ones to notice the measurement flaw in Lord, Ross, and Lepper's study. It is noted in Taber and Lodge (2006). Five other replications (with varying levels of fidelity to the original protocol) swap out the self-assessed attitude change measure for a so-called "direct" measure (Pyszczynski, Greenberg, and Holt 1985; Miller et al. 1993; Kuhn and Lao 1996; Munro and Ditto 1997; Corner, Whitmarsh, and Xenias 2012), which takes the difference between pre- and post-treatment measures of the level of attitudes to estimate changes "directly." In our replication that also used the direct measure, subjects were asked these two questions, once before treatment and once after treatment:

1. Which view of capital punishment best summarizes your own? [7-point scale, 1: I am very much against capital punishment, 7: I am very much in favor of capital punishment],
2. Does capital punishment reduce crime? Please select the view that best

summarizes your own. [1: I am very certain that capital punishment does not reduce crime, 7: I am very certain that capital punishment reduces crime]

The direct measurement strategy ameliorates the response substitution problem by relieving subjects of the cognitive burden of assessing hard-to-imagine counterfactuals. None of the five replications that use this approach found that changes in the direct measurements taken before and after the treatment information were different for proponents and opponents.

The second and more troubling problem is the lack of random assignment. It turns out that the Lord, Ross, and Lepper study isn't actually an experiment, if we take the definition of an experiment to be a procedure in which units are randomly assigned to treatment conditions with known probabilities between zero and one (Gerber and Green 2012). In Lord, Ross, and Lepper (1979), subjects weren't randomly assigned to see the treatment information *or not*; everybody saw both the pro and con information. The order was randomized, but we're not interested in the effects of the order the information was presented in, we're interested in the effects of the information itself. The lack of a randomly formed control group means that we can't characterize how subjects would have responded had they not seen pro or con information at all.

While the previous replications of Lord, Ross, and Lepper (1979) corrected the first problem, none of them used random assignment either. The replication that Andy Guess and I designed fixed both problems. We used random assignment to the content of studies subjects were asked to read as well as the direct measurement strategy. We also included the biased self-assessed change measure so we could embed an exact replication of the original design within our amended protocol.

The Guess and Coppock (2020) Replication Study

We recruited 682 subjects to participate in our study from Mechanical Turk (MTurk), a common source of online convenience samples. In our paper, we defend the use of that sample by pointing out that MTurk subjects are far more varied than 1970s Stanford undergraduates. In chapter 4, I'll offer some further defenses of the platform, including evidence that results of experiments conducted with MTurkers tend to correspond nicely with the results of the same experiments conducted on nationally representative samples. But we didn't know any of that at the time. The main reason we used MTurk is that we were graduate students and MTurk was within our budget.

We followed the original experimental protocol as closely as possible, but we made three important changes:

1. Lord, Ross, and Lepper assigned all subjects to see one pro study and one con study. We randomly assigned the content of the two studies subjects could see. The first study could be pro, con, or *null*. The null studies claimed to find inconclusive results on the effect of capital punishment on crime. We chose to use the null study condition rather than a pure control condition so that we could maintain parallelism with the original study's self-assessed attitude change measurement strategy. In retrospect, the inclusion of a pure control condition would have been useful, even if we could only have compared the treatment conditions to the pure control on the "direct" outcome measure.

2. We "modernized" the treatment stimuli. The exact wordings from the original study are no longer available. Our own replication of the study is based on a replication conducted by Joseph Lau and Diana Kuhn, who at one point had access to the original materials but no longer had them when we came calling in 2015. So our study is something of a photocopy of a photocopy. We updated the publication dates of the fictitious studies and we remade the figures using modern statistical software (that part was especially fun).

3. We used both "direct" and "self-assessed" measures of attitude change. As we'll see, both measures tell the same story once we compare responses according to the randomly assigned groups.

In both the original and the replication, the treatment stimuli were relatively complicated. Subjects were first given a "results card" with a research finding and were asked some intermediate questions. These results cards were like very short abstracts of academic articles. For example, here's the "results card" from the time series version of the pro-capital punishment study:

Kroner and Phillips (2012) compared murder rates for the year before and the year after adoption of capital punishment in 14 states. In 11 of the 14 states, murder rates were **lower after** adoption of the death penalty.

This research supports the deterrent effect of the death penalty.

And here's the results card from the cross-sectional version of the anti-capital punishment study:

Palmer and Crandall (2012) compared murder rates in 10 pairs of neighboring states with different capital punishment laws. In 8 of the 10 pairs, murder rates were **higher** in the state with capital punishment.

This research opposes the deterrent effect of the death penalty.

After the results card, subjects read quite a bit more about each study and saw a table and graph, both of which conveyed the same information. As an example, figure 2.1 shows two of the graphs used.

Replication Study Results

First, I'll show that we can recover very similar answers from our replication study if we analyze our data using the same procedures as the original authors. Table 2.2 presents the average self-assessed attitude change across proponents and opponents in an analogous format to table 2.1. Focusing on the "Combined" rows, we see that proponents report a total of 2.7 points of change in the pro-capital punishment direction and opponents report exactly the opposite: 2.7 points of change in the anti-capital punishment direction. The same pattern holds for changes in beliefs about the deterrent efficacy of capital punishment. When the replication data are analyzed as in the original article, we recover the same misleading result that attitudes appear to polarize. In fact, things appear to have gotten worse over time, as the magnitudes of the "changes" have increased by about a point over their 1979 values.

Figure 2.2 shows the same data summarized in table 2.2 but also includes the null study condition. The visual display of the data helps interpretation immensely. The average self-reported change by treatment condition is plotted in triangles for proponents and circles for opponents. These averages are overlaid on the raw data. We see that for both proponents and opponents, self-reported attitude change is higher in the pro condition than in the null condition and higher in the null condition than in the con condition. When we connect those group averages with lines, we see clearly visible parallel lines for both dependent variables and for

Murder Rate in 14 States for One Year Before and After Adoption of Capital Punishment
Reproduced with permission from Kroner and Phillips (2012)

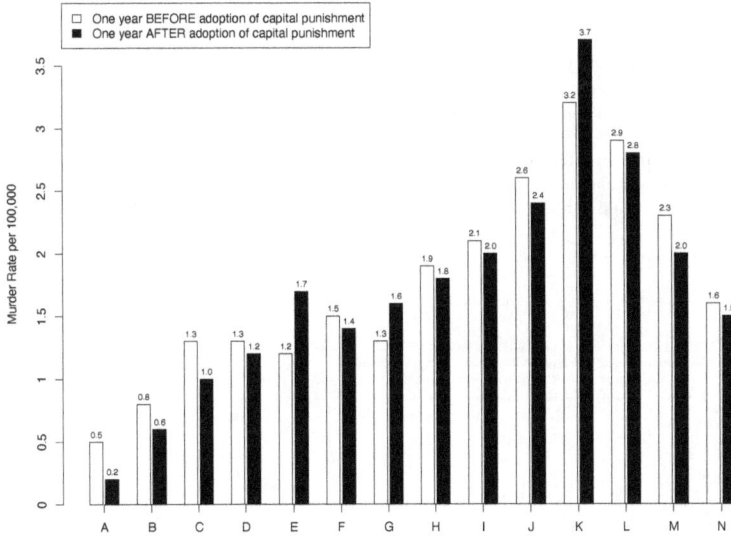

□ One year BEFORE adoption of capital punishment
■ One year AFTER adoption of capital punishment

Murder Rate in 2012 for Neighboring States with and without Capital Punishment
Reproduced with permission from Palmer and Crandall (2012)

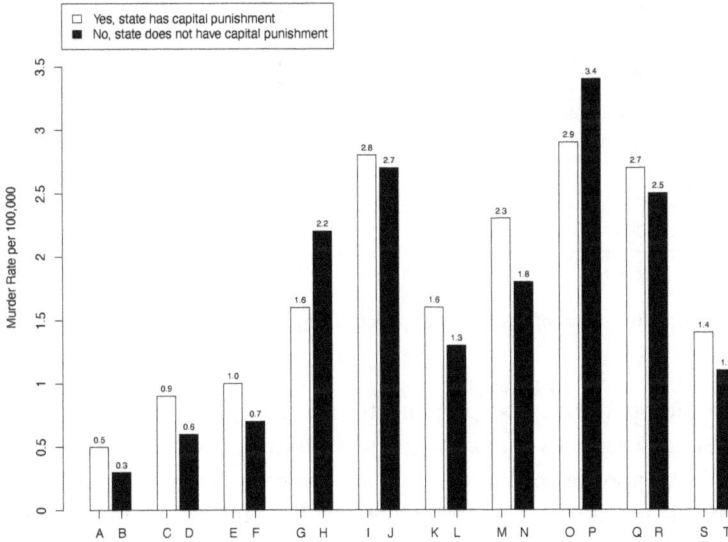

□ Yes, state has capital punishment
■ No, state does not have capital punishment

FIGURE 2.1. Graphical treatments used in Guess and Coppock's (2020) replication of Lord, Ross, and Lepper (1979): (a) pro–capital punishment (time series), (b) anti–capital punishment (cross-sectional)

TABLE 2.2 **Reanalysis of Guess and Coppock (2020) à la Lord, Ross, and Lepper (1979)**

	Proponents	Opponents
Change in attitudes toward the death penalty		
After pro-capital punishment study	0.0	−2.3
After anti-capital punishment study	2.7	−0.4
Combined	2.7	−2.7
Change in beliefs in deterrent efficacy		
After pro-capital punishment study	−0.7	−2.7
After anti-capital punishment study	2.8	−0.2
Combined	2.1	−2.9

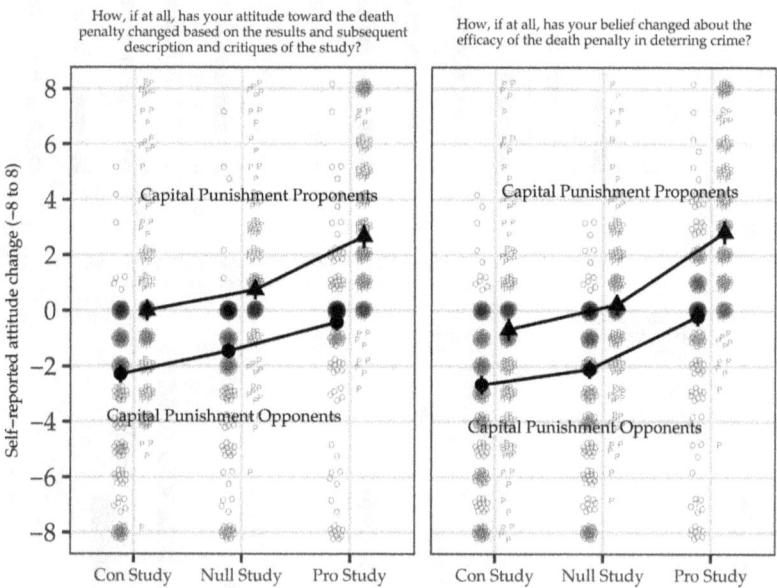

FIGURE 2.2. Reanalysis of Guess and Coppock (2020): Self-assessed outcome measure

both the opponents and proponents. The pro-versus-con difference is statistically significant at $p < 0.05$ in all four opportunities. We get exactly the opposite conclusion when we compare subjects across the randomly assigned partition. Instead of backlash, instead of attitude polarization, instead of *making things worse*, the treatments persuaded both proponents and opponents in the direction of information.

The next set of results shows that this conclusion does not depend on using the "self-assessed" or the "direct" measure of attitude change.

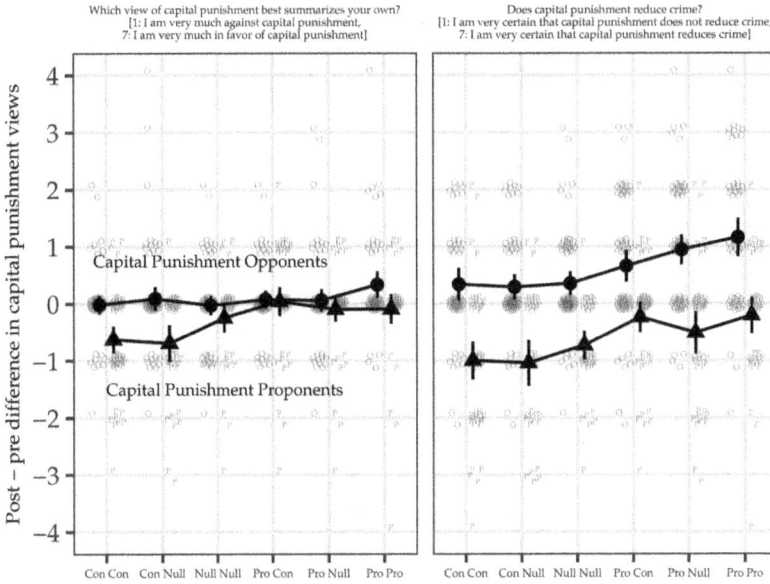

FIGURE 2.3. Reanalysis of Guess and Coppock (2020): Direct outcome measure
Note: Data from 682 MTurk respondents. Proponents' responses are plotted with the letter P and opponents' responses with the letter O.

Figure 2.3 has the direct measure (i.e., the post measure minus the pre measure) on the vertical axis and the "dosage" of pro or con information on the horizontal axis (recall that the post measure was only asked after subjects saw both studies to which they were randomly assigned). In the left facet, the effects of treatment on beliefs exhibit a parallel pattern: the slope for both proponents and opponents is positive. The pattern for the effects on attitudes (left facet) is somewhat murkier. Opponents move some, but not much, whereas proponents move in the standard direction: the more pro information they get, the more supportive they become. The summary conclusion from our replication study is that information does not cause proponents to move in one direction and opponents in the other. On the contrary, both groups of subjects update in the direction of information.

Biased Assimilation

Lord, Ross, and Lepper used the term "biased assimilation" to describe the phenomenon that people don't like evidence with which they

TABLE 2.3 **Biased assimilation in the original and replication studies**

Reproduction of Lord, Ross, and Lepper (1979), table 1		
	Proponents	Opponents
	Mean ratings of how well the two studies had been conducted	
Pro-capital punishment study	1.5	−2.1
Anti-capital punishment study	−1.6	−0.3
Difference	3.1	−1.8
	Mean ratings of how convincing the two studies were as evidence on the deterrent efficacy of capital punishment	
Pro-capital punishment study	1.4	−2.1
Anti-capital punishment study	−1.8	0.1
Difference	3.2	−2.2

Guess and Coppock (2020) replication		
	Proponents	Opponents
	Mean ratings of how well the two studies had been conducted	
Pro-capital punishment study	3.6	0.1
Anti-capital punishment study	1.5	2.6
Difference	2.1	−2.5
	Mean ratings of how convincing the two studies were as evidence on the deterrent efficacy of capital punishment	
Pro-capital punishment study	3.4	−1.0
Anti-capital punishment study	0.1	1.3
Difference	3.0	−2.3

disagree. The term is a little misleading because it implies that disliking evidence means that it doesn't get "assimilated" into subject attitudes— but as we'll see, even evidence we don't like can exert persuasive influence on attitudes. The authors provide direct evidence of "biased assimilation" in their original table 1, reproduced here in the top half of table 2.3. When asked to rate quality, subjects rated the congenial studies more highly than the counter-attitudinal studies. The bottom half of the table shows that this same pattern holds in our replication study as well—the "difference" rows line up especially well.

To some, findings like these show that people "reject" evidence with which they disagree and that people are therefore impervious to information that contradicts their views (e.g., Kahan, Jenkins-Smith, and Braman 2011). My interpretation is different. To me, this evidence shows that people *actually do* have prior beliefs that they *actually believe*. Capital punishment proponents actually think that the death penalty has a deterrent effect, so they naturally reason that studies purporting to show the opposite are more likely to be incorrect.

To my mind, this is how reasonable people should interpret new information. If you encounter a ridiculous claim, you're likely to think it's wrong. The claim is ridiculous because it contradicts your priors—that's what it means to characterize a claim as ridiculous in the first place. For example, suppose I learn of a randomized controlled trial that claims door-to-door canvassing has an absurdly large and negative −20 percentage point effect on turnout. I am likely to think something went seriously wrong in the design or analysis of the study, because the estimate so deeply contradicts my priors, which hover around the +2 percentage point mark, depending on electoral context (Green, McGrath, and Aronow 2013). Even if I were able to verify key details of the design and analysis, I would still be skeptical of the study, though perhaps I would shade my posterior beliefs (my updated beliefs after reading the study) about the average mobilizing effects of door-to-door canvassing down a fraction. Similarly, these capital punishment proponents and opponents infer that the counter-attitudinal studies are of low quality precisely because they think they are incorrect!

Chapter 7 will provide an explicitly Bayesian accounting of the "biased assimilation" process that follows this logic. For now, we can just appreciate the tension between the biased assimilation finding and the evidence of persuasion in parallel. Even though people don't *like* some evidence, they can nevertheless be persuaded by it.

Summary

This chapter has shown that an influential social psychology study from the 1970s yielded misleading conclusions. The claim in the original paper is that exposure to the same information can lead to attitude polarization. The authors argue that people are biased in how they evaluate evidence, which leads them to use any evidence, regardless of its content, to reconfirm and strengthen their previously held attitudes.

The original claim is not supported by the empirical results, for two main reasons. First, we can't just ask subjects to report the causal effect of a treatment on their attitudes and beliefs. Under the response substitution theory, proponents weren't saying they support capital punishment *more* because of the anti-capital punishment study; they were saying they support it *anyway*. One way to fix this problem is to use direct measurement of attitudes before and after exposure to information. Like the other replicators before us, when we use the direct measure, we find no evidence of attitude polarization.

The deeper critique, however, is that in order to understand the effects of information on attitudes and whether those effects are different for different kinds of people, we need to randomly assign exposure to that information. Random assignment ensures a fair test. Under random assignment, we can compare the treated to the untreated to estimate the effects of information. These two criticisms aren't just methodological finger-wagging. Instead, they expose how flaws in the research design lead to flaws in the conclusions.

CHAPTER THREE

Definitions and Distinctions

The goal of this book is to convince you of the persuasion in parallel hypothesis: the treatment effect of persuasive information on target policy attitudes is small, positive, and durable for everyone.

In this chapter, I'll lay out precisely what I mean by "treatment effect," "persuasive information," "target policy attitudes," "small," "positive," "durable," and "everyone." Along the way, we will distinguish persuasive information from group cues and target policy attitudes from attitudes about non-target policies or attitudes about the message or messenger. With these definitions and distinctions in hand, we will arrive at a theory of which kinds of messages are expected to generate positive or negative attitude changes among which groups.

Treatment Effect

Both in everyday life and in quite a bit of scholarship, we're loose with the word "effect." People use it to describe a particular phenomenon ("the Doppler effect") or descriptive differences between groups ("the effect of partisanship on attitudes"). I'm going to use it in an exclusively *counterfactual*, causal sense. The treatment effect for a particular individual is the difference in outcomes between two parallel universes: one in which the individual is treated and one in which the individual is not treated. The outcomes a person would express in each parallel universe are called *potential outcomes*, and they form the basis of the Neyman-Rubin causal model (Neyman 1923; Rubin 1974).

Under this model, individuals are endowed with potential outcomes, only one of which they ever express. In the simplest case, an individual i harbors only two potential outcomes. The treated potential outcome is called $y_i(1)$ and the untreated potential outcome is called $y_i(0)$. The difference between them is often written with the Greek letter tau: τ_i is defined as $y_i(1)$ minus $y_i(0)$. The little i subscripts indicate that these values are for an individual i, and do not refer to average causal effects like the "average treatment effect" (or ATE), which is what some people sometimes confusingly refer to as "the" treatment effect. Every person has a treatment effect, and nothing in the definition prevents treatment effects from being different from one person to the next.

The potential outcomes model helps to clarify a deep problem that we face every time we try to understand causality. We can only ever observe $y_i(1)$ or $y_i(0)$, but not both. The fact that you can't observe a unit in both its treated and its untreated state is sometimes called the fundamental problem of causal inference (Holland 1986). This huge problem has no solution for individual-level causal effects.

Sometimes we think we can "see" causality by just observing people at time 1, treating them, then observing again at time 2. This line of thinking motivates the "direct measure" described in chapter 2. The direct measure works if we assume that people first express their control outcome, then later express their treated outcome. In mathematical notation, the time 1 outcome can be written $y_{i,t1}$ and the time 2 outcome can be written $y_{i,t2}$. In order to see causality by watching units over time, we would need to assume the following: $y_{i,t1} = y_i(0)$ and $y_{i,t2} = y_i(1)$. In words, this assumption would require that the time 1 outcome be exactly equal to the untreated potential outcome and the time 2 outcome be exactly equal to the treated potential outcome.

The trouble is that this assumption could be correct (as is probably true in some physics experiments), but it could also be wrong (as in most social science studies). The main reason that this assumption tends to break down in social science studies is that the outcomes at time 1 and time 2 may plausibly differ for reasons other than the treatment in question. For example, in a panel study of political attitudes, the same individual might express high approval of the president in wave 1 but middling approval at wave 2. This change might be due to a persuasive treatment like criticism from the opposition party transmitted through the media, but it could also be due to increased political disaffection. Because all treatments move together in time, isolating the causal effect of any one particular treatment can be extraordinarily difficult. We encountered this problem in the studies of repeated cross-sectional surveys in chapter 1: opinions may change over time, but we don't know which treatment or treatments out of the many possibilities are responsible.

To demonstrate the persuasion in parallel hypothesis, I'm going to rely on evidence from randomized experiments. The main advantage of randomized experimentation is that we can justify the most consequential statistical assumptions by design, rather than by theory or conjecture. These experiments don't overcome the fundamental problem of causal inference, but they do allow us to make confident claims about various average causal effects.

We need to take a brief tour through a jumble of acronyms to distinguish between kinds of inquiries (sometimes called estimands, quantities of interest, or targets of inference). Bear with me on these, because the distinctions between these various terms will make it easier to talk about backlash and persuasion in parallel. These terms are gathered together in table 3.1 for easy reference.

We've already alluded to the average treatment effect, or ATE. It's the average value of all of the individual treatment effects. If we have a sample of N units, then the ATE is defined as $\frac{\sum_{i=1}^{N} \tau_i}{N}$. Taking the average does not mean that we're *assuming* that the treatment effect is the same for each person; we're just defining the ATE as the average of a set of individual treatment effects, whatever that average is. Sometimes an average is interesting to know and sometimes not. As a general rule, averages are less interesting when the things that are being averaged together are very dissimilar from each other. Put more plainly, if half the subjects experience positive effects and the other half negative effects, the fact that the average treatment effect is close to zero might not be of particular theoretical interest.

In addition to the overall average treatment effect, we might also consider *conditional* average treatment effects (CATEs). A CATE is the average treatment effect conditional on membership in a particular subgroup. For example, the ATE among capital punishment proponents is a CATE. CATEs can also mask substantial variation within subgroups and therefore can be as theoretically uninteresting as the ATE. In chapter 2, we estimated the CATE among capital punishment proponents,

TABLE 3.1 **Distinctions across three inquiries**

Full name	Shorthand	Definition	Description
Individual-level treatment effect	τ_i	$y_i(1) - y_i(0)$	Difference between the treated and untreated potential outcomes; the fundamentally unobservable effect of treatment for an individual unit i
Average treatment effect	ATE	$\dfrac{\sum_{i=1}^{N} \tau_i}{N}$	The ATE is the average of all individual-level treatment effects τ_i in the set of N units under study
Conditional average treatment effect	CATE	$\dfrac{\sum_{i=1}^{N} \tau_i * c_i}{\sum_{i=1}^{N} c_i}$	The CATE is the ATE among a subgroup of units defined by a condition c, which equals 1 when the condition is met and 0 otherwise.

but of course that group is not a monolith: proponents could vary among themselves in their responses to treatment. One of our most important goals here is to learn whether there exists a subgroup that updates their attitudes in the "wrong" direction. To that end, we would like to estimate CATEs that exhibit within-group homogeneity. The art of choosing what to condition on is key. If we can figure out the sources of variation in treatment response and condition on them, then we might have a shot at estimating the theoretically important CATEs.

We sometimes talk about treatment effect *heterogeneity* versus *homogeneity*. Treatment effects are heterogeneous if the treatment effect for one unit is different from the treatment effect for another. Treatment effects that are homogeneous are exactly the same for everyone. But because of the fundamental problem of causal inference, we can never know the treatment effect for any individual person, so we can never directly test whether the treatment effects for two different individuals are the same (homogeneous) or different (heterogeneous). What we can do instead is ask whether the CATEs for different subgroups of people are different from each other. If they are deemed to be different by a hypothesis test, we can affirm the presence of treatment effect heterogeneity.[1] Unfortunately, if the CATEs *aren't* shown to be different, we can't affirm treatment effect homogeneity, which is an asymmetry that will hound us throughout the book. This problematic potential for "hidden moderators" is discussed in greater detail in chapter 4.

Another way to state the persuasion in parallel hypothesis is that, in the main, the CATEs of persuasive information are all similar to each other and to the overall ATE. In other words, I hope to convince you that treatment effects in response to persuasive information are mostly homogeneous. I'm going to rely on subgroup analysis to establish that claim, hoping that I'm picking the most theoretically relevant subgroups. The unhappy truth is that we may never know if I've succeeded in doing so because it's impossible to know if I have measured every attribute that could contribute to heterogeneity.

Persuasive Information

In the studies that follow, persuasive information is the main causal variable of interest and is the randomly assigned treatment in each experiment. In everyday political communication, persuasive information can arrive in many formats, like tweetstorms, traditional TV ads, newspaper articles, or radio interviews. I think of a single "dose" of persuasive information as being approximately equivalent to the average political advertising appeal. In the experiments, persuasive information arrives as text alone, text with images, or a short video. Persuasive information need not be correct, so this definition includes both true information and false information (misinformation).

Some readers may be annoyed that I define the sorts of treatments under study as "persuasive information," since one of the things we want to know is whether persuasive information is indeed persuasive. A term like "targeted information" might get us out of this bit of circularity (is persuasive information persuasive?), but that term has its own problems, as some readers might imagine that what is being targeted is people, rather than attitudes. Nevertheless, I need to distinguish persuasive information from other kinds of information. Since it will turn out that this special kind of information does in fact persuade, the name "persuasive" information fits nicely.

What makes persuasive information different from non-persuasive information is that it has both a *target* and a *direction*. Non-persuasive information lacks a target, a direction, or both. The target of information is the relevant attitude or belief. A speech in which a politician lays out their vision for immigration reform targets the beliefs about the quality of the reform and the attitude of policy support for the reform. If the persuasive information is a speech about immigration, non-target attitudes would include things like attitudes toward tax policy or support for same-sex marriage. Non-target and target attitudes may of course be correlated with one another, but they are theoretically distinguished on the basis of the treatments that do or do not target them.

Like Hopkins and Mummolo (2017) before us, my collaborator Don Green and I find that while persuasive treatments definitely move target attitudes, they have basically no effects whatsoever on non-target attitudes (Coppock and Green 2022). We use this result to argue that attitudes are not "dynamically constrained." Dynamic constraint is a concept introduced by Converse (1964) to describe a process by which a change in one attitude causes knock-on changes in other ideologically related attitudes. Since we find that treatments do move target attitudes but not non-target attitudes, we conclude that attitudes are not shaped by dynamic constraint. However, buying that line of argumentation is not required in order to agree that the distinction between target and non-target attitudes is meaningful.

As an illustration of this point, consider figure 3.1, which shows an additional analysis of the op-eds study discussed in chapter 1. Earlier, we described the effects of just one of the op-eds (Rand Paul's flat tax piece), but subjects could actually have been exposed to one of five op-eds, each advocating a different libertarian policy position. We measured five separate attitudes, one corresponding to each op-ed. I've standardized those outcomes by dividing all outcomes by the standard deviation of the control group responses to make for a cleaner comparison of effect sizes across outcome variables. The main focus of the figure is the effect of each op-ed on its target attitudes versus its effect on the non-target attitudes. For example, the top row shows the effect of the "Amtrak" op-ed on five outcomes in the MTurk version of the experiment. Crudely speaking, it had a moderate effect on Amtrak attitudes, but basically no effect on the attitudes not targeted by the Amtrak op-ed. More precisely, the op-eds move opinion on target attitudes by an average of about 0.4 standard units (SDs), but the average effect on non-target attitudes is tiny (0.02 SDs).

The *direction* of persuasive information describes how the target attitude is *supposed* to change. Direction can be positive or negative and is assumed to be the same for all recipients. The direction of information is a property of the treatment itself. As maintained by motivated reasoning theorists, positive information could in principle have positive effects for some but negative effects for others. To test such a claim, we need to agree in advance about what the "correct" direction of information is, and this direction needs to be the same for all individuals.[2]

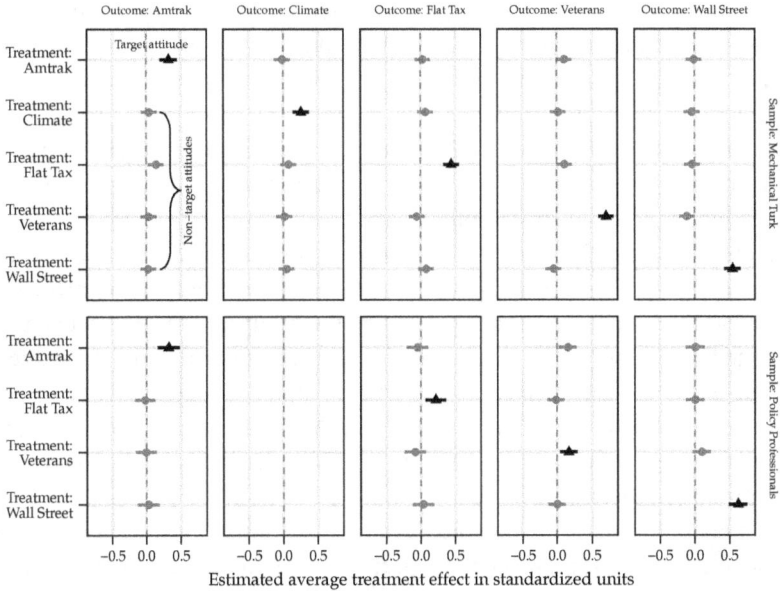

FIGURE 3.1. Effects of persuasive information on target and non-target attitudes
Note: Data from Coppock, Ekins, and Kirby (2018). Estimated average treatment effects on target attitudes are represented with triangles and effects on non-target attitudes with circles. Treatment effects are expressed in standard units to facilitate comparison across outcomes. The treatments move their targeted attitudes in the intended direction but do not move non-target attitudes.

Group Cues Are Not Persuasive Information

The largest category of political messages I exclude from the definition of persuasive information is group cues. Group cues provide information about which groups prefer what, but they don't include affirmative arguments for or against a policy. Instead of giving substantive reasons to support or oppose a policy, group cues just communicate what policies *other people* support or oppose.

In this way, group cues are theorized to work as a heuristic or an information shortcut (Brady and Sniderman 1985; Popkin 1991). The cue informs voters that their in-group prefers policy A. Since they agree with their in-group on most things, they infer from this cue that if they were to look into policy A, they would probably prefer it too. Voters pass on the hard work of learning about the policy and instead skip straight to increasing their support for policy A. The reverse works in a similar fashion. If the cue informs voters that their out-group prefers policy A, they reason that since they disagree with their out-group on most things, they would disagree with them on policy A if they spent effort learning about it.

People have multiple, overlapping group identities that can express themselves according to race, religion, class, gender, language, age, education, profession, geography, or other attributes. In-group and out-group cues probably work for all of these groups, though the strength of cue is likely related to the strength and quality of group membership as well as the specific relationship between the group and the policy issue at hand (e.g., Mason 2018, chapter 6). For example, one might imagine a religious cue in which people learn where a religious group stands on an issue. Members of the group might update their views in line with the cue, whereas people who do not like the group might update in the opposite direction (Albertson 2015).

Political scientists who study American politics have focused on a particular kind of group cue, the party cue, and have found that indeed, such treatments have heterogeneous effects: a party cue that Democrats support policy A will increase support for the policy among Democrats but decrease support among Republicans (Bullock 2019). In *Follow the Leader*, Lenz (2013) points out how troubling the effects of party cues are, since under standard political accountability models, voters should punish party leaders for adopting positions they don't hold, not adopt those positions themselves.

The prototypical demonstration of the effects of party cues is an experiment in which subjects are randomly exposed to cues that signal the positions taken by one or both of the major parties on a candidate or policy issue. A very early example of a party cue (quasi-) experiment comes from a 1982 poll of Californians that asked for voters' opinions about whether state supreme court justices should be retained or not. The resulting data were analyzed in at least three academic articles: Squire and Smith (1988), Smith and Squire (1990), and Mondak (1993). Control subjects were asked for their opinions without any cue. Treatment subjects were informed as to which governor appointed the justices before they were asked for their opinions.[3]

The results of the quasi-experiment are presented in figure 3.2. For Justices Broussard, Kaus, and Reynoso, the interpretation is clear. The cue that the justices were appointed by Governor Jerry Brown (a Democrat) mildly increases support among Democratic respondents and

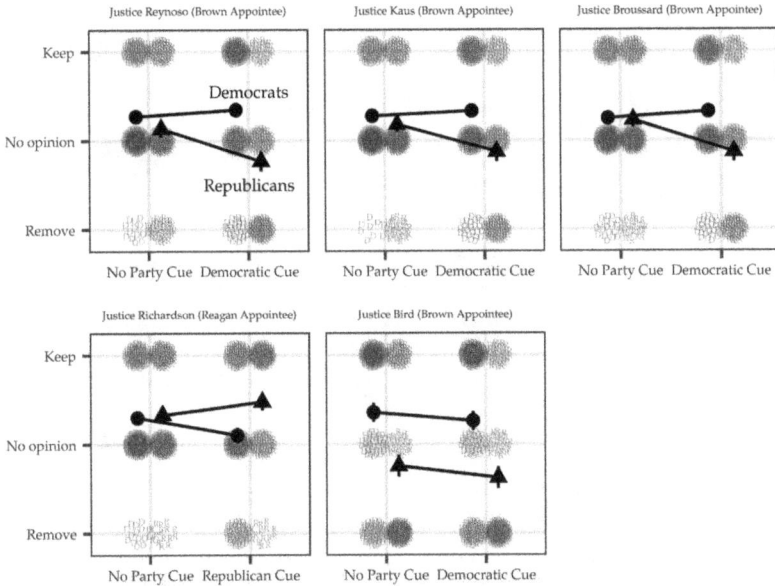

FIGURE 3.2. Reanalysis of 1982 California poll party cue experiment
Note: The 1,007 subjects in the 1982 California poll experiment were quasi-randomly assigned to hear which governor (Governor Brown, a Democrat, or Governor Reagan, a Republican) had appointed each justice to the state supreme court before expressing their support or opposition to the justices' retention. With the exception of Justice Bird (see text for possible explanation), party cues polarize opinion.

dramatically decreases support among Republican respondents. For Justice Richardson, the pattern is the same, but in the opposite direction. The cue that Richardson was appointed by Governor Ronald Reagan (a Republican) increases support among Republican respondents and decreases support among Democratic respondents. The effects for Justice Bird are small and statistically insignificant for all groups. The explanation given by Mondak (1993) and hinted at in Squire and Smith (1988) is that because of extensive news coverage of Justice Bird at the time, many respondents would already have been exposed to repeated party cues about her before taking the survey.

A more recent example comes from Nicholson (2012), who studied the effects of Democratic and Republican cues in favor of two policies: one on foreclosure that would provide relief for at-risk homeowners, and a second on immigration that would ensure a path to citizenship for noncitizens currently living in the US. Figure 3.3 shows the results of the

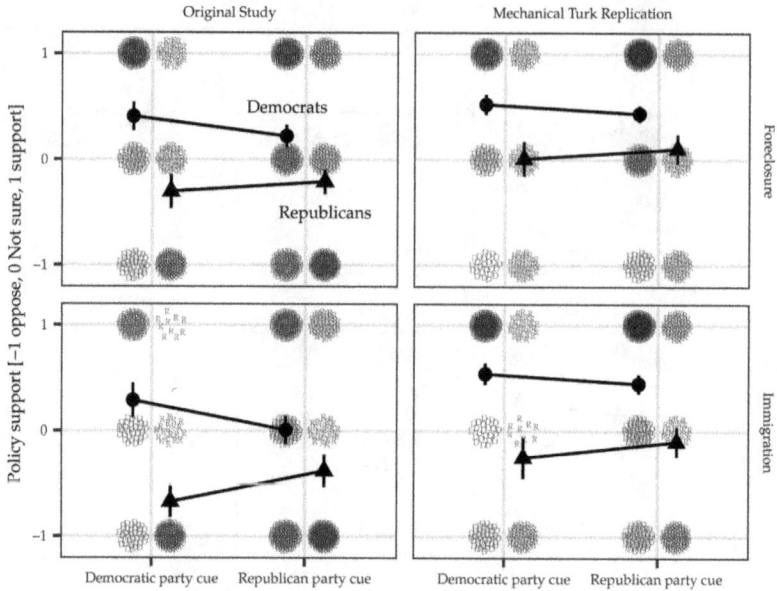

FIGURE 3.3. Reanalysis and replication of Nicholson (2012)

original study as well as an exact replication I conducted on Mechanical Turk. In both samples (and both policies), Democratic subjects who saw a Democratic cue supported the policy more than Democratic subjects who saw a Republican cue. For Republican subjects, this pattern was reversed. Unlike the effects of persuasive information, which are mostly homogeneous, the effects of group cues are often heterogeneous. Learning that Democrats like a policy makes Democratic respondents like the policy more but makes Republican respondents like it less (and vice versa).

Sometimes this pattern of treatment effect heterogeneity is attributed to a phenomenon dubbed "partisan motivated reasoning," according to which Republicans don't like the policies proposed by Democrats because they are motivated to keep their opinions consistent with their party identity (Bolsen, Druckman, and Cook 2014). The negative effects of the out-group cue are attributed to this motivated response rather than to the heuristic "information shortcut" account described above.

Since both theories predict oppositely signed treatment effects of party cues depending on partisan identification, some scholars have turned to how the magnitude of the effects varies with the level of political sophistication to adjudicate between them. Under the partisan motivated reasoning account, those who are high in political sophistication should be most influenced by party cues since they are theorized to have the strongest motivation to defend their partisan identities. Under the heuristic account, those higher in political sophistication should give less weight to "information shortcuts" because they know more about the content of policies. Bullock (2019) shows that the existing record on sophistication as a moderator of the effects of party cues yields some evidence in favor of the heuristic account, no evidence in favor of the partisan motivated reasoning account, and a sizable stack of evidence showing party cues work about the same for those with high and low levels of sophistication (see also Tappin, Pennycook, and Rand 2020a).

My own interpretation of the heterogeneous effects of group cues sides with the heuristic account rather than the partisan motivated reasoning account, though I grant that the observational equivalence of the two theories renders an empirical demonstration of one over the other more or less out of reach. I'll offer a more thorough critique of motivated reasoning in general in chapter 7, but for now I'll say that oppositely signed effects of group cues emphatically do *not* constitute evidence against the persuasion in parallel hypothesis, as group cues and persuasive information are separate classes of information treatments.

It is difficult to characterize how much of the political information space is filled with group cues versus persuasive information, and furthermore, the distinction between them is not always clear. In some cases, persuasive information might carry with it clues about the group membership of the speaker and their preferred policies. If a subject can infer group membership from the persuasive message, then some of the heuristic processes associated with group cues could apply to persuasive information as well. Further, group cues are often accompanied by at least a small dose of persuasive information, e.g., "Republicans prefer policy A for reason X." That said, a large portion of political communication is done "on the merits." Newspapers are filled with opinion pieces and editorials that make affirmative arguments for and against policies; they don't simply rehearse who is on what side of a dispute. And they may have good reason to omit the group cue information, since explicit group cues clearly turn off out-group members. This dynamic may explain why candidate advertisements rarely emphasize (or even mention) party (Neiheisel and Niebler 2013) and partisans sometimes masquerade as independents (Klar and Krupnikov 2016).

One important theoretical question concerns how the effect of persuasive information changes in the presence versus the absence of group cues. It could be that group cues "dominate" such that once people know where their group stands, information has no room to maneuver. On the other hand, persuasive information is always delivered within a broader information context in which people have at least vague knowledge of which groups support which policies. Since persuasive information can influence attitudes under those circumstances, it seems reasonable to imagine it could still do so when such knowledge is made more salient via a group cue. Two studies that have investigated this question empirically find that persuasive information continues to influence opinion even in the presence of party cues (Boudreau and MacKenzie 2014, 2018). Related work finds that while party cues certainly affect policy attitudes, they do not change the subject's relative ranking of alternative policies (Nicholson 2011; Bullock 2011).

Policy Attitudes and Beliefs

Our main focus will be the effects of persuasive information on a particular set of dependent variables: namely, the policy attitudes and beliefs that are the target of the persuasive information. The nature of attitudes has been the subject of intense study and debate within social psychology and political science alike, so this section will linger a moment on some of the important details of attitude theory as they relate to persuasion.

An attitude is a "learned predisposition to respond in a consistently favorable or unfavorable manner with respect to a given object" (Fishbein and Ajzen 1975, 10). Importantly, attitudes are *affective*. They represent a standing evaluation of an attitude object. Again, following Fishbein and Ajzen (1975), a belief "links an object to an attribute," with some level of certainty. They give the example of the belief "Russia is a totalitarian state," which links the object "Russia" to the attribute "totalitarian state." Fishbein and Azjen argue for an information processing model in which attitudes are based on the salient beliefs about an attitude object, i.e., that beliefs are causally prior to attitudes. Under this view, information treatments first change beliefs about an object, which then change attitudes toward that object. For instance, a treatment that increases the belief that Russia is a totalitarian state should decrease attitudes toward (affective evaluations of) Russia.

The dominant model of the survey response is the expectancy value model of attitudes (Ajzen and Fishbein 1980; Nelson, Oxley, and Clawson 1997; Chong and Druckman 2012). Under this model, subjects give a "top of the head" survey response that is the average of the considerations (also called belief-elements) that float to the surface as a respondent prepares to select one response over another (Taylor and Fiske 1978; Zaller 1992). I'll rely on a mildly tweaked version of this model, building on the variant described in Zaller (1992) as the "Receive-Accept-Sample" (RAS) model.

We'll leave aside the "receive" and "accept" parts of the RAS model and focus on the "sample" part.[4] Under this model, at the very moment of answering a survey question, a respondent takes a random sample of the attitude-relevant considerations that happen to be cognitively accessible and averages them. Each consideration is sampled with a different probability, reflecting differences in the relative accessibility of each consideration. Zaller uses the resulting variation in attitudes to explain "response instability," or the documented pattern that the same survey subjects, responding to the same survey questions, sometimes give different answers. They give different answers because different considerations happened to be sampled.

The weighted sampling analogy is a helpful heuristic (especially for analysts accustomed to thinking in terms of survey sampling methods!), even if it is not literally true. The analogy insists on the idea that the way considerations combine is *stochastic*, not fixed. People don't harbor a single, true attitude just waiting to be tapped by a survey taker. Instead, they take a quasi-random draw from a distribution of attitudes when they are asked for their opinion. Even if the real functions that people use to combine considerations are more complex and idiosyncratic, the analogy to weighted sampling accommodates two important features of the model: some considerations are more salient or accessible than others, and attitudes might bounce around as a result.

Respondents combine their considerations via a quasi-random process into a *latent* attitude, which I'll call y_i^*. The "*" notation indicates that this variable is not directly observable to the researcher. A latent attitude is translated into a measured attitude via a survey question Q: $y_i = Q(y_i^*)$. The latent attitude is the output of the process of combining the considerations that come to mind when a respondent thinks of an attitude object—"what do I think of increasing foreign aid?" The measured attitude is the piece of information recorded in a dataset when a respondent answers a survey question like "On a scale from 1 (very strongly oppose) to 7 (very strongly support), how strongly do you oppose or support increasing foreign aid?"

Measurement error occurs whenever measured attitudes differ from latent attitudes.[5] Survey measurement of attitudes is almost certainly riddled with measurement error. Respondents need to somehow condense their possibly amorphous and barely considered latent attitude toward a particular policy into the scale that researchers have provided for them. How should a subject choose a "5" versus a "6" on a 1–7 Likert scale? It's my hunch that subjects somehow understand what researchers are really asking for and try to be helpful. Respondents assist in the complex task of projecting latent policy attitudes (that do not exist on any particular scale) into the available response options. *Of course* the attitudes are measured with error, because we stretch and shear them into artificial measurement spaces. Nevertheless, these scales sort of work because people who actually do support policies tend to choose higher values, and people who actually do oppose policies choose lower values. When survey questions are designed well, we can hope that at the very least, latent and measured attitudes are positively correlated.

To translate this idea into formal notation, let's imagine that respondent i has k considerations indexed as $c_{i,1}$, $c_{i,2}$, . . . , $c_{i,k}$. Considerations can carry negative or positive valence: positively valenced considerations cause attitudes to become more positive, and negatively valenced considerations cause them to become more negative. The weights attached to each of the k considerations are written as $w_{i,1}$, $w_{i,2}$, . . . , $w_{i,k}$. The weights are sampling inclusion probabilities that can vary between zero and one: if w_k is 0.5, then c_k has a 50 percent chance of being sampled. If c_k is 1.0, then the consideration is always sampled. If it's 0.0, the consideration is never sampled.

As an example, imagine that a survey respondent i has $k = 10$ considerations, seven of which are positive and three of which are negative. All of the considerations have weights of at least 0.5, but the negative ones have slightly larger weights:

$$\mathbf{c}_i = c_{i,1}, c_{i,2}, c_{i,3}, c_{i,4}, c_{i,5}, c_{i,6}, c_{i,7}, c_{i,8}, c_{i,9}, c_{i,10}$$
$$= 1, 1, 1, 1, 1, 1, 1, -1, -1, -1$$
$$\mathbf{w}_i = w_{i,1}, w_{i,2}, w_{i,3}, w_{i,4}, w_{i,5}, w_{i,6}, w_{i,7}, w_{i,8}, w_{i,9}, w_{i,10}$$
$$= 0.5, 0.5, 0.5, 0.6, 0.6, 0.6, 0.7, 0.7, 0.7, 0.8$$

If we simulate this sampling process thousands of times, we don't just find one attitude for subject i; we see a distribution of possible attitudes, visualized in figure 3.4. On the left side of the plot we see the full distribution of latent attitudes. Most of the considerations are positive, so most of the time the latent attitude is positive. Rarely—but sometimes—only the three negative considerations are sampled, resulting in a latent attitude of −1. One defect of the sampling analogy is that we might be tempted to think that the "true" attitude is the average of this distribution and that the points above and below the average are random deviations, like sampling error around a population mean. That interpretation may have some use, but it obscures the fact that the above- and below-average values are just as "true" as the average value. On the right side of the plot, we map the latent attitudes into measured attitudes using a 1–7 Likert scale. This mapping is accomplished by the respondents themselves. They have to figure out which response option comes closest to the latent attitude they came up with this time. The figure imagines a more or less faithful mapping. Higher values of the latent attitude are never mapped to lower values of the measured attitude, for example. However, sometimes higher and lower values of the latent attitude are mapped to the same measured attitude, resulting in some (mild in this case) measurement error.

We can use this model to think about how persuasive information and group cues can affect attitudes. Persuasive information can operate most directly by giving people new considerations to think about when evaluating their latent attitudes. New positive considerations should have a positive impact on attitudes, and new negative considerations should do the opposite. Some kinds of persuasive treatments might not actually add new considerations, but might instead change how the existing considerations combine. Emphasis frames (Druckman 2001) are hypothesized to affect responses by "changing the weights," not the considerations themselves. Most persuasive treatments probably do a little of both adding new considerations and altering what is most salient when thinking about an attitude object.

Group cues also operate by adding new considerations. But instead

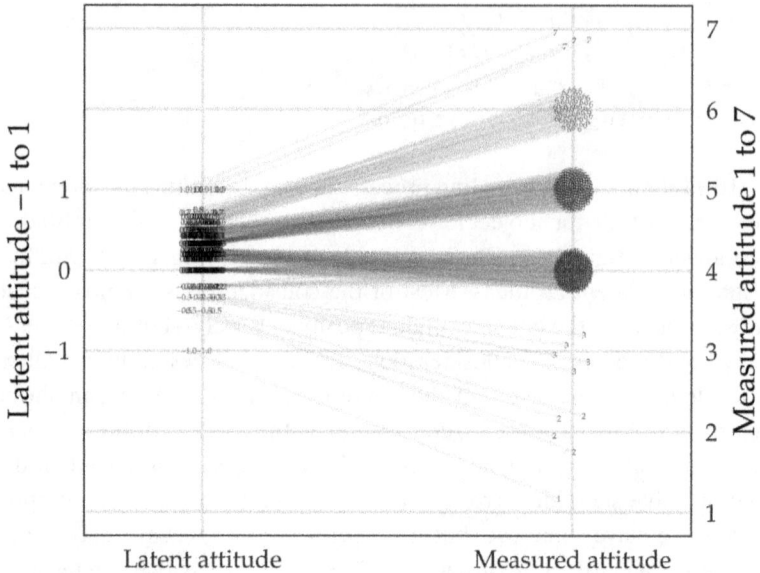

FIGURE 3.4. Illustration of the attitudes model
Note: This visualization of the attitudes model illustrates both response instability and measurement error. The subject's latent attitude can change depending on which of 10 considerations are sampled. The measurement procedure imperfectly maps the latent attitude into a measured attitude.

of adding new arguments for or against a policy, they add new considerations about which groups believe what. For in-group members, learning that their group supports a policy is a positive consideration, but it is a negative consideration for out-group members. Group cues may also serve to signal which considerations are the important ones, so group cues may also operate by changing how considerations are combined.

Affective Evaluations of Messages and Messengers

A word on what we are *not* measuring as the outcome variable in these experiments. Sometimes in experiments in which subjects are randomly assigned to see persuasive information or not, the outcome variable is some sort of rating of the information itself or the source from which the evidence came. For example, Kahan, Jenkins-Smith, and Braman (2011) show that subjects are less likely to agree that a source is an "expert" when that source presents counter-attitudinal arguments and evidence. The authors of that piece interpret this pattern as affirmative evidence for a "cultural cognition" model of information processing in which people reject evidence that is not congenial to their cultural worldview. Alternatively, we might interpret this more straightforwardly as evidence that people think those who disagree with them are wrong. In any case, we seek to measure the effect of persuasive information on attitudes about policies, not attitudes about the information itself.

As alluded to in chapter 2, people who give low ratings to sources or evidence with which they disagree can nevertheless be persuaded by them. For example, Nyhan et al. (2019) conducted an experiment in which subjects were randomly assigned to read either an article that repeats the uncorrected (and false) statement by President Trump in 2016 that crime in America was on the rise, or an article with the same statement corrected by FBI statistics that show crime was decreasing. Trump voters rated the article with the correction as less accurate; Clinton voters rated it as more accurate. Despite the two groups having oppositely signed effects on the perceived accuracy of the article, *both* groups update strongly about the American crime rate, always in the direction of information. Since both effects can occur simultaneously, we can't use ratings of the messenger or the message itself to study persuasion.

Positive

Positive means that the treatment effect on attitudes and beliefs is "in the direction" of the persuasive information. Negative means that the treatment effect is "away" from the direction of treatment. This distinction underscores why it's so crucial that the treatment information have a direction, because otherwise it's meaningless to say the treatment effect is positive.

Sometimes, the estimated average treatment effect will be close to zero, but it will be estimated with a fair amount of uncertainty. Sometimes the estimate itself is a negative number, but this shouldn't concern us too much. Negative estimates that are not statistically significant do not count as good evidence in favor of backlash. In recent years, scholars have fiercely debated whether the concept of statistical significance does more harm than good because it divides up effects as "real" or "noise" on the basis of an arbitrary threshold like $p \leq 0.05$ (e.g., Benjamin et al. 2018; McShane et al. 2019). However, to be sure that a treatment induces a negative treatment effect, at least for some subjects, we need some certainty threshold above which we can all agree that the true average effect in that group is in fact negative. Traditional hypothesis testing procedures provide a framework for doing so, so we'll proceed with it while acknowledging its shortcomings. Opponents of statistical significance should take some heart, though. The focus in this book will be almost exclusively on estimates and their precision, not on hypothesis tests.

Small

The treatment effects of information are small. The typical persuasive treatment—e.g., an op-ed, a speech, or an advertisement—has an (immediate) effect on opinions of about 5 percentage points. If you were 10 percent likely to support a policy (that is, not very much), a treatment might make you 15 percent likely to support it. Fifteen percent is more than 10 percent, but it's still not very likely. If the outcome is not binary, but is instead on a continuous scale, effects on the order of a tenth of a standard deviation are common. According to some classifications like Cohen's d (Cohen 1988), such effects are considered small. Effects are small because the typical information treatment adds only a handful of considerations to the mix already present in a person's mind, and the typical framing treatment only slightly alters how existing considerations are combined.

In some domains, of course, a 5-percentage-point effect might be considered enormous. Moving to a 95 percent success rate from a base rate of 90 percent in a lifesaving medical procedure would of course be of huge consequence. Political campaigns would be thrilled to discover a message that causes a 5-point shift in vote choice. Within the study of policy attitudes and opinions, however, such effects are considered relatively small.

Small effects make sense. If persuasive effects were larger, say more on the order of 30 percentage points than 5, we would constantly be flip-flopping our opinions in response to the latest argument we heard. Even the most open-minded among us don't completely switch positions after each conversation. Persuasive information causes small, marginal changes in opinion.

Durable

A major concern in the study of political persuasion is that the sorts of persuasive attempts that are so common in everyday political life may be ephemeral. When a person is exposed to a thirty-second advertisement in the middle of an engrossing television show, it's reasonable to imagine that the advertisement went in one ear and out the other. A similar critique has been leveled at survey experiments (Gaines, Kuklinski, and Quirk 2007). If a persuasive treatment can induce an average treatment effect of 5 percentage points immediately after treatment but the effect dissipates within a matter of minutes, the treatment may not be of great political importance.

The claim that the treatment effect of persuasive information is durable comes from survey experiments in which I measure attitudes both right after treatments are deployed and again after ten days. On average, I find that treatment effects are approximately half their original magnitude after ten days. In the one study I conducted that examined attitudes thirty days out, I found a remarkable degree of persistence. Broockman and Kalla (2016) found that a ten-minute doorstep conversation about transgender people had positive effects that endured for over three months. Green, Wilke, and Cooper (2020) showed that the effects of video dramatizations of violence against women on incidents of violence and willingness to report persisted at least eight months. Far more research is required to better understand the variation in over-time treatment effect decay, but for the moment we can at least say that treatment effects don't evaporate minutes after respondents are treated.

Everyone

So far we've said that treatment effects of persuasive information on policy attitudes and beliefs are positive, small, and durable. My claim is that these patterns are more or less universal. While we differ from person to person on many dimensions, our ability to update our opinions in response to persuasive information appears to be commonplace and shared.

That being said, I've only studied American adults who speak English and take surveys. I'm very sure that if I were to expose people who do not speak English to some of these treatments, their opinions would not change, for the simple reason that they wouldn't understand the first thing about them. I would bet, however, that if we translated the treatments into a language they do speak, we'd observe a similar pattern. I haven't shown this in a study, but it's my hunch. Because English-speaking Americans who take surveys are so wildly different from one to the next—and treatment effects are so homogeneous among *them*—I feel comfortable extrapolating from the American context to others, although confirmation of this hunch will have to await future experimentation.

More important than cross-linguistic differences, however, is the idea that there is a subset of the population that is fact-resistant. Depending on which side of the political divide you happen to be on, you may think that your hardest-core opponents are the ones who simply won't listen to reason. It may be uncomfortable to imagine that they too are able to update their opinions in response to information. Another common view is that it's easier to change the minds of people who are uncertain than those of people who are certain (e.g., Tesler 2015). Indeed, you may yourself be convinced that your mind is made up on most issues. All I can say is that I do not find evidence that any particular subgroups are impervious to persuasion.

Summary

This chapter has spent a long time on each of the words in the persuasion in parallel hypothesis that the treatment effect of persuasive information on target policy attitudes is small, positive, and durable for everyone. Distinguishing each of these terms from related terms has led to some auxiliary claims that go beyond the persuasion in parallel hypothesis, like the effect of persuasive information on non-target attitudes or the heterogeneous effects of group cues. Table 3.2 brings these predictions together in a three-by-two matrix. The rows of the table correspond to the three kinds of outcome variables: target policy attitudes, non-target policy attitudes, and attitudes toward the message and messenger. The columns of the table refer to the two kinds of political messaging treatments we've considered: persuasive information and group cues.

The persuasion in parallel hypothesis is in the upper left cell of the table: it concerns the effects of persuasive information on target attitudes.

TABLE 3.2 **Summary of predictions**

Outcome: Attitude	Treatment: Persuasive information	Treatment: Group cues
Affective evaluations of target policy	The effects of persuasive information on target policy attitudes are small, positive, and durable for everyone (this book).	The effects of group cues on target policy attitudes are positive for in-group members and negative for out-group members (Squire and Smith 1988; Bullock 2011; Nicholson 2012)
Affective evaluations of non-target policies	The effects of persuasive information on non-target policy attitudes are very close to zero (Hopkins and Mummolo 2017; Coppock and Green 2022)	The effects of group cues on non-target attitudes are presumably close to zero. I am unaware of direct evidence supporting this prediction.
Affective evaluations of the message and messenger	The effects of persuasive information on message and messenger attitudes are positive for policy proponents and negative for policy opponents (Kahan, Jenkins-Smith and Braman 2011; Nyhan et al. 2019)	When the message includes an endorsement of the group cue, the effects on message and messenger are positive for in-group members and negative for out-group members, presumably because the endorsement implies group affinity. I am unaware of direct evidence supporting this prediction.

The other treatment-outcome pairings in the matrix are interesting too, but they do not directly address the central concern of how people update their attitudes in response to new information.

Table 3.2 is useful for countering some empirical challenges to the persuasion in parallel hypothesis. If we find evidence that people dislike messages and messengers when the message is counter-attitudinal, we haven't shown that they "reject" counter-attitudinal information in the sense of not updating their targeted attitude in the appropriate direction. If we find evidence that people respond to group cues in opposite directions depending on their group membership, we haven't shown that they are motivated reasoners, just that they can make efficient use of information shortcuts. In order to falsify the persuasion in parallel hypothesis, we need to find evidence of oppositely signed treatment effects of persuasive information on target attitudes. The panel survey experiment design described in chapter 4 is well suited to finding such evidence, if indeed the hypothesis is incorrect.

CHAPTER FOUR

Research Design

To demonstrate that the treatment effect of persuasive information on target attitudes is small, positive, and durable for everyone, I will draw on evidence from a series of panel survey experiments, a research design that features random assignment of treatments and over-time measurement of attitudes. This chapter explains the attractive properties of panel survey experiments and also admits some ways in which they tell us less than we would want them to. This foray into the design details becomes somewhat technical in parts, so busy readers can skip ahead to the results in chapter 5 if they wish. That said, this chapter contains my response to many of the common objections people have raised when I've shared this work: Why aren't you doing mediation analysis? Are you saying the persuasive effects are exactly equal for all people? What does "parallel" even mean? For responses to those questions and more, read on.

I'll employ the *MIDA* framework I developed with Graeme Blair, Jasper Cooper, and Macartan Humphreys (Blair et al. 2019) to describe the panel survey experiment design. *MIDA* is an acronym for the four elements of a research design: a causal *M*odel of the world, an *I*nquiry about that model, a *D*ata strategy according to which researchers will gather or generate data, and an *A*nswer strategy according to which researchers will summarize the realized data to generate answers to the inquiry.

Briefly, the causal model I have in mind is the expectancy value model of attitudes described in chapter 3. The inquiries are the conditional average treatment effects of information on policy attitudes, conditioning on a series of characteristics like pre-treatment policy support, partisanship, ideology, and demographic attributes. The data strategy involves three elements: sampling schemes (some probability samples, some convenience), assignment protocols (almost exclusively simple random assignment to conditions with equal probabilities), and measurement procedures (multiple waves of survey questions measuring pre-treatment characteristics and post-treatment policy attitudes). The answer strategy flows directly from the data strategy: conditional average treatment effects are estimated by comparing *across* the randomly assigned partitions *within* the covariate subgroups.

These panel survey experiments are built to confront three core inference problems, with varying degrees of success: causal inference, descriptive inference, and generalization inference.

First, panel survey experiments tackle causal inference with random assignment, since in these experiments exposure to persuasive information can be directly controlled by the researcher. When treatments are not assigned at random, inferences are dogged by the possibility that those who do and don't come to be treated express different outcomes for reasons other than the treatment itself. In nonrandomized studies, we have to assume that we have figured out all the ways units might differ in advance of receiving the treatment, so we can compare treated and untreated units that *don't* otherwise differ. After all that, we have to convince skeptics that these assumptions are correct. Random assignment is much easier because we can rely mostly on experimental design rather than mostly on unverifiable assumptions.

Second, we have a descriptive inference problem insofar as measured attitudes are not equal to latent attitudes. The survey format allows us to measure attitudes by asking subjects about them. Answers to survey questions are imperfect measures of latent policy attitudes, but are perhaps preferable to alternatives that seek to infer attitudes on the basis of observed behavior or physiological responses. Inducing people to express their latent attitudes in closed-ended surveys can be more or less crude depending on the quality of the question. When questions are well designed, we assume that measured attitudes are positively correlated with latent attitudes. Further, in a panel survey experiment, subjects are interviewed multiple times post-treatment, allowing us to measure the evolution of attitudes over time. Exploiting the panel structure of the experiments introduces many additional design and analysis complications that I'll leave aside for now and pick back up in chapter 6.

Third, we seek to make inferences about Americans in general, which means we need to generalize the inferences we make from the few thousand people we do study to the millions of other people we don't. Survey experiments conducted on national probability samples are often praised because they marry the "internal validity" of an experiment with the "external validity" of a representative survey (Mutz 2011)—i.e., such studies will recover good estimates of population average treatment effects. That's true, but it's not representativeness *per se* we need in order to support the claim that persuasive information has positive effects for everyone. We need to do more than show that the average effect in the population is positive; we need to show that the average effects among the theoretically relevant subdivisions of the population are positive too. For that reason, within-sample subject diversity is especially important for this study, and we can achieve such diversity with both probability and convenience samples.

The remainder of this chapter will describe in detail each of the four elements of the panel survey experimental design (model, inquiry, data strategy, answer strategy) as they apply to the persuasion in parallel hypothesis.

Model

Chapter 3 laid out most of the elements of the causal model of persuasion I have in mind. At its core, the model presumes that persuasive information is one among many factors that influence policy attitudes. The effect of persuasive information is mediated by considerations (the belief-elements that come to mind when forming a latent attitude) and possibly by other psychological processes beyond considerations. Both observed and unobserved background factors influence three important variables: exposure to information, the set of mechanisms through which information affects attitudes, and the attitudes themselves. Figure 4.1 gives a representation of this model as a directed acyclic graph (DAG). DAGs were developed by Judea Pearl and his collaborators as a method for encoding some beliefs about causal structures. (See Pearl 2009 for a highly technical discussion of DAGs, or Pearl and Mackenzie 2018 for a gentler introduction.) For now, the important things to know

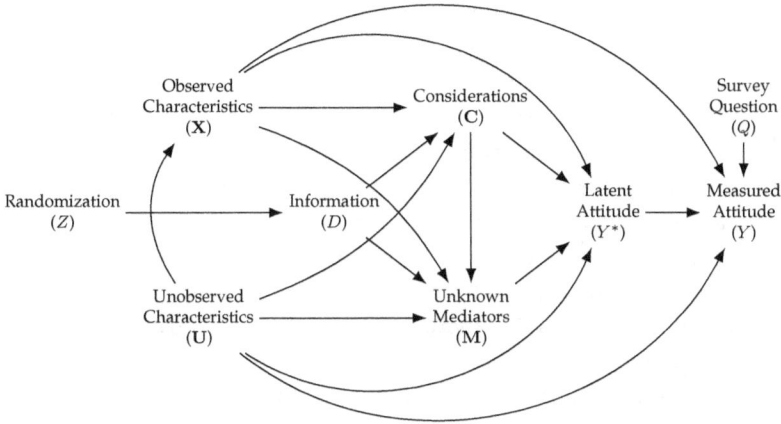

FIGURE 4.1. Model of persuasive information and policy attitudes in the panel survey experiment design

when reading a DAG are that the points are called nodes and the arrows between them are called edges. If an edge leads from node A to node B ($A \rightarrow B$), we know that according to the theory encoded in the DAG, variable B is causally affected by variable A.

Moving from left to right, let's take each node in the DAG in turn. Z is the assignment to information controlled by the researcher, and D is the treatment information itself whose effects on attitudes we're trying to learn about. No edges lead into Z because it is randomly assigned. An edge leads from Z into D because being assigned to see information absolutely does affect whether a unit actually sees information. No other edges lead into D besides Z, because in survey experiments where noncompliance isn't a problem, other causal variables don't interfere with the successful application of treatment.

X is the set of characteristics about subjects that we can measure. This set includes demographic characteristics like age, gender, race, and ethnicity; social characteristics like education, income, and religious affiliation; political characteristics like partisanship and interest in politics; and psychological variables like "need for cognition" (Cacioppo and Petty 1982) and personality. These are the pre-treatment variables that show up in a dataset if we measure them. By contrast, U is the set of *unobserved* characteristics about subjects that do not appear in any datasets but are nevertheless real. The set of things in U is immense—it includes the full life experience and circumstance of subjects. To contemplate the sort of things that might be in **U**, think about a person who has your same demographic, social, political, and personality characteristics. That person might be a work colleague or someone you knew from school. Despite being very similar in these measured characteristics, I'm sure that you differ in thousands of unmeasured ways, some of which are unimportant but others of which are consequential. The arrow connecting **U** to **X** signifies that the measured variables all have causal determinants, but they are possibly unknown and definitely unobserved. If we manage to measure something in **U**, then it joins its measured cousins in **X**, but there will always be other variables in **U** that elude measurement.

Information D affects latent policy attitudes Y^* through intermediate variables, or mediators. The variables along the path from information to latent attitudes represent *information processing.* Zaller's (1992) "Receive-Accept-Sample" model (described and elaborated in chapter 3) posits that considerations **C** are the key intermediaries in information processing. Information treatments add new considerations and framing treatments change the functional form (the weights) according to which they are combined into latent attitudes. Alternative theories of information processing offer different points of view on what other variables **M** may mediate the effects of D on Y^*. Theories of motivated reasoning posit that various cognitive and affective processes condition how information is incorporated into attitudes. Bayesian theories of information processing propose that people interpret evidence according to a likelihood function and that the resulting likelihood is combined with a prior attitude to generate a posterior attitude. I've grouped these mediators under the label **M** and described them as "unknown," for reasons I will describe in chapter 7, along with fuller discussions of motivated and Bayesian reasoning.

In addition to the influence of information (however it may be mediated), the latent attitude Y^* is also affected by **X** and **U**. The measured attitude Y is obviously affected by the latent attitude Y^* and by the survey question Q we use to measure attitudes. It's perhaps unfamiliar to think of survey questions and latent attitudes as jointly causing the measured attitude, but the graphical representation helps to tease out these subtleties. We also allow **X** and **U** to affect the measured outcome separately from the latent outcome because we could imagine that different kinds of people (attentive versus inattentive, for example) might respond to the survey question differently, even if they had the same latent attitude.

The arrows that are missing from DAGs are equally if not more important than the arrows that are present, since the absence of an arrow between two nodes encodes the substantive assumption that neither variable affects the other. No edges lead into the assignment Z and survey question Q, which is justified because they are both directly set by the researcher in the data strategy. An important further assumption is that Q only affects the measured attitude Y and not the latent attitude Y^* or any of the other variables in the causal process that result in the latent attitude. Substantively, this assumption means that Q is not itself a treatment that changes considerations or how they are combined. If this assumption is wrong (Q does change attitudes), we still learn about the effect of the treatment D since the assignment is randomized, but it does color our interpretation.

Inquiry

Inquiries are questions that can be stated in terms of the model. The model represented in figure 4.1 could support many different research questions. We might be interested in the descriptive question of how variables in $\mathbf{X}$ covary with Y. We might want to study the measurement properties of Q, i.e., how strongly related the measured variable Y is to the latent variable Y^*. We might be interested in studying the mediators through which D affects Y.

My inquiry concerns the total effect of D on Y and how it might vary from individual to individual. It's the total effect because the primary interest is not each of the pathways by which D affects Y, but instead the whole effect, regardless of how it may be transmitted. The theoretical claim from chapter 3 was that the effect of persuasive information is small, positive, and durable for everyone. Stated in terms of the model, that claim is

$$\tau_{large} > y_i^*(D = 1) - y_i^*(D = 0) = \tau_i^* > 0, \forall_i$$

This expression says that the difference between the treated and untreated potential outcomes (τ_i^*) is smaller than some "large" value τ_{large} but is bigger than zero. Notice that the potential outcomes are defined with respect to the latent attitude and that the claim is about every subject *i*. Evaluating this claim would require knowing the value of τ_i^* for all subjects—so our inquiry is the vector of individual-level treatment effects.

As a theoretical target of inference, this inquiry—the full set of individual-level effects—is unrivaled. It is exactly what the claim is about and would be wonderful to know. However, no research design could ever yield such knowledge. First, it would require supernatural powers of measurement, amounting to the ability to peer directly into subjects' minds to recover Y^* without help from a survey question Q. Second, it would require a godlike talent for perceiving parallel universes, since in order to know τ_i^*, we'd need to know both $y_i^*(1)$ and $y_i^*(0)$ the latent potential outcomes. Last, we'd need to be able to perform these miracles for all people, past, present, and future. For mere mortals, the fundamental problems of causal inference, descriptive inference, and generalization inference get in the way.

In light of these insuperable limitations, we might redefine our inquiry to be the *average* treatment effect (ATE) on the *measured* attitude:

$$ATE = \frac{\sum_1^N y_i(1) - y_i(0)}{N}$$

This inquiry is defined not with respect to the latent attitude Y^*, but instead with respect to the measured attitude Y. Even though it's still defined in terms of potential outcomes, only one of which we get to see, this inquiry can be well estimated using standard experimental designs. The treatment group reports a random sample of the $y_i(1)$'s, so we can construct an unbiased estimate of the *average* $y_i(1)$; the control group reports a random sample of the $y_i(0)$'s, so we can estimate the average $y_i(0)$ as well. We estimate the ATE by taking the difference between the average $y_i(1)$ and the average $y_i(0)$.

But this inquiry has now swung too far in the other direction. The ATE on the measured attitude is of course interesting, but it doesn't get to the heart of persuasion in parallel, because we need to demonstrate that the effect is similar for different types of people. For this we turn to conditional average treatment effects, or CATEs. A CATE is just an ATE among a subgroup of subjects, usually defined in terms of the values of the variables in **X**.

I'll consider CATEs according to many subdivisions. In some cases, I have pre-treatment measures of policy support, so I can divide the subject pool into policy-specific proponents and opponents. In other cases, I don't have access to the pre-treatment level of support, but I have the next best thing: subject partisanship. Because so much political disagreement in America occurs along partisan lines, subject partisanship is highly predictive of policy support in many (but not all) domains. In addition to policy support and partisanship, I will estimate CATEs by age, gender, race, ideology, and education.

The CATEs themselves form the inquiry. If they are positive (i.e., in the direction of information) and small, then we will have generated evidence in favor of the main claim. If for some treatments the CATE is positive for one subgroup but negative for another, we will have evidence against persuasion in parallel.

Because the CATEs are defined over groups of subjects and not at the individual level, this inquiry is necessarily second best. Even if the CATEs according to the covariates I have measured are all positive, I can't rule out the possibility that some individual subjects experience negative treatment effects, but I just don't have access to a covariate that distinguishes these subjects from others. This problem has no solution, because the set of possibilities is immense and checking them all would be impossible. I take comfort in the fact that most proposals for other ways to subdivide the population are correlated (often strongly) with the political and demographic covariates that I do use.

What about Mediated Effects?

The model in figure 4.1 posits that the effect of information on attitudes is mediated by considerations and by other potential intermediate variables. I've chosen to focus on the total effect of information on attitudes, inclusive of any and all mediation, rather than on the fraction of the effect that is due to considerations or other mediators.

The main reason why is that empirically demonstrating causal mediation is extraordinarily difficult if not impossible. Estimators of mediation quantities are prone to bias (Bullock, Green, and Ha 2010; Bullock and Ha 2011; Gerber and Green 2012), except when the usually implausible assumption of "sequential ignorability" is met (Imai et al. 2011). Sequential ignorability is so named because it requires that a *sequence* of variables be as-if randomly assigned. First, the treatment variable (in our case, exposure to persuasive information D) must be as-if randomly assigned. This requirement is easily satisfied by actually randomly assigning exposure to treatment. This first assumption is encoded in figure 4.1 by the absence of edges leading from any of the variables (including U and X) into Z. Second, within each treatment condition, the value of each mediator itself must be as-if randomly assigned (possibly after statistical adjustment for the observed variables in X). This second ignorability assumption is not justified in any way by the random assignment of the treatment. To justify making this second assumption, we have to imagine that there are not variables in U that affect both the mediators and the outcome. This isn't a matter of controlling for more variables; it's a matter of asserting that there are no more variables to control for. In terms of figure 4.1, this assumption amounts to deleting the edge from U to M. The quality of the inferences about the mechanisms by which treatments influence outcomes depends crucially on whether this second requirement of the sequential ignorability assumption is met. In my own experience, I have rarely been convinced of a sequential ignorability assumption. If the researchers were worried enough about ignorability of the treatment variable to go to the trouble of assigning it at random, it seems inconsistent to brush off those concerns when it comes to the mediators.

What about Differences-in-CATEs?

The title of the book is *Persuasion in Parallel*, which implies more than just positive effects for everyone: it implies that the effects are similarly sized. Taken literally, the title means that the effects are not just similar, but identical. The standard approach for assessing such a claim would be to specify an additional set of inquiries, the *differences-in-CATEs*, and to show that they are close to zero. Differences-in-CATEs are perfectly natural targets of inference, and we definitely have the technology to estimate such differences and to report whether or not they are significant.

I resist the focus on differences-in-CATEs for three reasons.

First, they have no causal interpretation, since the variables we condition on are pre-treatment covariates that are not randomly assigned. If we find that proponents and opponents exhibit different responses to treatment, we can't say that this difference is caused by the differences in initial policy views. The difference is a descriptive quantity, not a causal quantity. We can of course be interested in descriptive inquiries, so this reason on its own isn't sufficient.

A second, slightly better reason is that the statistical power to detect differences-in-CATEs (power is the probability of finding a statistically significant difference) is typically abysmal. In a two-arm experiment with a binary outcome and a binary covariate that evenly divides the sample, we would need about 3,000 subjects to achieve 80 percent power to detect a 10-percentage-point difference-in-CATEs. A 10-point difference in effects is huge, and most differences-in-CATEs are likely to be smaller than that. In other words, another reason to spend less effort on differences-in-CATEs is that our experiments do a noisy job of measuring them.

The third reason to not overemphasize the differences-in-CATEs is subtler and strikes at the heart of what it means for treatment effects to be homogeneous or heterogeneous. It turns out that the measurement scale itself can determine whether two CATEs are the same or different. In one scale the effects may be deemed homogeneous while in another scale they are found to be heterogeneous.[1]

What Does Parallel Even Mean?

Very frustratingly, these shifting sands of what it means for treatment effects to be either heterogeneous or homogeneous throws the very concept of parallel shifts in attitudes into disarray. What is parallel in one scale might not be parallel in a different scale. The choice of scale then determines whether the hypothesis is supported or not, which is obviously unsatisfying.

To see this, imagine that treatment effects are homogeneous in the latent scale: $y_i^*(0) + \tau^*$. In words, this expression means that the treated outcome is the control outcome plus a constant τ^* for all units, which is to say that effects are exactly homogeneous. But we don't get to see Y^*, we only get to see Y, the attitude as measured by a survey question Q. Let's imagine that Q is a function that returns 1 or 0 depending on whether Y^* is above a cutoff c:

$$Q(y_i^*) = \begin{cases} 1 & \text{if } y_i^* \geq c \\ 0 & \text{otherwise} \end{cases}$$

With a binary outcome like this, we can divide up subjects into four groups according to their potential outcomes, as shown in table 4.1. Following the labels given in Humphreys and Jacobs (2015), an adverse type is a subject who would respond with 1 if they were not treated but with 0 if they were treated. Adverse types have a treatment effect of −1. Bene-

TABLE 4.1 **Possible types when measurements are binary**

Type	$y_i(0)$	$y_i(1)$	τ_i
Adverse	1	0	−1
Beneficial	0	1	1
Chronic	0	0	0
Destined	1	1	0

ficial types, on the other hand, express a 0 if untreated but a 1 if treated, for a positive treatment effect of +1. Chronic types express 0 regardless of their treatment status, and destined types express 1 regardless of their treatment status, so both chronic and destined types have a treatment effect of 0.

In our example, all subjects have a (positive) treatment effect of exactly τ^* in the latent scale, but not all are in the "beneficial" category according to the measured scale. The chronic types are those whose untreated potential outcomes are well below the cutoff—they express a zero in both cases. The opposite holds for the destined types—their y_i (0) was already equal to 1, so it appears according to the measurement that nothing changed. It's only those subjects who are just below the cutoff for whom the treatment causes a change in measured outcomes. Even though treatment effects are homogeneous in the latent scale, they are heterogeneous in the measured scale.

The problem is not restricted to binary outcomes, either. If the outcome is measured on a 1–7 Likert scale and there are two treatment conditions, there are $7^2 = 49$ subject types (we'll skip writing them out and giving them clever names). Unless by some crazy coincidence the sample is exclusively composed of subjects whose treatment effects (in terms of the measured outcomes) are exactly the same, then we might conclude that persuasion does not occur in parallel.

This issue extends directly to the comparison of conditional average treatment effects. To make things concrete, consider the example cooked up in figure 4.2. In the left facet, we see the latent treated and untreated outcomes for Democrats and Republicans. The CATEs for both groups are set to 0.2 SDs. When the latent attitudes get measured, however, different proportions of each group are shifted across the binary measurement cutoff at 0 on the latent scale. In the right facet, we see that the CATEs expressed in the measured outcomes are twice as large for Republicans as for Democrats, even though the treatment "re-

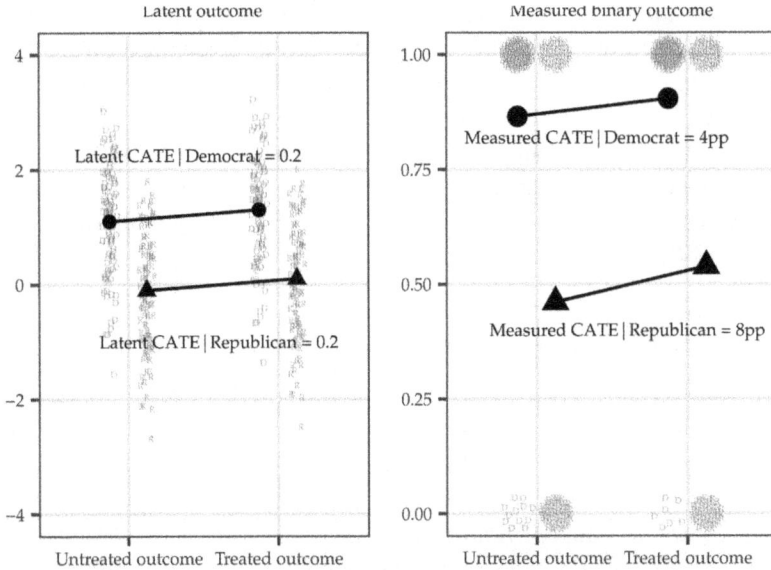

FIGURE 4.2. CATEs on measured outcomes can be different even if CATEs on latent outcomes are equal

ally" affects both groups by exactly the same amount. This doubling is a consequence of the measurement scale, not of any actual differences in treatment response.

What's the upshot of all this? I think it means we have to be generous with our conceptualization of "parallel." When I say that persuasion occurs in parallel, I don't mean that literally every subject has exactly the same response to treatment, and I don't mean that every group of subjects has exactly the same CATE. As the preceding example showed, the ground can shift beneath our feet about what "sameness" even is. We will need to fall back on a largely qualitative sense of when two CATEs are sufficiently similar that it's scientifically useful to say that they are about the same. In general, we pick outcome scales that have the property that changes at the low end of the scale are qualitatively similar to equivalent changes at the high end of the scale. Indeed, some measurement models *assume* that changes of the same size have the same substantive meaning, so measurement scales are constructed or selected so that they have this property.

To preview my approach to this problem, my data strategy will measure treatment effects in the "raw" measurement scales in the hope that the measurement scales were chosen well in the first place. I will describe treatment effects on binary outcomes in percentage points and treatment effects on Likert scales in scale points. In a few cases, I will standardize outcomes by dividing all outcomes by the standard deviation in the control group. Since this is a linear transformation, it doesn't alter the relative magnitudes of the CATEs. While I think this overall approach makes good sense, I also acknowledge that interpretations might differ.

What about Hidden Moderators?

Focusing on CATEs will allow us to assess whether effects are similar for many different *groups* of people, but of course we can't know how the effects vary across the different people *within* those groups. The fact that groups classified on the basis of partisanship, ideology, race, gender, age, education, or prior attitudes experience similar conditional average treatment effects does not mean that every single member of those groups responds to treatment identically. It's possible that even within groups that seem homogeneous with respect to their baseline attitudes, some unmeasured dimension distinguishes the persuadable from the unpersuadable. Not only is it possible, it must almost certainly be true that such a moderator exists but goes unrecorded in my experiments.

To see this, let's briefly return to the model of types in table 4.1. Destined types always respond $y_i = 1$ regardless of whether they get the treatment or not. Chronic types always respond $y_i = 0$. It's only the Adverse and Beneficial types that actually change their views in response to treatment: A types experience a negative effect while B types experience a positive effect. The average treatment effect in a group of people is equal to the proportion of B types minus the proportion of A types.

The hidden moderator is the "type" variable itself. If only we could reliably measure whether people are A, B, C, or D types, we could partition people into those who can be persuaded and those who can't be. The reason we can't just ask subjects to report their type is the fundamental problem of causal inference. None of us, not even the subjects themselves, knows for certain how they would have responded had the treatment been set to a different level.[2]

At best, we can search for variables that *correlate* with type, because those variables either causally determine or merely predict what type a person is. Many theories of persuasion offer proposals for such variables, but we lack clear theory or evidence for a moderator that predicts treatment effect heterogeneity across a reasonably broad class of treatments and outcomes. My hunch is that if ever such a moderator is discovered, it will not be a trait-type variable like personality, trait emotions, moral foundations, or need for cognition. The reason for my skepticism is that I suspect that whether or not a person is a B type will vary depending on characteristics of the treatment and characteristics of the outcome. Someone who is persuadable on one issue might not be persuadable on another, so person-constant variables are unlikely to solve the mystery. It's possible that a special three-way match between an argument, an issue, and a person is required for successful persuasion, though of course predicting when that special match will arise would be extraordinarily difficult.

The true hidden moderator may also be a mundane consequence of how we measure outcomes with surveys. Surveys ask subjects to map their latent attitudes into discrete survey categories. The idiosyncratic thresholds subjects use when rendering their survey responses might then be the missing variable that distinguishes types. Those thresholds are not obviously theoretically interesting in and of themselves. For example, if minor tweaks to the wording of a question perturb whether subjects' latent potential outcomes fall above or below a threshold, then whether a subject is a B or a D type is more an artifact of measurement than a politically important characteristic.

Despite all this hand-wringing about what is and is not possible to know about individual-level treatment effects, it's worth remarking on the political importance of the group-level effects we can estimate. Grant for the moment that the share of A types is close to or exactly zero because we don't think backlash occurs. Groups then are made up of people who either support the policy regardless of treatment (D types), oppose the policy regardless of treatment (C types), or support the policy if and only if they get the treatment (B types). Since average treatment effects are small, we know that groups are mostly made up of C and D types. Opposing political groups typically have very different shares of C and D types. Most Republicans will "chronically" oppose liberal policies while most Democrats are "destined" to support them. Under the persuasion in parallel hypothesis, both partisan groups have something in common: they all count a small number of B types in their ranks, but we lack the information to predict which ones they are. The political implication is that we should attempt to persuade broadly rather than expend effort trying to microtarget the *B* types.

Data Strategy

The data strategy encompasses what researchers *do* in the world to collect or generate information about it. The data strategy includes three basic elements: sampling (how units are chosen to be included in the study), assignment (how units are assigned to treatment conditions), and measurement (the survey questions and any standardization or post-data-collection transformations).

Sampling of Subjects

Nearly all of the subjects in the survey experiments that follow were recruited via online survey platforms. Table 4.2 enumerates the studies and indicates the source of subjects.

The highest-quality (and most expensive) source used in this book is the survey firm GfK, which produces nationally representative samples through a combination of probability sampling from their large panel of subjects and post-stratification weights. All of the GfK samples were collected in collaboration with Time-sharing Experiments for the Social Sciences (TESS), a program funded by the National Science Foundation. In terms of the demographic variables measured by the census, the (weighted) GfK samples are very close to national targets. Whether the samples are nationally representative in terms of unobservable variables is a matter of conjecture. The weights might account for the important drivers of selection into the GfK panel, but they might not. For example, if the politically interested are more likely to take surveys even after accounting for observable demographics, even high-quality samples like those constructed by GfK may not be perfectly representative.

The lowest-quality (and least expensive) survey platform I used is Amazon's Mechanical Turk (MTurk) platform. The main purpose of the MTurk platform is to serve as an online labor market for small digital tasks like tagging photos or entering data. Social scientists were drawn to MTurk because the platform enabled them to pay for another small digital task—answering an online survey—quickly and easily. MTurk

TABLE 4.2 **Sample sources and sizes for 23 persuasion survey experiments**

Original studies

Capital punishment	Redesign of Lord, Ross, and Lepper (1979)	MTurk workers	686
Gun control	Guess and Coppock (2018)	GfK panelists	2,678
Minimum wage	Guess and Coppock (2018)	MTurk workers	1,169
Newspaper op-eds	Coppock, Ekins, and Kirby (2018)	Policy professionals	2,181
		MTurk workers	3,571

Replications and reanalyses

Expert economists	Johnston and Ballard (2016)	Original study reanalysis (GfK)	2,071
		MTurk replication	2,985
Frame breadth	Hopkins and Mummolo (2017)	Original study reanalysis (GfK)	3,318
		GfK replication	3,213
		MTurk replication	2,972
Free trade	Hiscox (2006)	Original study reanalysis	1,610
		GfK replication	2,123
		MTurk replication	2,972
		Lucid replication	3,504
Immigration frames	Brader, Valentino, and Suhay (2008)	Original study (GfK)	354
		MTurk replication	2,138
Patriot Act	Chong and Druckman (2010)	Original study (Bovitz)	1,302
		MTurk replication	1,891

TESS reanalyses

Drone strikes	Kreps and Wallace (2016)	Original study (GfK)	2,394
Income inequality	Trump and White (2018)	Original study (GfK)	1,020
Job loss	Mutz (2017)	Original study (GfK)	1,011
Political equality	Flavin (2011)	Original study (GfK)	2,015
Venue effects	Gash and Murakami (2009)	Original study (GfK)	1,022

samples have been criticized from every conceivable angle. The samples skew young, male, and liberal (Huff and Tingley 2015). Some scholars are concerned that MTurk is overfished (Stewart et al. 2015), that some respondents have become professional survey-takers (Chandler et al. 2015), and that respondents may be especially prone to sensitivity biases that may distort answers toward socially preferred responses (Behrend et al. 2011).

These concerns have to be balanced against the mounting evidence that survey experiments conducted with MTurk samples return similar answers to experiments conducted on nationally representative samples. An early entry in this literature is Berinsky, Huber, and Lenz (2012), which presented successful replications of classic political science survey experiments on the platform. Mullinix et al. (2015) and Coppock (2019) compared modern social science experiments conducted on the TESS platform to MTurk replications, and both found a high degree of correspondence. Coppock, Leeper, and Mullinix (2018) found that this correspondence extends beyond overall average effects to the average effects within subgroups defined by demographic categories. If a national probability sample finds a large treatment effect among Republicans, our best guess is that an MTurk sample will find a large treatment effect among Republicans too.

One study uses Lucid, another source of online convenience samples. Lucid is an aggregator of survey respondents from many sources. The main advantage of Lucid over MTurk is its ability to quota sample subjects to match census margins. In Coppock and McClellan (2019), my co-author Oliver McClellan and I validate the use of Lucid for survey experiments by replicating the same experiments Berinsky, Huber, and Lenz (2012) used to validate MTurk.

In large part, the discussion of whether the sample is representative (in the sense of approximating a random sample of the US population at a given moment in time) is beside the point. To begin with, even the samples that are constructed to be representative must be reweighted using statistical models that are only as good as their assumptions. So-called representative samples are usually just assumed to be representative after statistical adjustment; we don't know that they actually are. Secondly, MTurk workers are people too, and I expect them to be susceptible to persuasive information just like everyone else. In Coppock and McClellan (2019), we borrow the "fit-for-purpose" framework from the survey sampling literature to argue that what matters most for survey experiments is whether the theoretical claims *also* apply to the people in the survey, even if the people in the survey look different, on average, from the national population. Since the theoretical expectation here is that everyone responds to persuasive information by updating their attitudes in the direction of information, the theory applies to MTurkers and respondents on Lucid as well as it does to the kinds of people who respond to a nationally representative survey.

Assignment of Information

By far the most important feature of the data strategy used in these experiments is random assignment. Subjects couldn't choose what persuasive information to see, nor were all subjects deterministically assigned to read the same information. *Some* but not *all* subjects were exposed to the persuasive information, and who saw what was determined by random chance.

The substance of the persuasive information varies from study to study, as described in table 4.2. The table is split into three sections. The top panel shows the experiments that I designed (or redesigned, in the case of the capital punishment study) with coauthors. These studies were specifically designed with the estimation of the conditional average effects of persuasive information in mind. The middle panel collects together a set of five studies that were designed by others for their own purposes. I both reanalyze the original data for these five studies and replicate the experiments on fresh samples.[3]

Replication has many benefits. First and foremost, replicators benefit enormously from the original authors' care and expertise. These studies are all well designed and address important political science questions, as evidenced by their placement in nice journals. Coming up with clear persuasive information treatments and appropriate outcome measures is time-consuming and theoretically challenging. I am grateful to be able to build on the effort of others. Second, replications like these hold most design features constant while varying the subjects (and the research team). In a commonly used framework, the similarity of units, treatments, outcomes, and settings determines the extent to which findings generalize across settings (Cronbach 1982, 1986). The replications in this book are exact in the sense that the treatments, outcomes, and settings are identical across study versions. I use precisely the same treatment stimuli and outcome questions as the originals. Since all studies are conducted online, the settings are as similar as possible. Under the assumption that I incorporated all these important design features in my replication (and that minor things like fonts and button shapes are irrelevant), the only difference should be the subjects themselves. This feature allows us to explore effect heterogeneity by sample type. Third, because I have access to the original datasets as well as my replication datasets, I can analyze originals and replications using the exact same answer strategy. Sometimes the results of original studies and replications can diverge because original authors and replicators answer slightly different questions, but that problem is avoided here. Finally, the large number of original-replication pairs collected here serves as a kind of meta-replication. We can see if the original-replication correspondence observed for one pair replicates in the others.

The bottom panel of table 4.2 lists five studies that I reanalyzed but did not replicate myself. The main reason to include these studies is to defend against the criticism that I just happened to pick a set of studies to replicate for which the persuasion in parallel finding holds. To pre-empt this concern, I went looking for more persuasion studies.

The social scientific record is bursting with examples of survey experiments in which a persuasive treatment is allocated at random. A full accounting of all such experiments would be prohibitively time-consuming, so I restricted my search for persuasion experiments to the vast cache of experimental datasets at Time-sharing Experiments for the Social Sciences (TESS). Funded by the National Science Foundation, TESS helps researchers conduct studies on nationally representative samples of the US. National samples are extremely expensive to collect, so TESS offers a vital public service to researchers who want to scale up their survey experiments beyond online convenience samples. TESS also has two other great features beyond generous funding for survey experimenters. First, all proposals for TESS are peer-reviewed and revised prior to data collection, so these studies tend to be well theorized and well designed. Second, TESS makes all raw study data publicly available on their website one year after collection, so we can mine the TESS website for persuasion experiments and reanalyze them using a common set of procedures.

I selected a set of TESS studies and preregistered (before seeing the data) how I would reanalyze them at the registration archive hosted by Evidence in Governance and Politics (egap.org). The main selection criterion was that the randomized treatment had to be persuasive information. Persuasive information is information that has a *target* and a *direction* (see the definition given in chapter 2). This criterion ruled out many kinds of experiments on TESS. List experiments are a tool for measuring the prevalence of a sensitive item, so they were out. Conjoint experiments are for measuring multidimensional preferences over things like job candidates, politicians, or policies, not the effect of persuasive treatments. Vignette experiments typically ask subjects to react to a scenario or judge the reactions of others in a scenario. Some experiments on TESS randomly assign subjects to write an essay about their self-identity or a time that they experienced a particular emotion. While these treatments may influence attitudes, the treatments themselves don't aim to move a target policy attitude in a particular direction. Finally, many persuasion experiments on TESS feature explicit partisan cues, which are also ruled out by the definition of persuasive information.

In the interest of full disclosure, I preregistered the reanalysis of twelve studies, but only two of those twelve are included here. Upon closer inspection of the designs, I found that the other ten did not meet the definitions laid out in chapter 3. The treatments weren't persuasion treatments in the sense of having both a target attitude and a direction, or if they were, in some cases the experiments didn't measure the target attitude, usually because studying persuasion was not the main goal of the original researchers. Two replications is not enough, so I then added three more TESS studies that did meet the inclusion criteria. None of these choices was made on the basis of the results; nevertheless, I wish I had spent more effort on the pre-analysis plan to be sure of the set of studies. I can, however, report that I followed the planned analysis procedures for each study faithfully, even though the set of studies included is not what I had planned.

Measurement of Policy Attitudes

The studies use a variety of survey questions to measure latent attitudes. Most are Likert scales like "Do you favor or oppose raising the federal minimum wage? [1: Very much opposed, 7: Very much in favor]." The set of studies includes four-, five-, and seven-point scales, reflecting the heterogeneity in previous authors' measurement preferences. Some outcomes are binary, such as "Do you favor or oppose increasing trade with other nations? [0: oppose, 1: favor]." In one case, the outcome is a properly continuous policy preference: "What do you think the federal minimum wage should be? [$0.00–$25.00]"

The outcomes as measured probably vary in terms of how well they correlate with the latent attitudes they are designed to measure, though because we don't have access to the latent attitude, we can't tell which ones are better or worse.

A common objection to survey measurement of attitudes in experimental studies is that apparent treatment effects might be due to a "demand effect" wherein treatment group subjects feel compelled to give the answer they think experimenters want to hear. While demand effects have certainly occurred,[4] the most recent scholarship appears to show that they are rare in survey experimental work (White et al. 2018; Mummolo and Peterson 2019; De Quidt, Haushofer, and Roth 2018). Alternatively, survey measures might be distorted by sensitivity bias wherein subjects falsely report their attitudes for fear of judgment by the researcher or others. With my collaborators Graeme Blair and Marga-ret Moor, I tried to assess the extent of this problem by comparing sup-posedly bias-free estimates from list experiments with direct questions, finding limited evidence of sensitivity bias except in cases where subjects had a legitimate reason to worry about someone finding out their an-swers (Blair, Coppock, and Moor 2020). The studies reported here were conducted anonymously online and did not touch on obviously sensitive topics, so I think sensitivity is not likely to be an important source of bias.

Answer Strategy

The answer strategy describes how the data will be summarized once it has been collected in order to render an answer to the inquiry. Methods textbooks overflow with an abundance of answer strategies to choose from; they all have their strengths and weaknesses.

Because these studies all feature random assignment, we can rely on the bread-and-butter answer strategies of difference-in-means and Or-dinary Least Squares (OLS), estimated among subsets of the data de-pending on pre-treatment covariates like partisanship and proponent/opponent status. The reason to use OLS is to adjust for pre-treatment outcomes in order to increase the precision of the treatment effect es-timates, not to adjust for confounding factors (Gerber and Green 2012, chapter 4). The treatment variable is not confounded by those factors be-cause it is randomized.

As described in the data strategy section, some of the outcomes are binary and some are ordinal. Many scholars were taught in their quan-titative methods courses that OLS is not appropriate in such cases and that analysts should opt for generalized linear models like logit, probit, or ordered probit instead. I will decline to estimate such models for two main reasons. First, those procedures rely on additional modeling as-sumptions that are not rooted in the design (Freedman 2008). Second, there is nothing wrong with the difference-in-means or OLS estimates. They are both consistent for the ATE (or CATE) regardless of the out-come space. The common methods advice to use nonlinear models for binary or ordinal outcomes may or may not apply in other research set-tings, but it need not be followed in the case of experiments when the in-quiry is an average causal effect.[5]

In addition to the statistical results, the principal way I will summarize these experiments is graphical. Wherever possible, I will display the experiments using a design-based statistical graph. I coined the term "design-based statistical graph" in Coppock (2020) to refer to visualizations that convey a study's design and results together as opposed to figures that show results only. For these experiments, conveying both design and results entails overlaying group means and confidence intervals on top of the raw data. We get a sense of distribution of the outcome, how random assignment was carried out, and how the data were analyzed.

Summary

This chapter has characterized the panel survey experiment design in terms of its model, inquiries, data strategy, and answer strategy. The theoretical half of the design (the model and inquiries) uses a theory of how attitudes respond to information to define targets of inference. In the empirical half of the design (the data and answer strategies), we invite subjects into the survey environment, measure their pre-treatment covariates, randomly assign them to different levels of persuasive information, then estimate the conditional average treatment effects on target attitudes. Along the way, I've also given defenses against some common objections to the design choices I did and did not make. Without further ado, chapter 5 will present the results of this design, applied many times over.

CHAPTER FIVE

Persuasion Experiments: Originals, Replications, and Reanalyses

This chapter collects together a large set of persuasion survey experiments (twenty-three in total) and analyzes them first separately as case studies and then together in a meta-analysis.

Why case studies first? Each study attempts to persuade using different treatment information, and each measures outcomes using different survey questions. Simply calling them all persuasion studies and mixing them together in a meta-analysis blender would inappropriately average over the particularities of each individual experiment. Many of these experiments were originally written up in full 10,000-word journal articles that explained the nuances of how the treatments and outcomes map onto the theoretical subtleties in the relevant social scientific literature, the reasons why the experimental results should inform our thinking outside the confines of the study itself, and the study's limitations. In my own retelling of each experiment, I'll try to find a middle ground between a single number summary and the full 10,000 words.

This collection of studies is obviously not representative of all persuasion survey experiments ever conducted. It is neither a census of all such studies, nor is it anything resembling a random sample of them. Even if it were, there would remain the further concern of whether the survey experiments that have been conducted are themselves representative of survey experiments *not yet* conducted, which is presumably a main concern of a researcher contemplating running a new experiment. My hope is that both the diversity and the quantity of studies presented here convinces you that at the very least, these findings generalize to a broad set of persuasion experiments, even if the boundaries of that set are not known precisely.

I will present the main results in three groups. The first is a set of three original experiments that my collaborators and I designed and conducted ourselves. The second is a group of five experiments that were originally designed and conducted by other researchers and that I replicated on new samples. A major benefit of this second set of studies is the ability to see the original and replication results side by side. The third is a group of five experiments by other researchers funded by the Time-sharing Experiments for the Social Sciences (TESS) organization. The purpose of this third group is to serve as an "out-of-sample" test. I had already learned from the experiments in the first and second groups that persuasion in parallel is a good description of how people respond to persuasive information. These five extra studies show that the empirical patterns discovered in the first two sets of studies apply more broadly to other persuasive information treatments.

After describing all three groups of studies using the procedures outlined in chapter 4, I'll present two sets of additional analyses. The first is a (slightly unorthodox) meta-analysis that shows that conditional average treatment effects of persuasive information are strongly correlated across subdivisions of the population. Simply put, if we find large positive effects for Democrats, we should expect to find large positive effects for Republicans as well. The second set concerns what happens when a persuasive information treatment is countered by an opposing message. The summary of this set of analyses is a little anticlimactic: they appear to mostly cancel each other out.

Three Original Persuasion Experiments

Original Study 1: Guess and Coppock (2020) — Minimum Wage

This minimum wage study was the first experiment Andy Guess and I designed after our replication and extension of Lord, Ross, and Lepper (1979). As is typical for graduate students designing their first experiments, we made things far more complicated than they should have been. All subjects saw two videos, but which two in particular was determined at random. Subjects could be assigned to a placebo condition or one of *twelve* treatment conditions. We had selected four YouTube videos on the subject of raising minimum wage: two videos in favor and two videos against. We got to twelve conditions by taking all 4 choose 2 = 6 combinations of the four videos, then randomizing which video subjects saw first. We can address some of the confusion introduced in the data strategy with a fix in the answer strategy. I'll focus only on three groups of subjects: those who saw both anti-minimum wage videos, those who saw both pro-minimum wage videos, and those who saw the two placebo videos.

The anti-minimum wage videos articulated the standard Econ 101 arguments against wage floors. Because employers are expected to respond to the higher price of labor by purchasing less of it, minimum wage laws may raise wages for some but are theorized to have the unintended consequence of causing some low-wage workers to lose their jobs. The pro-minimum wage videos acknowledged this argument but cited the empirical work in economics that showed no reduction in employment following the introduction of minimum wage laws. After subjects watched the videos, we measured two outcomes: their preferred minimum wage in dollars per hour from $0.00 to $25.00 and their support for increasing the minimum wage on a seven-point scale. On the basis of these same questions, asked in a pre-survey conducted ten days before treatment, we categorized subjects as minimum wage proponents or opponents.

The results are shown in figure 5.1. For proponents, the two pro videos (relative to the two anti videos) increased the preferred minimum wage by $3.24 (robust standard error: $0.40) and the support for raising it by 0.84 scale points (SE: 0.19 points). For opponents, the effect on the preferred minimum wage was smaller ($1.04, SE: $0.65), but the effect on support for raising the minimum wage was almost identical, at 0.88 scale points (SE: 0.32 points). The figure makes clear that minimum wage proponents and opponents—regardless of which videos they saw—definitely still disagree with one another. The triangles (for proponents) are substantially higher than the circles (for opponents). Nevertheless, the effects of the videos themselves are quite similar across the two groups. In addition, the average difference between the negative treatment and the placebo is always negative; the average difference between the positive treatment and placebo is always positive. These differences are statistically significant in four out of eight opportunities. In no cases do we have any evidence of "incorrectly" signed effects.

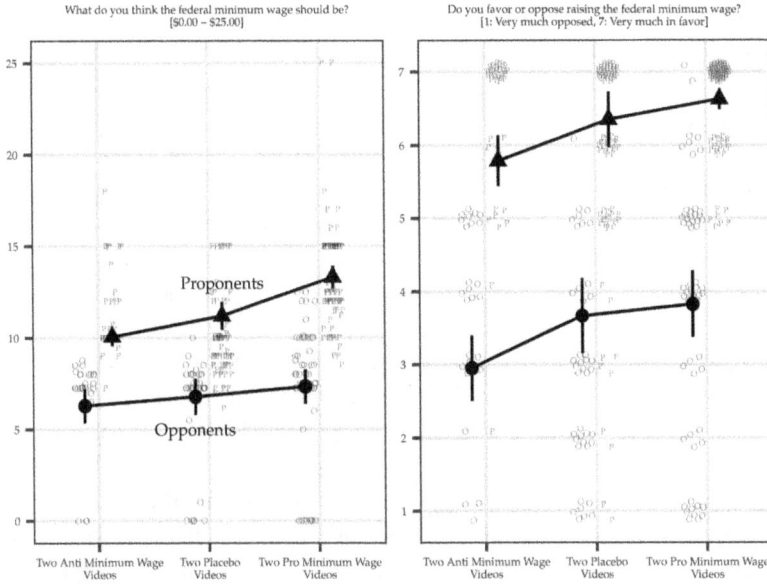

FIGURE 5.1. Reanalysis of Guess and Coppock (2020): Minimum wage

Original Study 2: Guess and Coppock (2020)—Gun Control

Andy Guess and I had learned from the minimum wage study that persuasion in the direction of information was possible. We'd also learned from the capital punishment replication and extension that people could be persuaded by treatments that resembled short descriptions of social scientific articles. We were sensitive to the possibility that the minimum wage was an "easy" issue and that opinions may therefore have been easily manipulable. While I'm not sure I still buy that line of argumentation (what makes an issue easy or hard?), we nevertheless wanted to see if our results from the capital punishment and minimum wage studies would hold up for the incontrovertibly contentious issue of gun control.

We were extremely fortunate to have secured a grant from Time-sharing Experiments for the Social Sciences to run this experiment on a nationally representative sample (gathered by GfK) as a two-wave study. In wave 1, we gathered pre-treatment measures that allowed us to identify gun control proponents and opponents. In wave 2, we randomly assigned subjects to a control condition or to see one of two fabricated studies on the effects of gun control. The anti-gun control study claimed that gun-related crimes were higher in states with stricter gun laws; the pro-gun control study claimed the opposite. All subjects were debriefed by email after the conclusion of the study with the real data, which are inconclusive on the matter.

The results of our study are shown in figure 5.2. Once again, all of the treatment effects estimates are correctly signed. In no case does seeing the pro information cause people to become *less* supportive of gun control, nor does the anti information cause increases in support. The largest effect is among gun control proponents. When they see the anti-gun control study, they become less supportive of stricter gun laws, by 7.4 percentage points (SE: 2.2 points). Proponents are of course still quite supportive of stricter laws, but they update slightly in the direction of information. The largest effect for opponents is the effect of the pro study, which comes in at 3.1points. The standard error around that estimate is 4.1 points, so the estimate is not statistically significant.

Our conclusion from this study is that our treatments weren't *wholly* ineffective at changing minds on the issue of gun control. If anything, our subjects were more receptive to arguments from the other side than they were to arguments from their own side. While our treatments had

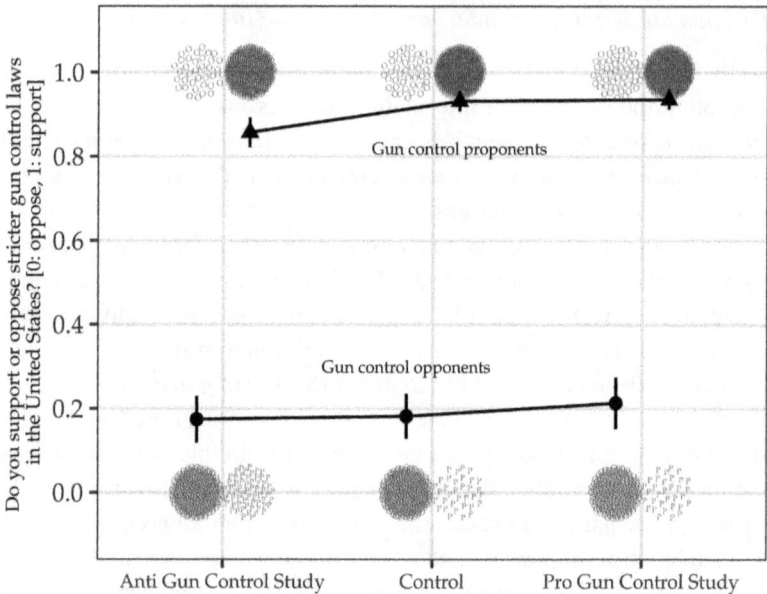

FIGURE 5.2. Reanalysis of Guess and Coppock (2020): Gun control

mostly small effects on opinion, they had similarly small effects for both opponents and proponents. In no case did we find evidence that trying to persuade people about gun control was counterproductive in the sense of reinforcing initial positions.

Original Study 3: Coppock, Ekins, and Kirby (2018) — Newspaper Op-Eds

Next we revisit the newspaper op-eds study that we've already encountered twice before now. In chapter 1, we saw how Rand Paul's *Wall Street Journal* opinion piece was effective at increasing support for a flat tax. The op-ed worked for Republican and Democrat respondents among DC policy professionals and Mechanical Turk workers alike. In chapter 3, I used this study to make the point that target and non-target attitudes are different; the op-eds move the target attitudes but do nothing to change the non-target attitudes. We'll actually encounter this study one more time after this, when we discuss the persistence of persuasion effects in chapter 6.

The main reason we keep returning to this study is because it is so large. Emily Ekins, David Kirby, and I surveyed over 3,500 Mechanical Turk workers and just under 2,200 DC policy professionals. Instead of concocting treatments using fabricated studies, we used real op-eds placed in national outlets like the *New York Times*, *USA Today*, the *Wall Street Journal*, and *Newsweek*. Many survey experiments use short, to-the-point treatments that make a single argument. These op-eds were full length: the shortest was about 400 words and the longest about 1,000. The op-eds covered a wide range of topics and advocated libertarian policy positions on infrastructure spending, climate change, taxes, veterans' healthcare, and Wall Street.

Figure 5.3 shows the results, separated out by op-ed, sample, and subject partisanship. In every case, the group that read the op-ed held opinions closer to the libertarian position than those of the control group. In thirteen of the fourteen opportunities (corresponding to each of the slopes depicted in the figure), the difference is statistically significant. The summary implication from figure 5.3 is that people across the political spectrum can be influenced by detailed policy arguments. They may *disagree* with the authors of the op-eds—and indeed the figure provides clear evidence that many subjects in the treatment and control conditions do—but they can change their minds, at least a little bit.

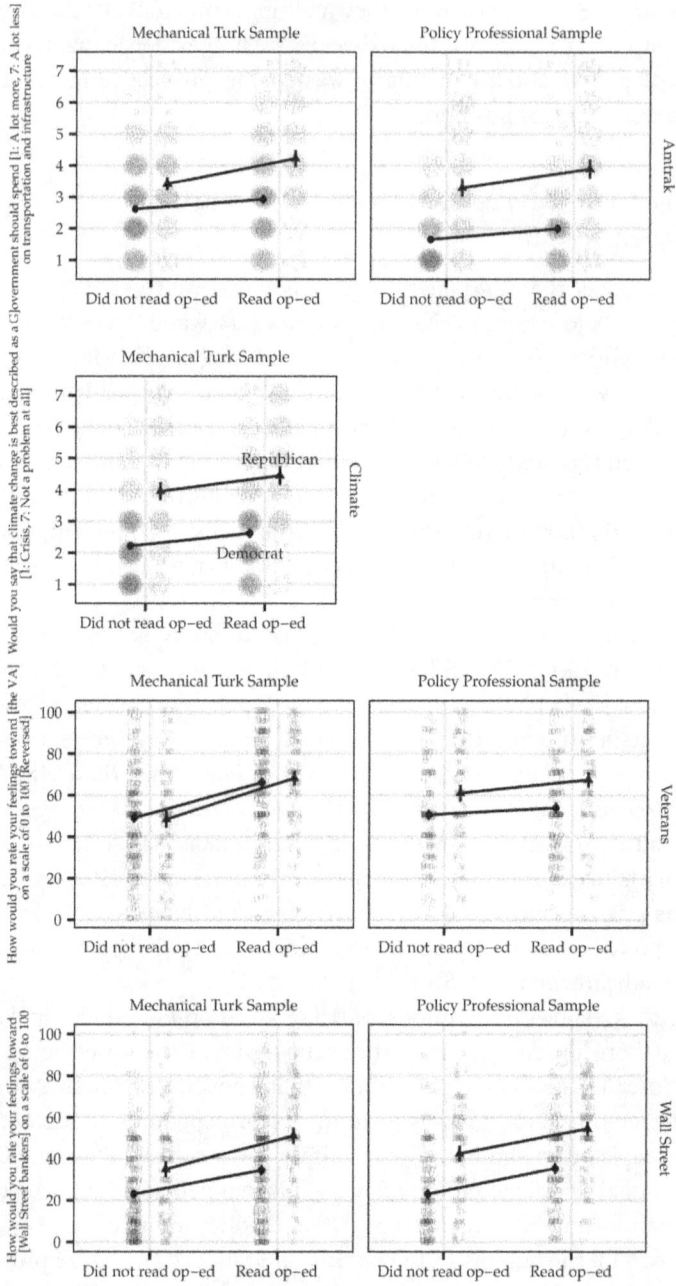

FIGURE 5.3. Reanalysis of Coppock, Ekins, and Kirby (2018): Newspaper op-eds

Reanalysis and Replication of Five Persuasion Experiments

So far we've seen the experiments that my collaborators and I designed ourselves. Now we're going to turn to experiments designed by other scholars who were forward-thinking enough to make their replication datasets publicly available for others to learn from. This second set of experiments will come in five pairs of two studies. In each of these cases, I will both reanalyze the original experiment and report a replication conducted on one or more new samples.

In nearly every case, the analyses of the original and replication experiments come to very similar results, so this is not at all a story about replication failures. Instead, the pattern that emerges is that despite drastic differences in sample composition—a sample of Mechanical Turk workers differs considerably from the national population along nearly every demographic dimension we measure—we find similar treatment effects across original and replication versions of the same experiment. This cross-sample replication is another version of persuasion in parallel. Just as Democrats and Republicans have different baselines but update by similar amounts, so too do MTurkers and members of the general public.

Reanalysis and Replication 1: Chong and Druckman
(2010)—Patriot Act

Chong and Druckman (2010) studied the effect of large doses of statements that cast the Patriot Act legislation in a positive or negative light. In the "strong pro" condition, subjects read six statements like "The Patriot Act enhances domestic security through counterterrorism funding, surveillance, border protection, and other security policies" and "The Patriot Act includes less known provisions including funding for terrorism victims and their families." In the "strong con" condition, the statements were more critical: "Under the Patriot Act, the government has access to citizens' confidential information from telephone and e-mail communications" and "Since its passage, the Patriot Act has been challenged in federal courts on the grounds that many of its provisions are unconstitutional." The main outcome measured support for the Patriot Act on a 1–7 Likert scale.

The left facet of figure 5.4 shows a reanalysis of the original study

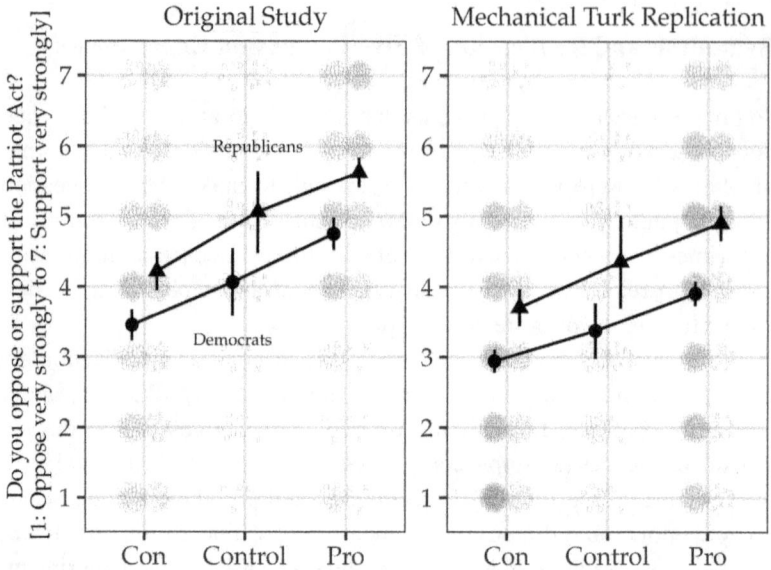

FIGURE 5.4. Reanalysis and replication of Chong and Druckman (2010): Patriot Act

conducted by Chong and Druckman using a nationally representative sample collected in December 2009. On the right is a replication I conducted with an online convenience sample of MTurkers in March 2015. The difference between MTurkers in 2015 and Americans in 2009 can be seen directly by comparing the control groups in each study. Democrats *and* Republicans on MTurk support the Patriot Act less than their nationally representative counterparts, by about half a scale point. This difference could be due to drift over time or it could be due to unmeasured differences between partisans on the two platforms.

In both versions the treatments were *strongly* effective in changing subjects' views of the Patriot Act. Comparing the group assigned to read the con messages to the group assigned to read the pro messages, we see an average difference of about one entire scale point. For comparison, this is approximately the same size as the average difference between the Republican and Democratic points of view in the control group. These magnitudes were replicated with startling consistency in the MTurk version. This experiment, both in the original and in the replication, shows very clearly that people update their views on the Patriot Act in parallel.

Reanalysis and Replication 2: Brader, Valentino, and Suhay (2008) — Immigration Frames

Next up, we consider an experiment originally reported in Brader, Valentino, and Suhay (2008). This study measured the effect of news stories about immigrants on attitudes toward immigration. The news stories cast immigrants in either a positive or a negative light. The experiment also varied the home country of the immigrant, but we'll average over that dimension in this reanalysis.

Figure 5.5 again shows large baseline differences between the subjects in the original study (a nationally representative sample collected in 2003) and in the MTurk replication. The original study participants were, on the whole, very negative toward immigration. On average, the MTurk participants were also negative toward immigration, but somewhat less so. Comparing the negative news story groups to the positive news story groups, we see a very clear pattern—subjects in the positive groups support immigration more than subjects in the negative groups. This pattern holds for Republicans and Democrats in both samples.

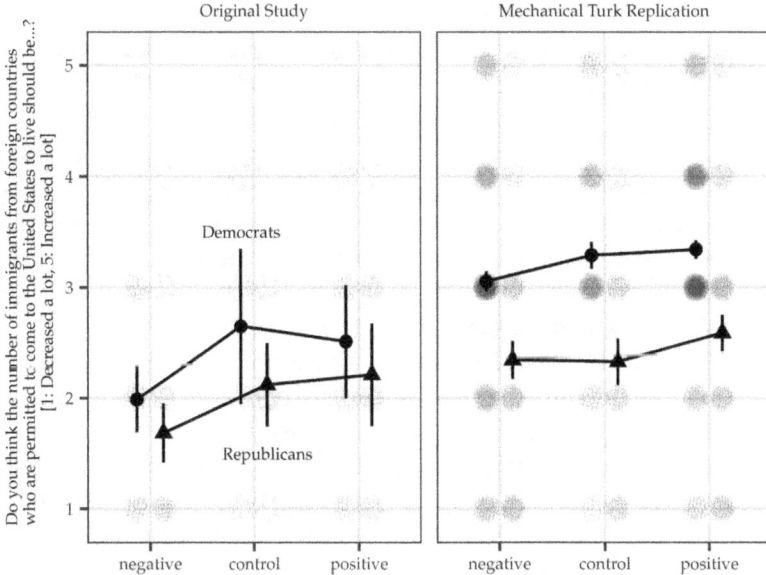

FIGURE 5.5. Reanalysis and replication of Brader, Valentino, and Suhay (2008): Immigration frames

We can try to use the control group to get some traction on the question of which treatment (the positive or the negative news stories) was "doing more work," though the picture is somewhat muddy. Focusing on the MTurk replication (which had a far larger sample size, as indicated by the greater number of points on the plot), we see that the negative treatment was especially effective for Democrats and the positive treatment was especially effective for Republicans. What's odd, though, is that this is the *opposite* of the motivated reasoning prediction, which would contend that only congenial treatments would be effective. In this case, it was the *counter-attitudinal* treatments that were slightly more effective in persuading people. We don't observe this same pattern in the original study (nor anything similar in the Patriot Act experiment above), so we shouldn't make too much of this point except to note that it's absolutely not predicted by the (directional) motivated reasoning accounts of information processing. Even on the complicated and fraught issue of immigration, we see that people are at least a little bit persuadable.

Reanalysis and Replication 3: Hiscox (2006) — Free Trade

We turn next to four versions of an experiment on trade preferences first reported in Hiscox (2006): the original, and replications conducted on MTurk, a nationally representative sample collected by GfK, and a second online convenience sample obtained from Lucid. Subjects in the control group were asked: "Do you favor or oppose increasing trade with other nations?" Subjects in the "Expert" condition saw this additional text before answering the same question: "According to the *New York Times*, almost 100 percent of American economists support increasing trade with other nations. In 1993 over a thousand economists, including all living winners of the Nobel Prize in economics, signed an open letter to the *New York Times* urging people to support efforts to increase trade between the United States and neighboring countries."

This treatment caused substantial shifts in opinion in all four samples, among both Democrats and Republicans. The effects are on the order of 10 to 15 percentage points and are in all cases "no-doubters." We barely need statistical tests to demonstrate that indeed, this heavy-handed expert treatment increases the fraction of survey subjects that favors trade (fig. 5.6). This result is very robust and does not depend on the partisanship of the subjects or how the experimental sample was constructed. Of course subjects of different partisan backgrounds differ on trade—

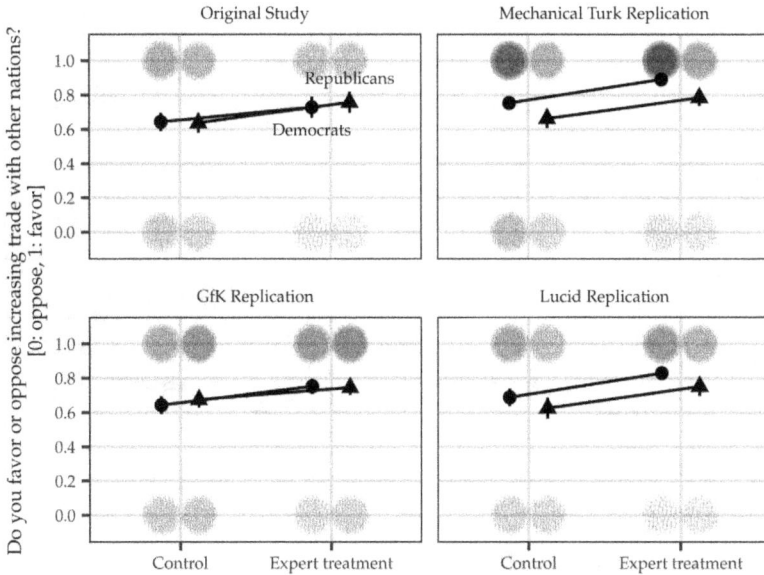

FIGURE 5.6. Reanalysis and replication of Hiscox (2006): Expert treatment

and so do participants recruited from different survey platforms—but these groups do not differ meaningfully in how they respond to the expert treatment.

The study in Hiscox (2006) was a two-by-four factorial, as the Expert versus Control comparison shown in figure 5.6 was crossed with a "valence" treatment. Valence could take on four values: control, positive, negative, or both. Subjects in the positive condition were told "Many people believe that increasing trade with other nations creates jobs and allows Americans to buy more types of goods at lower prices," whereas subjects in the negative condition were told "Many people believe that increasing trade with other nations leads to job losses and exposes American producers to unfair competition." Control subjects saw neither statement, and subjects in the "both" condition saw both statements. For now, I'll focus on the positive and negative treatments, but we'll consider the "both" condition in the section below on "Two-sided Messages" when we discuss the consequences of competing persuasive treatments.

The results are shown in figure 5.7. The pattern of results for the negative treatment is unambiguous. Regardless of sample or partisanship, the

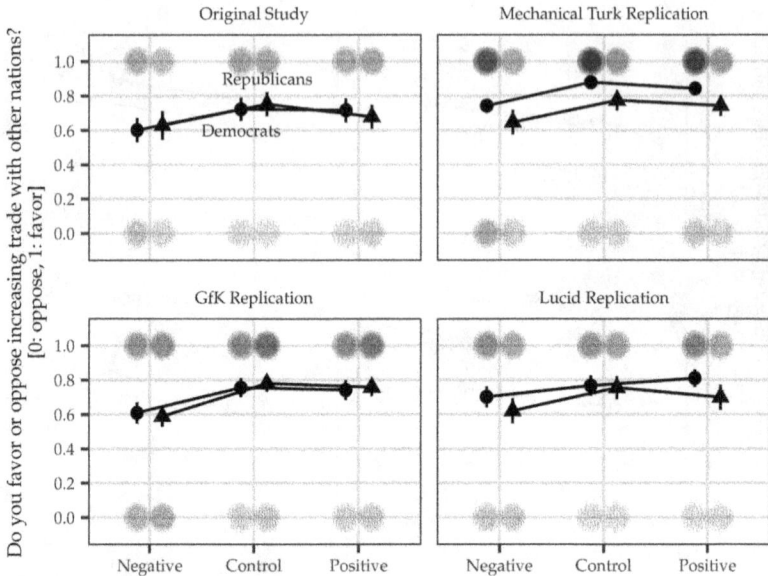

FIGURE 5.7. Reanalysis and replication of Hiscox (2006): Valence treatments

negative treatment substantially decreases support for trade. The effects are on the order of 12 to 14 percentage points, depending on the subgroup and sample. The effects of the "positive" treatment, however, are very curious. The effects are always small, but they are sometimes positive, sometimes null, and occasionally negative. I don't understand why this happens, but the behavior of the positive treatment is consistently strange across all four samples, so I don't think this is a fluke. One possible explanation is that the positive statement may have a "thou doth protest too much" quality that triggers a negative response. The honest truth is that this result is puzzling to me. I don't count this as a "backlash" effect, however, because that would require oppositely signed effects for different subgroups. Here, both Republicans and Democrats exhibit the same unexpected behavior.

Reanalysis and Replication 4: Johnston and Ballard
(2016) — Expert Economists

The study reported in Johnston and Ballard (2016) extends the reach of the "expert economist" treatments to other economic issues beyond trade. In the control condition, subjects were asked for their views on immigration, health care, trade with China, taxes, and the gold standard. In the treatment condition, subjects were told economists' views on each issue before they gave their own positions. Just as in the original study and replications of Hiscox (2006), the expert treatment exerts a powerful and unambiguous pull on subjects' attitudes. In the expert treatment condition, subjects gave answers that agreed with the economists' position far more, sometimes by as much as 20 percentage points. This pattern holds for all five issues and both samples (see fig. 5.8).

Reanalysis and Replication 5: Hopkins and Mummolo (2017) — Frame Breadth

For our final replication and reanalysis, we'll turn to a creative study reported in Hopkins and Mummolo (2017). This study, which was designed to estimate the effects of an argument on non-target attitudes, was a source of inspiration for the Coppock and Green (2020) study of dynamic constraint described in chapter 3. Hopkins and Mummolo find that their treatments mostly move target attitudes and mostly don't move non-target attitudes. Here we'll examine the effects of their treatments on target attitudes, again splitting respondents by partisanship.

Subjects were randomly assigned to read statements by US senators on the topics of crime, health care, the stimulus bill, or terrorism. In the original study conducted with a nationally representative sample, subjects read statements on two randomly chosen topics; in the replication, subjects were assigned to read a statement on just one topic. This small data strategy tweak simplifies the answer strategy somewhat while holding the inquiry constant. The outcome variables were preferences about spending for all four subject areas, indicated on a seven-point scale from 1: Decreased a lot to 7: Increased a great deal.

We see in figure 5.9 that the argument to decrease stimulus spending indeed decreases stimulus spending preferences, and that the counterterrorism argument is effective in increasing counterterrorism preferences. These effects are similarly sized for Republicans and Democrats. The other two treatments had mostly null effects on spending preferences — and they aren't differently null by partisan identification.

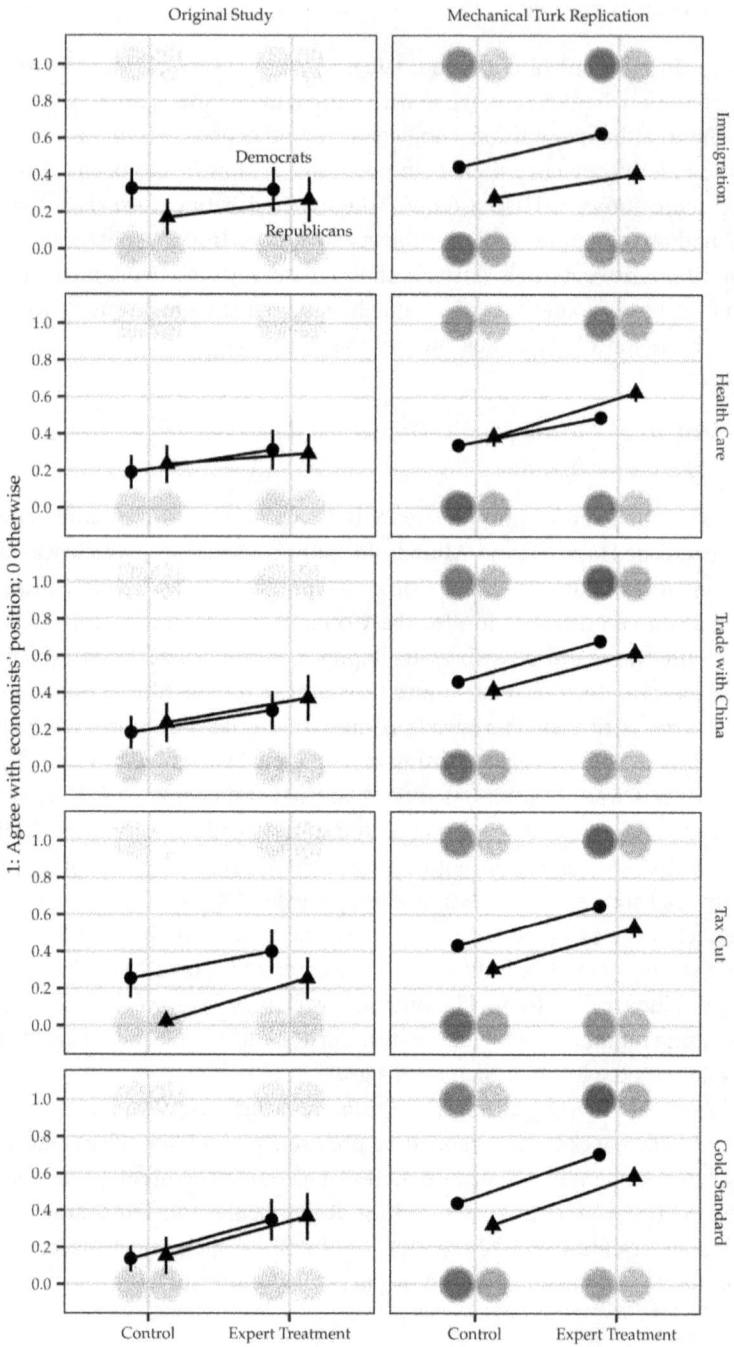

Original Study   Mechanical Turk Replication

1: Agree with economists' position; 0 otherwise

Immigration · Health Care · Trade with China · Tax Cut · Gold Standard

Control   Expert Treatment   Control   Expert Treatment

FIGURE 5.8. Reanalysis and replication of Johnston and Ballard (2016): Expert economists

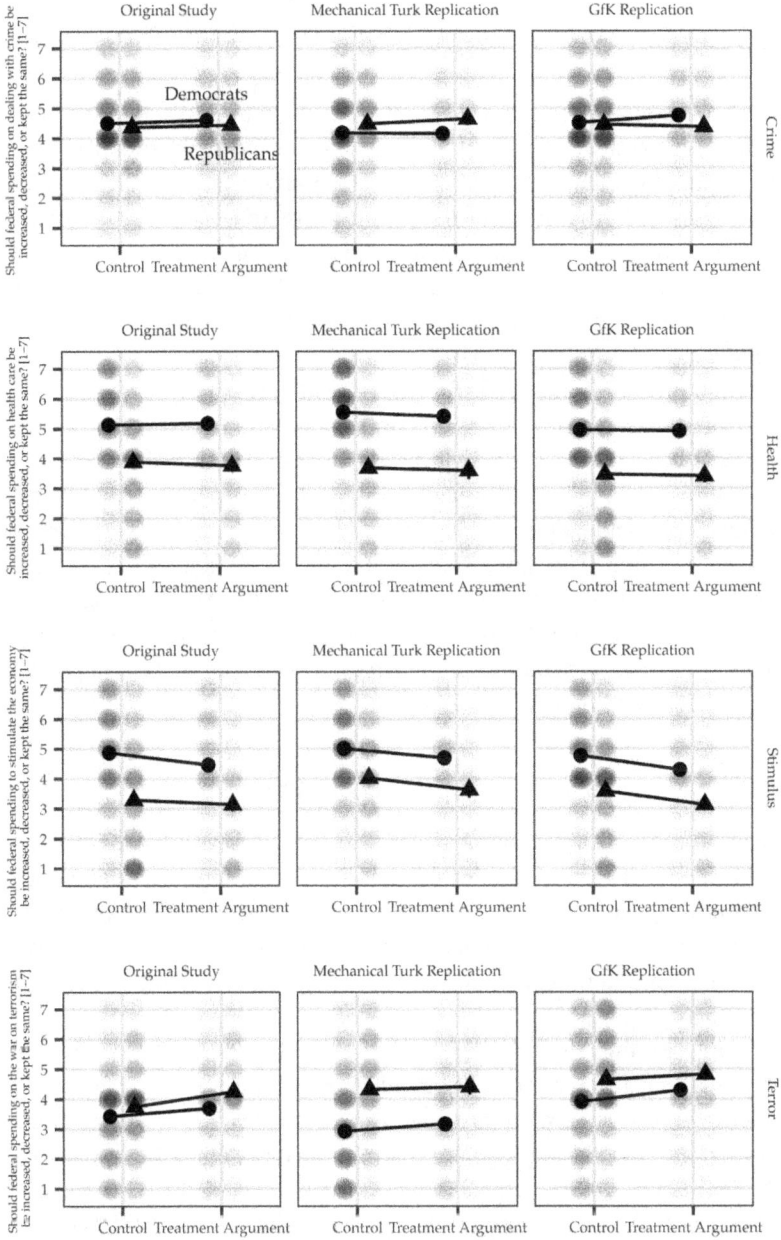

FIGURE 5.9. Reanalysis and replications of Hopkins and Mummolo (2017): Frame breadth

Reanalyses of Five TESS Studies

In this section, we're going to bolster the external validity of the persuasion in parallel finding by reanalyzing five persuasion experiments conducted by others on nationally representative samples. These five experiments address wildly different substantive areas: gender discrimination in hiring, the role of money in politics, the status of drone strikes in international law, job losses due to trade, and income inequality in the US. They have in common that the treatments target policy attitudes or beliefs.

Up until now, I've been estimating CATEs by one of two covariates: opponent versus proponent status on the basis of a pre-treatment measure of the target attitude, or subject partisan identity. For these next five studies, I'm going to expand this set of covariates to partisanship, gender, race, and education. These analyses will therefore bolster external validity along two dimensions. Not only will we be looking at a fresh sample of studies, we'll also be considering new ways of slicing up the subjects. This approach (at least partially) addresses the concern that the mostly homogeneous CATEs by partisanship might mask important heterogeneity by other characteristics.

Reanalysis 1: Gash and Murakami (2009)—Venue Effects

Gash and Murakami (2009) explore "venue effects," or the idea that public support for a policy will differ depending on which democratic institution enacted it. Specifically, does support differ depending on whether the policy was mandated by a legislature, the courts, or by voters via referendum? The policy in this experiment was gender-based hiring practices.

Control group subjects were asked: "Do you agree or disagree with the idea that these companies should not be able to give special consideration to women when making hiring decisions?" In three randomly formed treatment groups, subjects were informed that either the courts, the legislature, or voters at the ballot box had decided that companies could not consider gender when hiring. The subjects then indicated their agreement or disagreement with that choice on a one-to-four scale.

Figure 5.10 shows that uniformly, regardless of which political venue made the decision, treatment subjects agreed with the policy much

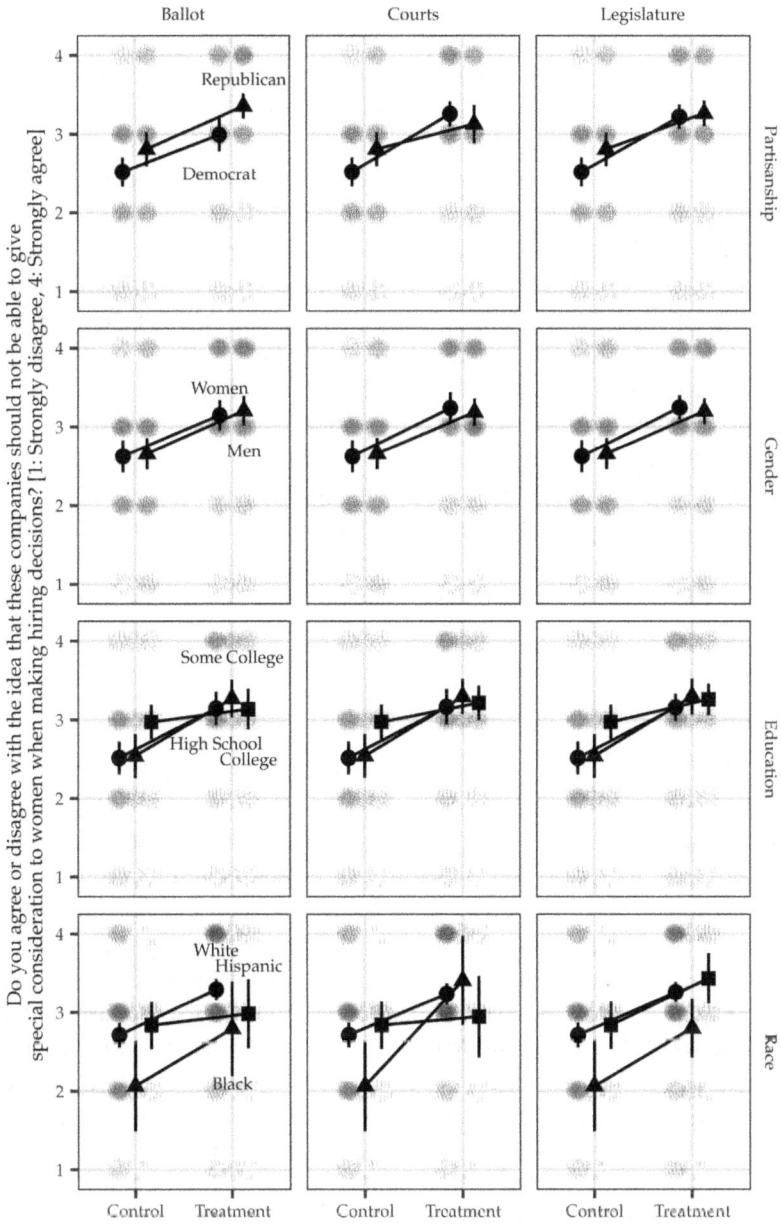

FIGURE 5.10. Reanalysis of Gash and Murakami (2009): Venue effects

more than control subjects. This pattern can be appreciated by looking across columns of facets: all the slopes are similarly positive for the *Ballot*, *Courts*, and *Legislature* treatments. Comparing across rows shows that this pattern holds not only among Republicans and Democrats, but also among men and women, the well and less well educated, and Black and White Americans. We see some evidence that the treatment effect is somewhat smaller for those with at most high school education—but this group definitively does not like the policy *less* when treated.

In many ways, these treatments are similar to the "expert" treatments in Hiscox (2006) and Johnston and Ballard (2016). In all cases, subjects are informed that other people—people who have looked into the matter, like economists who are supposed to know, or the courts, the legislators, or the voters—have come to a judgment about the topic at hand. Finding out that others have made this judgment may lead subjects to infer that perhaps they too would come to the same conclusion if they knew all the facts. In this way, treatments that rely on source cues are another form of information shortcut. Interestingly, these source cues are not hypothesized to generate treatment effect heterogeneity the way group cues are.

Reanalysis 2: Flavin (2011)—Political Equality

In this next study, Flavin (2011) examines how support for political equality changes depending on how it is defined to the survey subject. The control group subjects were asked, "Some people think that the United States should place a greater emphasis on promoting political equality. How about you, do you strongly support, somewhat support, neither support nor oppose, somewhat oppose, or strongly oppose promoting political equality?" Treatment group subjects answered the same question, but "political equality" was defined more precisely: "By political equality we mean making sure elected officials listen and respond to the opinions of all citizens equally—whether they are rich or poor, black or white, male or female—when making important policy decisions." This small change, which really just restates the definition of equality, dramatically increases support for promoting political equality. Figure 5.11 shows that the CATEs of this treatment hover around 0.8 scale points, which is far larger than the difference between the subgroups themselves at baseline.

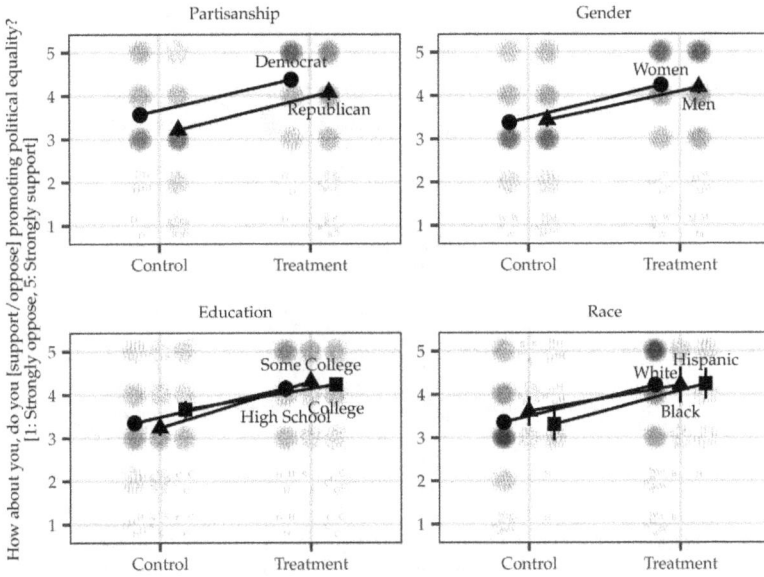

FIGURE 5.11. Reanalysis of Flavin (2011): Political equality

Reanalysis 3: Kreps and Wallace (2016) — Drone Strikes

Kreps and Wallace (2016) considered the effect of informing subjects that drone strikes violate international law on their support for strikes. Figure 5.12 shows unequivocally that subjects support drone strikes far more if they are told they do not violate international law than if they are told the opposite. Labeling drone strikes as illegal versus legal (with respect to international law) clearly reduces support for strikes across all demographic groups shown here. The effects aren't enormous, with the average effect hovering around 0.2 scale points, which is about the same magnitude as the average difference between Republicans and Democrats. None of the groups likes drone strikes more because they heard strikes violate international law (thank goodness).

Reanalysis 4: Mutz (2017) — Job Loss

Mutz (2017) reports an experiment in which subjects are asked to read a vignette about Michael Morrison, a fictional steel mill worker in Illinois. Control group subjects are told he loses his job, but treatment

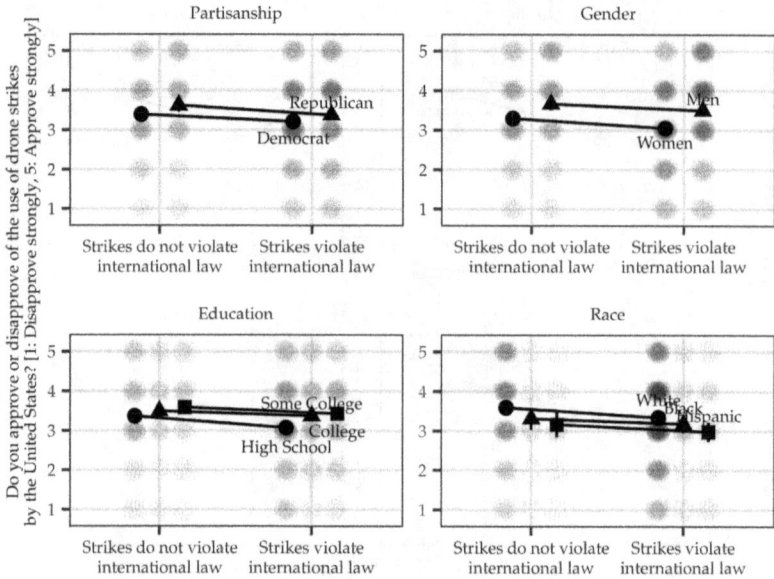

FIGURE 5.12. Reanalysis of Kreps and Wallace (2016): Drone strikes

group subjects are told that he loses his job due to trade with China. The vignette explains that "Of the 74 machines that were operating in the factory, 63 are now operating in China." This change to the Morrison vignette has very small effects on subjects' views of free trade (see fig. 5.13). It very mildly increases opposition to free trade (the average effect is 0.07 scale points on a 1-to-4 scale), though this effect is not statistically significant. We do not observe differential effects by demographic subgroup. The coefficient for the middle category of education is slightly negative, but not statistically significantly so.

Reanalysis 5: Trump and White (2018) — Income Inequality

Our last entry in this parade of persuasion experiments is a fun one. Trump and White (2018) make very clever use of the vertical axis to develop two visualizations of income inequality in the US over time, as reproduced in figure 5.14. Graphs A and B show the same time series, but the treatment version restricts the vertical axis to values between 35 percent and 50 percent, whereas the control version shows the entire range from 0 percent to 100 percent.

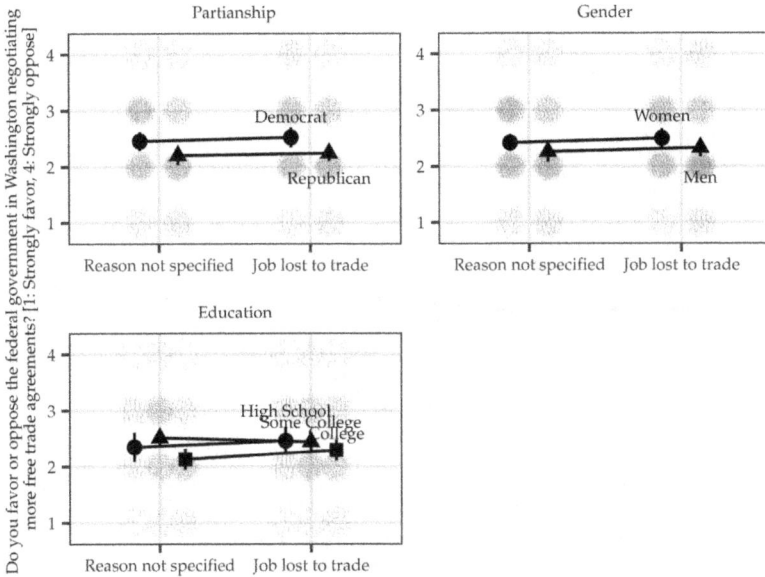

FIGURE 5.13. Reanalysis of Mutz (2017): Job loss

The article focuses on the difference in "system justification" attitudes caused by the treatment graph versus the control graph. Estimates of this effect are close to zero, regardless of how system justification is measured. However, the graphs do cause large differences in beliefs about how income inequality has changed over time. Figure 5.15 shows large effects for all demographic subgroups—the effects are close to 25 percentage points in nearly all cases. It may be that changing beliefs about income inequality doesn't change system justification, but it is very clear that the graphical presentation of data matters enormously for the beliefs subjects hold about empirical truths.

Meta-analysis

If the persuasion in parallel hypothesis is true, it means that the conditional average treatment effects of persuasive information are similar for different groups of people. If a treatment effect is large for Democrats, we should expect it to be large for Republicans as well. If an effect is close to zero among men, we should expect effects among women to be close to zero too.

United States: Income Inequality Over Time

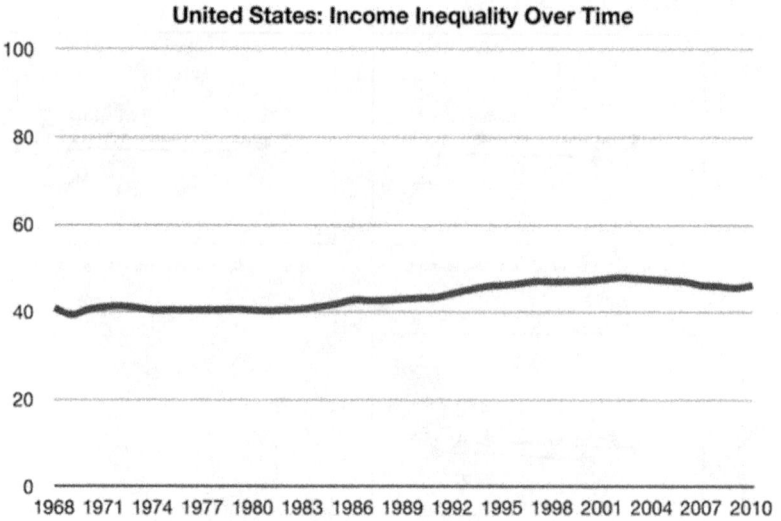

United States: Income Inequality Over Time

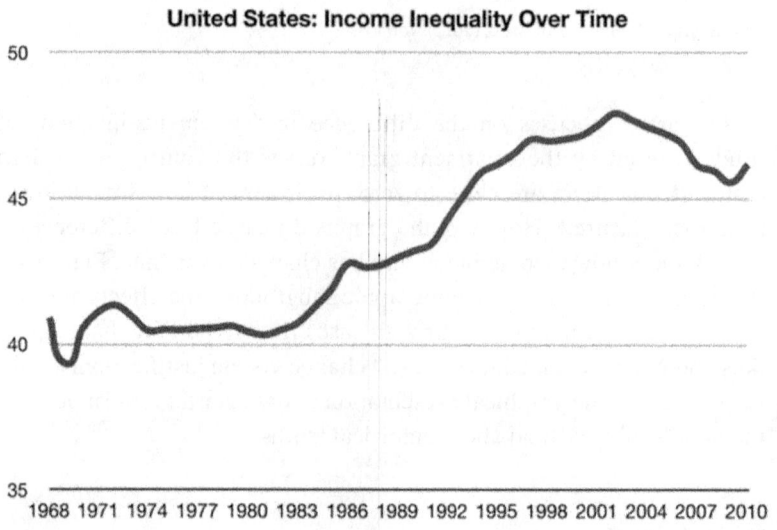

FIGURE 5.14. Treatments in Trump and White (2018)

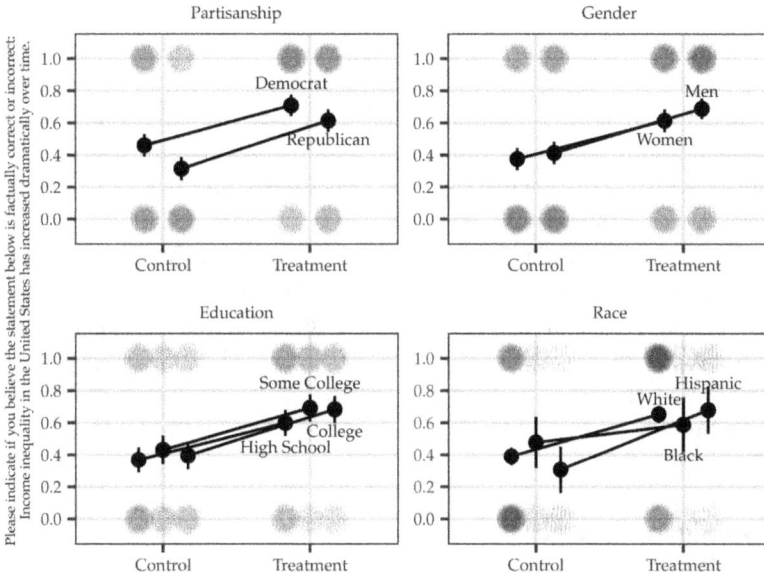

FIGURE 5.15. Reanalysis of Trump and White (2018): Income inequality

Figure 5.16 summarizes the experimental evidence in favor of this claim. Each facet is a scatterplot of the conditional average treatment effects for the set of experiments we've seen in this chapter. The vertical and horizontal axes show the CATEs for non-overlapping subsets of each study sample. So that we can more easily compare them, all the CATEs have been standardized by dividing by the standard deviation in the control group. A datapoint at [0.5, 0.5] in, say, the partisanship facet refers to an experimental contrast in which the effect for Republicans was 0.5 standard deviations and the effect for Democrats was 0.5 standard deviations as well. Each point is estimated with some sampling variability, so we have 95 percent confidence intervals in each direction.

The overwhelming pattern from this plot is that treatment effects are *strongly* correlated across subdivisions of the population. The estimated correlations are 0.86 (partisanship), 0.80 (ideology), 0.62 (race), 0.92 (gender), 0.62 (age), and 0.70 (education). The correlations are smaller for comparisons that include smaller subgroups, since CATEs will typically be estimated with more uncertainty when sample size is smaller, and that uncertainty will bias the correlations toward zero. Indeed, these

raw correlations are all the more impressive because they are attenu-
ated by the "measurement error" due to sampling variability. If we knew
these CATEs with certainty, the correlations would be higher than estimated. In my view, the main reason that we see such extraordinary correspondence in treatment response is within-study treatment effect homogeneity. If a treatment effect is 0.5 SDs for one group, it's likely to be
close to 0.5 for the next group.

Figure 5.16 is the big payoff from slogging through the definitions
and distinctions in chapter 3, the design details in chapter 4, and what
my colleague Josh Kalla dryly called the "death-march" of experiments
presented in the first half of this chapter. In my view, figure 5.16 is evidence that the persuasion in parallel hypothesis is correct and holds
quite broadly.

Two-Sided Messages

Suppose you now agree that in response to persuasive information, people update their views in the direction of information at least a little bit.
Because political information is often contested by opposing messages,
a reasonable next question to ask is how people respond to two-sided
doses of persuasive information.

Two-sided communications are, by their nature, a bundle of at least
two treatments, one in favor of a policy position and another against it.
We have seen so far that positive arguments usually move people in a
positive direction and negative arguments move people in a negative direction. The most straightforward prediction, therefore, is that the bundle of treatments will operate in an additive fashion. If we add the positive effects of the positive treatment to the negative effects of the
negative treatment, we will arrive at the total effect of the bundle. To
the extent that the two sides of the argument are approximately equal
in strength, the additive model predicts that two-sided communications
will tend to have effects that are close to zero for all subjects. If one
treatment is stronger, the total effect will be in the direction of the stronger treatment.

An intriguing alternative is that the presence of multiple messages allows people to pick and choose among them. In particular, some psychological models predict that people will give greater weight to messages with which they agree than to messages with which they disagree.

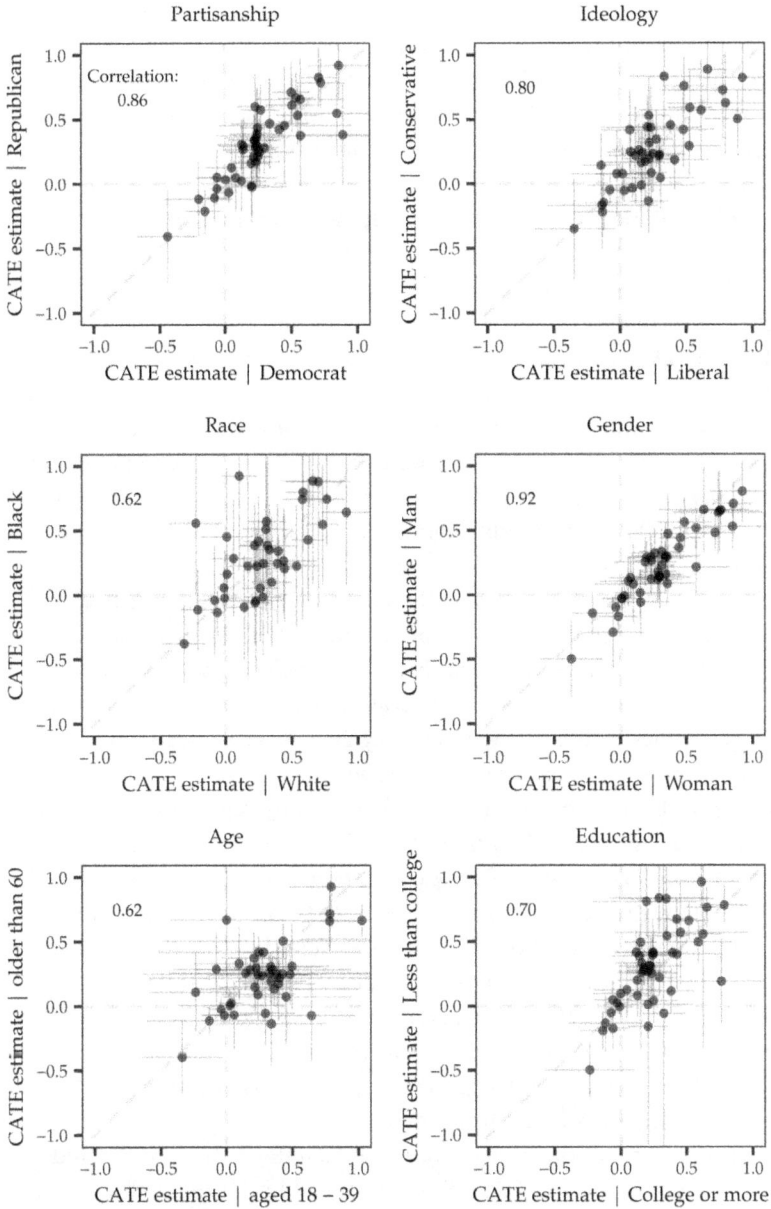

FIGURE 5.16. Correlation of CATEs across demographic subgroups

By "give greater weight" I mean these theories predict that the treatment effect of the pro-attitudinal message will be stronger than the effect of the counter-attitudinal message. If this perspective is correct, then a two-sided bundle of persuasive information will have heterogeneous effects, because subjects "pick and choose" from the set of persuasive arguments presented to them. People who are predisposed toward a policy will become more supportive; the opposite pattern will hold for people who oppose the policy. Various mechanisms have been proposed for this process, including the idea that people will vigorously counterargue the counter-attitudinal information, or alternatively, actively ignore it. As an example of this line of thinking, Zaller (1992, chapter 9) concludes from an observational study of support for the Vietnam War that "highly aware doves were able to resist the dominant pro-war message of this period in part because they were exposed to the countervalent antiwar message." Evaluating this empirical claim is of course very difficult because of the ever-present threat of unobserved heterogeneity in nonexperimental studies.

The experimental record on the effects of two-sided messages is, unfortunately, much thinner than the record on one-sided messages. Three of the studies that we have examined so far included a condition in which subjects saw both positive and negative messages on the same policy. These studies employed factorial designs in which subjects could see the positive message, the negative message, neither message, or both messages. Such experiments are often analyzed by regressing the outcome on each message and their interaction. The estimated coefficient on the interaction term describes how differently each factor affects the outcome in the presence versus the absence of the other. However, the interaction term itself is not our main interest here. Instead, we want to know the average effect of the "both" condition relative to the control condition, and whether those average effects have opposite signs depending on subjects' predispositions. For this reason, I will estimate the effects of the "both" condition using the same tools I used to analyze the one-sided messages earlier in the chapter.

If the effects of the both condition are similar for opponents and proponents (and are close to zero), then we will have support for the additive model. By contrast, if we find oppositely signed conditional average treatment effects, then we will have support for the "pick-and-choose" model. Because this is not a mystery novel, I'll just tell you now: I find strong support for the additive model and no support at all for the pick-and-choose view of the effect of two-sided messages.

Two-Sided Messages 1: Guess and Coppock's (2020) Redesign of Lord, Ross, and Lepper (1979) — Capital Punishment

Among our set of three, the first example of an experiment that employed a two-sided messaging treatment comes from Guess and Coppock's (2020) redesign of the Lord, Ross, and Lepper (1979) study described in chapter 2. Subjects in the *Null Null* condition saw two studies that found no conclusive link between capital punishment and crime; subjects in the *Pro Con* condition saw one study that claimed that capital punishment deters crime and a second that claimed the opposite. Figure 5.17 shows the distribution of responses in each condition to two outcomes. As shown in the left facet, the average effect of the two-sided message on support for capital punishment is very close to zero for both proponents (0.28 scale points, SE: 0.18) and opponents (0.10, SE: 0.11). The right facet shows a very similar effect on belief in the deterrent effect for opponents (0.30 points, SE: 0.17) and for proponents (0.50, SE: 0.18). My interpretation of these results is that the pro argument ever so slightly dominates the con argument, possibly because it may be harder to understand how capital punishment could lead to the unintended consequence of increasing crime.

Two-Sided Messages 2: Chong and Druckman (2010) — Patriot Act

Chong and Druckman's 2010 Patriot Act experiment provides a cleaner test of this theoretical proposition, for two main reasons. First, unlike in the previous study, the control group here is a pure control group that is exposed to no arguments about the Patriot Act. Second, the pro-Patriot Act and anti Patriot Act treatments are quite similar in strength, since they each consist of six easily digestible mini-arguments. The results of being exposed to both pro- and anti-Patriot act statements are shown in figure 5.18. The CATEs of the "both" treatment are indistinguishable from zero for Republicans and Democrats, both in the original study and in the Mechanical Turk replication. This example provides strong evidence in favor of the notion that the effects of two-sided messages are mostly additive. Figure 5.4 earlier in the chapter shows that the pro and con ar-

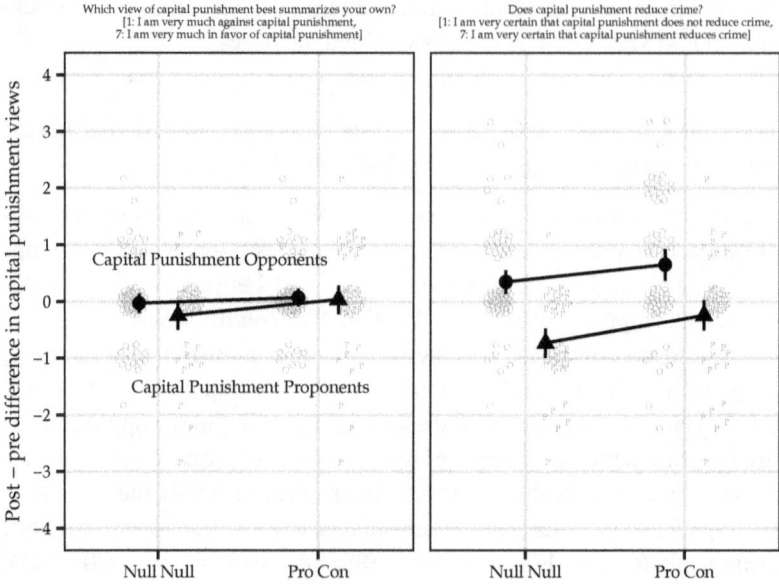

FIGURE 5.17. Two-sided messages in Guess and Coppock's (2020) redesign of Lord, Ross, and Lepper (1979): Capital punishment

guments each have strong effects on members of both major parties; this analysis shows that they cancel each other out when presented together.[1]

Two-Sided Messages 3: Hiscox (2006)—Free Trade

As a final example of a survey experiment that featured a two-sided message flow, we turn to Hiscox (2006), focusing on the pro and con free trade treatments. Subjects could be assigned to see the pro frame, the con frame, both, or neither. As in the previous examples, we'll compare the both condition to the neither condition. Figure 5.19 shows that the both condition *decreased* support for trade for both Republicans and Democrats in all four versions of the experiment, with the exception of the Democrats on Lucid. This result has to be interpreted alongside the relatively confusing pattern of results from the analysis of the one-sided messages. The anti-free trade argument worked as expected to decrease support; the pro-free trade argument was either ineffective or counterproductive in all versions of the experiment. I conclude from those results that for some reason, the pro- and anti-free trade arguments were not equally strong; under the additive model, then, it makes sense that negative treatment would overpower the positive treatment when presented together.

Two-Sided Messages Summary

Although we have far less information about the effects of two-sided messages than one-sided messages, the emerging consensus from these experiments is that two-sided messages behave in a mostly additive manner. When both arguments are about the same strength, they mostly cancel each other out. When one argument is stronger than the other, that strength differential will be reflected in the effect on policy attitudes. We do not see evidence in support of the idea that two-sided arguments work differently for different kinds of people because they get to pick and choose congenial arguments. Even in those cases in which there were glimmers of treatment effect heterogeneity, none of the instances from above suggest that the average effect of both arguments together could have one sign for one group of people but the opposite sign for another.

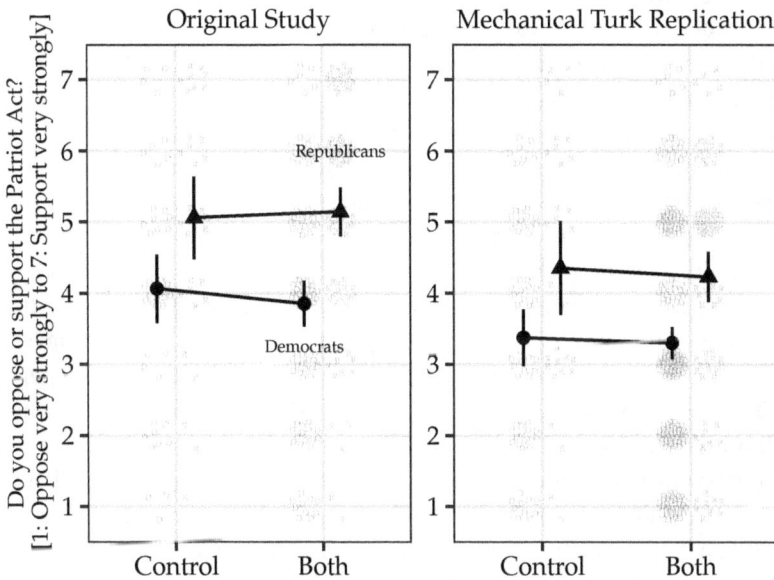

FIGURE 5.18. Two-sided messages 2: Chong and Druckman (2010), Patriot Act

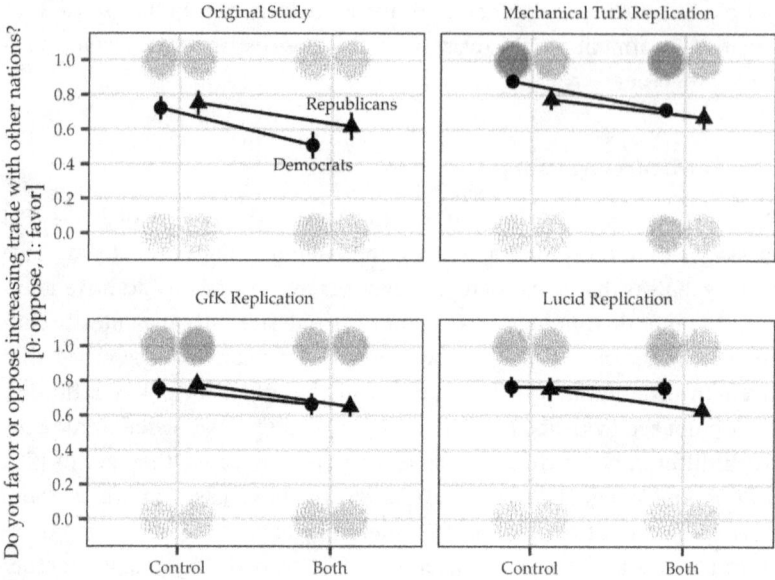

FIGURE 5.19. Two-sided messages 3: Hiscox (2006), Free trade

That being said, a major difficulty in evaluating the hypothesis that two-sided messages work differently for different people is statistical power. Suppose that the truth lies somewhere between the additive model and the pick-and-choose model. Suppose we have one-sided messages that are equally effective—e.g., when presented alone, the pro treatment causes a 0.2 SD shift in attitudes whereas the con treatment moves attitudes by −0.2 SDs. Now imagine that the effect is mostly additive, but subjects *do* pick and choose among the arguments, at least a little bit, because of their limited attention budgets. Suppose that when pro and con arguments are presented together, subjects downgrade the counter-attitudinal argument by 10 percent: proponents experience a treatment effect of $0.2 + 0.9*(-0.2) = 0.02$, whereas opponents experience a treatment effect of $0.9*0.2 + (-0.2) = -0.02$. Under standard assumptions, the sample size needed to distinguish an effect size of 0.02 from 0 with 80 percent power is 80,000; the sample size needed to distinguish a CATE of 0.02 from a CATE of −0.02 is bigger than that. Even if it's true that arguments don't *exactly* cancel, isolating these small effects from each other is plainly out of reach for the vast majority of survey experimental designs.

Summary

This chapter has pulled together empirical evidence on the effects of persuasive information from dozens of survey experiments. The main finding is an overall *lack* of treatment effect heterogeneity. Instead, survey respondents update their views in the direction of information: they are persuaded in parallel. The meta-analysis presented this homogeneity in a different way, by showing the strong correlation of CATEs across different subgroups. Finally, we checked what happens when persuasive information is presented with countervailing information. The summary finding is that information effects are mostly additive, so when subjects see arguments on both sides of an issue, the effects mostly cancel.

CHAPTER SIX

Persistence and Decay

The persuasion in parallel hypothesis holds that the treatment effect of persuasive information on policy attitudes and beliefs is small, positive, and durable for everyone. I hope that chapter 5 convinced you that the effects of persuasive information are at least small and positive among the subdivisions of the American population defined by demographics and partisanship. Left to demonstrate is that these effects are durable. In this chapter, I assess the durability of treatment effects by re-interviewing experimental subjects ten days after exposure to treatment and by comparing the relative persistence of different kinds of treatments. The summary finding is that treatment effects are, on average, one-third of their original magnitude after ten days. Not all treatments persist at the same rate. Arguments that provide new (and more) information exhibit stronger persistence than light-touch framing or priming treatments.

The durability of the persuasive effects of treatment is of huge importance to anyone who's ever tried to convince somebody of something. When you change someone's mind, you want their mind to *stay changed*. You hope the person now sees the issue the way you see it, adopting your perspective and logic for the long haul. At the same time, we all know people who claim to be convinced on a Monday but need reminding by Thursday.

The persistence of persuasive effects has clear implications for electoral campaigns. If the effects of even very persuasive messages evaporate within a few hours, then campaigns would be best served by not spending large amounts of money on early advertisements only to see those effects dissipate by election day. If, however, persuasive information can induce durable attitude change, the cumulative effects of two years' campaigning might have a substantial impact on election results.

The vast majority of the scholarly work on persuasion takes place in laboratory or survey environments, and a common criticism of such studies is that they uncover real but fleeting effects. If so, the causal relationships studied in survey experiments may be little more than laboratory curiosities with only minimal importance for the real world. In the words of Gaines, Kuklinski, and Quirk (2007, 6), "The implications of survey-experimental results for politics depend crucially on how long the effects last, with relevant periods measured in weeks, or months, not minutes."

Previous work has found mixed evidence on persistence. Those who find little or no persistence include de Vreese (2004), who shows that subjects exposed to "strategic" news about the enlargement of the European Union reported higher political cynicism (0.44 scale points, 5-point scale) than subjects who read news focused on the issues surrounding enlargement. This difference was almost nonexistent in a follow-up conducted one week later (0.02 scale points). Similarly, Druckman and Nelson (2003) find that a special-interests frame increased support for a bill by 0.71 scale points (7-point scale); ten days later this effect drops to 0.41.[1] Mutz and Reeves (2005) report that videos featuring uncivil discourse between politicians decreased political trust by 0.44 standard deviations relative to civil discourse videos, but that the difference (not reported) was no longer statistically significant approximately one month after treatment.

Some survey experiments have found clear evidence of persistence. Tewksbury et al. (2000) report that exposure to a pro-regulation news story increased support for the regulation of hog farms by 24 percentage points relative to an anti-regulation story; this difference remained at 25 percentage points three weeks later. Lecheler and de Vreese (2011) show that a positive economic benefit frame increased support for the inclusion of Bulgaria and Romania in the European Union by 1.1 scale points (7-point scale); this effect was 0.93 after a day, 1.35 after a week, and 0.81 after two weeks. Dowling, Henderson, and Miller (2020) find that even four weeks post-treatment a factual information treatment about the Affordable Care Act increased the accuracy of beliefs by 20 to 30 percentage points, but that the initially observed effects on opinions about the law had mostly dissipated. For context, consider Hill et al. (2013), who use an observational research design to estimate that the persuasive effects of TV ads in presidential elections lasted for at least six weeks.

In this chapter, I'll develop the model of attitudes and attitude change given in chapter 3 to include time. Under the elaborated model, persuasive treatments that provide subjects with new considerations are hypothesized to last longer than framing or priming treatments that only change how existing considerations are combined into latent attitudes. This model helps to explain the different persistence patterns across kinds of treatments and also hints at an explanation for the "hockey stick" pattern of persistence observed in one longer-term panel survey experiment.

Extending the Research Design through Time

In order to study persistence, we need to elaborate the research design as described in chapter 4, with changes to the model, inquiry, data strategy, and answer strategy.

Changes to the Model

According to a typology given by Baden and Lecheler (2012), *Accessibility* treatments are hypothesized to operate primarily by increasing the weight given to a particular consideration. Because such treatments only affect outcomes through the weighting scheme, they are hypothesized to be fleeting. *Applicability* frames also operate by changing the weights given to considerations, but do so by linking two attitudes, so that the considerations in common are given greater weight. This theoretical subtlety is interesting, but I will conceive of both accessibility and applicability treatments as changing how considerations are combined. By contrast, *information* treatments operate by adding new considerations (which arrive with their own emphasis).

The Baden and Lecheler (2012) theory does not draw out subtleties with respect to individual differences across subjects, though others have done so. Chong and Druckman (2010), for example, explore differences according to whether subjects use "memory-based" processing or are high in "need-for-evaluation." My main focus here is on differences across *treatments*, not differences across subjects, though at the end of the chapter we'll consider whether persistence in one case appears to differ depending on partisanship.

In chapter 3, we imagined that subject i has k considerations indexed as $c_{i,1}, c_{i,2}, \ldots, c_{i,k}$, each of which is sampled according to probability weights $w_{i,1}, w_{i,2}, \ldots, w_{i,k}$. We can elaborate this model by subscripting considerations by time. Now subject i has k considerations at time t indexed as $c_{i,t,1}, c_{i,t,2}, \ldots, c_{i,t,k}$, each of which is sampled according to time-specific probability weights $w_{i,t,1}, w_{i,t,2}, \ldots, w_{i,t,k}$.

If treatment is randomly assigned at time 1, then we can think of $y_{i,t=1}(Z)$ as the measured attitude that unit i would express immediately after treatment is or isn't applied. This measured attitude is a combination of the considerations at time 1, sampled according to the weights at time 1. $y_{i,t=2}(Z)$ is i's measured attitude ten days after treatment is or isn't applied, and is a function of the considerations and weights at time 2. Importantly, Z is not subscripted by time. We are interested in how treatments that occur at one point in time affect attitudes measured immediately and at later points in time. I am specifically not considering treatments that vary over time. Here we are dealing with a single treatment delivered at one moment in time and outcomes that are measured at multiple points in time.

Changes to the Inquiry

In chapter 4, I gave the standard definition of the average treatment effect inquiry as $ATE = \frac{\sum_1^N y_i(Z=1) - y_i(Z=0)}{N}$. We can define the average treatment effects at time 1 and time 2 analogously:

$$\text{ATE Time 1} = \frac{\sum_1^N y_{i,t=1}(Z=1) - y_{i,t=1}(Z=0)}{N}$$

$$\text{ATE Time 2} = \frac{\sum_1^N y_{i,t=2}(Z=1) - y_{i,t=2}(Z=0)}{N}$$

The main inquiry in this chapter is the *persistence ratio*, which is defined as the ratio of the ATE at time 2 to the ATE at time 1:

$$\text{Persistence Ratio} = \frac{\sum_1^N y_{i,t=2}(Z=1) - y_{i,t=2}(Z=0)}{\sum_1^N y_{i,t=1}(Z=1) - y_{i,t=1}(Z=0)}$$

This inquiry can be thought of as the fraction of the average treatment effect we observe at time 1 that is still apparent at time 2. If the ATE at time 2 is half as big as the ATE at time 1, the persistence ratio is 0.5.

The persistence ratio is subtly different from an alternative inquiry that we might call "average persistence":

$$\text{Average persistence} = \frac{\sum_{1}^{N} \frac{y_{i,t=2}(Z=1) - y_{i,t=2}(Z=0)}{y_{i,t=1}(Z=1) - y_{i,t=1}(Z=0)}}{N}$$

This quantity averages over the time 2 to time 1 effect ratios of each individual. Average persistence is, in many ways, a more natural inquiry than the persistence ratio, as the psychological processes hypothesized to be responsible for persistence take place at the individual level. If I could estimate it, I would prefer to target average persistence rather than the persistence ratio. Unfortunately, estimating average persistence is too hard, and perhaps even impossible without imposing strong modeling assumptions. Because of the fundamental problem of causal inference, we can't estimate the individual-level causal effects at time 1 or at time 2, so we can't estimate the individual-level ratio either.

Frustratingly, the persistence ratio is not equal to average persistence, because a ratio of averages is not, in general, equal to an average of ratios. As a result, the persistence ratio can sometimes be misleading or at least difficult to interpret. Imagine, for example, that half the sample has a treatment effect of 2 at time 1 but 1 at time 2; the other half has treatment effects of 1 at time 1 but 2 at time 2. For individuals in the first group, average persistence is $\frac{1}{2} = 0.5$; for individuals in the second group, average persistence is four times bigger: $\frac{2}{1} = 2$. The persistence ratio, however, is $\frac{1.5}{1.5} = 1$. In a situation like this, claiming 100 percent persistence would be misleading. The persistence ratio and average persistence don't have to disagree, of course. For example, if treatment effects were equal to 2 for everyone at time 1 and equal to 1 for everyone at time 2, then the persistence ratio would be the same as the average persistence: $\frac{1}{N}\sum_{1}^{N}\frac{1}{2} = \frac{1}{N}\sum_{1}^{N}1 / \frac{1}{N}\sum_{1}^{N}2 = 0.5$. Loosely speaking, if the patterns of persistence are similar across different kinds of subjects, the persistence ratio and average persistence will agree.

Changes to the Data Strategy

Studying how long the effects of persuasive treatments last should be straightforward. We just need to conduct experiments in which subjects

are randomly exposed to treatments, then we need to measure their political attitudes and beliefs at multiple subsequent points in time. The design is conceptually straightforward but logistically challenging because
of the difficulty and expense inherent in recontacting subjects, some of
whom we fail to recontact altogether. As I will discuss below, this missingness in the follow-up waves causes design headaches that qualify
some of the conclusions. These technical and statistical challenges help
to explain why, to date, relatively few survey experiments have employed
a panel design in which the same subjects are reinterviewed multiple
times post-treatment.

This chapter brings together evidence from twelve panel survey experiments. Four of the studies are replications, so the set of twelve com-
prises eight unique designs. Because the studies include multiple treatment conditions to which subjects could be assigned, I'll report the
persistence of thirty-eight separate treatments. In all cases, the time 1
outcome variable is collected in the same survey in which the treatment
was delivered. I'll refer to this measurement as "immediately" post-
treatment, although in most cases, subjects answered other questions in
between exposure to treatment and outcome measurement. The time 2
variable is collected approximately ten days after the time 1 survey. The
timing is approximate because I never initiated recontact on weekends
and because subjects sometimes only responded after two or three attempted recontacts. In only one case—the newspaper op-ed study discussed in chapter 1—were subjects recontacted a third time.

I have categorized the treatments into those that should exhibit stronger persistence and those that show weaker persistence, as shown in table
6.1. These categorizations are loosely based on whether the treatments
are primarily about changing the weights on existing considerations or
primarily about giving subjects new considerations. In a subset of the
studies (the replications of Hopkins and Mummolo 2017; Brader, Valentino, and Suhay 2008; Hiscox 2006; and Johnston and Ballard 2016),
these predictions were preregistered. For the others, the "predictions"
were made after the studies were completed, but I promise that I did not
make them on the basis of the results.

Whether or not these predictions are borne out is a very weak test of
the theoretical framework described above, mainly because the causal
variable in that theory (whether the treatment operates by changing the
weights or by changing considerations) was not directly manipulated. A
rigorous test of the theory would take a set of treatments and change

TABLE 6.1 **Persistence predictions for 12 panel survey experiments**

Study	Treatments	Prediction	Sample
Chong and Druckman (2010)	6 pro- or 6 anti-Patriot Act statements	Strong	Original Study (N = 825); MTurk Replication (N = 968)
Coppock, Ekins, and Kirby (2018)	Op-eds favoring libertarian policy positions	Strong	MTurk sample (N = 2,137); Policy professional sample (N = 1,276)
Guess and Coppock (2018)	2 pro- or 2 anti-minimum wage video clips	Strong	MTurk sample (N = 279)
Lord, Ross, and Lepper (1979)	2 pro- or 2 anti-capital punishment scientific studies	Strong	MTurk replication (N = 303)
Hopkins and Mummolo (2017)	Short policy statements by US senators	Weak	MTurk replication (N = 1,940); GfK replication (N = 2,426)
Brader, Valentino, and Suhay (2008)	Positively or negatively framed newspaper articles about immigration	Weak	MTurk replication (N = 1,498)
Hiscox (2006)	Statements about economists' preferred policies; short pro- or anti-free trade statements	Weak	MTurk replication (N = 1,442); GfK replication (N = 1,336)
Johnston and Ballard (2016)	Short statements about economists' preferred policies	Weak	MTurk replication (N = 2,115)

Ns refer to the number of subjects who participated in the Time 2 follow-up study and were assigned to conditions used in the persistence analysis.

only this variable. I tried hard to come up with such a design, but I found it very challenging practically. We would need to come up with a pair of treatments in which one operates through the weights and the other operates through new considerations, but they are otherwise identical. The treatments in this study vary on many dimensions, some of which may be correlated with these mechanisms. In this sense, whether the treatments are hypothesized to operate mainly through the weights or via new considerations is just a treatment-level covariate whose causal role we don't get to learn about since we don't directly manipulate it.

These predictions summarize my intuitions about which treatments ought to last longer. My intuitions are informed by the theoretical framework, but they are of course also influenced by other intangible reactions to and impressions of the treatment. My hope is that at a minimum, they help to inform a tentative first step into a typology of persuasive information treatments that predicts the persistence of their effects on attitudes.

Changes to the Answer Strategy

When discussing the duration of treatment effects, it is common to dichotomize effects into those that persist and those that do not (e.g., Druckman and Nelson 2003; de Vreese 2004; Mutz and Reeves 2005). For example, if a treatment caused a statistically significant shift in outcomes at time 1, but the time 2 estimate is not statistically significant, the treatment effect is said to "not persist." While this categorization may have some heuristic value, I think it probably paints too pessimistic a picture. Instead, in addition to reporting the time 2 estimate and standard error, I will directly estimate the persistence ratio and its standard error. I will build my estimate of the persistence ratio from the ratio of the time 2 to time 1 OLS average treatment effect estimates. Since the two ATE estimates are not independent, I obtain standard errors and build confidence intervals via the nonparametric bootstrap.

Estimation is complicated by attrition, or the unfortunate fact that not all subjects respond at time 2. Except in the unlikely scenario that missingness is uncorrelated with time 2 potential outcomes, our estimates may be biased away from the full-sample estimands. I address this problem by changing the inquiry ever so slightly. Instead of estimating effects among the full sample, I will shoot at the persistence ratio among a subset of subjects, the so-called always-reporters.[2] Always-reporters respond to the wave 2 survey regardless of what treatment condition they were assigned to. Never-reporters, as their name suggests, *don't* respond to the wave 2 survey, irrespective of treatment condition. Under the assumption that all subjects are either always-reporters or never-reporters (and not some other type, like if-treated reporters or if-untreated reporters), then we obtain consistent estimates of the persistence ratio for always-reporters. One piece of evidence that supports (but does not prove) this always-reporter assumption is that in all cases studied, the estimated average effects of treatment on missingness cannot be distinguished from zero—that is, we don't have direct evidence that some subjects are if-treated or if-untreated reporters. The upshot of this complication is that the estimates of over-time persistence only pertain to the always-reporters. For this reason, the time 1 ATE will be estimated among always-reporters only as well, which eases interpretation by holding the sample fixed across waves.

Results

Figure 6.1 presents the study-by-study standardized average treatment effects at time 1 (immediately post-treatment) and time 2 (ten days post-treatment) for all 12 studies. So we can focus on the magnitudes of the treatment effects rather than their signs, both time 1 and time 2 estimates have been multiplied by the sign of the time 1 estimate. The first and most obvious pattern is that most treatment effects decay. In 33 of 38 opportunities, the time 2 estimate is smaller than the corresponding time 1 estimate. This finding accords with the standard expectation that, regardless of the mechanism, effects should get smaller over time.

Different treatments experience different levels of decline. The pro-minimum wage videos, the flat tax op-ed, and the pro-capital punishment studies all had persistence ratios above 60 percent. Other treatments, such as the pro- and anti-Patriot Act conditions in the Chong and Druckman (2010) replication, had persistence ratios that could not be distinguished from zero. Curiously, the different replications of the Hiscox (2006) "expert" treatment generated very different persistence estimates: 49 percent on MTurk but 0 percent on Lucid. Some unobserved difference across the two versions may be responsible for this divergence, or it might simply be attributable to sampling variability. For those interested in the study-by-study persistence estimates themselves, they are presented at the end of the chapter in table 6.4.

Figure 6.2 visualizes the persistence ratio estimates themselves on the vertical axis and the time 1 estimates on the horizontal axis, with triangles for treatments with a weak persistence prediction and circles for treatments with a strong persistence prediction. The plot also overlays the meta-analytic estimates according to the predicted strength of persistence. The first thing to note about this plot is that, indeed, those treatments that were predicted to persist at a higher rate did so. Across all 12 studies, the average persistence ratio was about one-third, or 34 percent; that figure is 50 percent in the stronger persistence group and 20 percent in the weaker persistence group (see table 6.2).

The second feature to notice about figure 6.2 is that there is very little (if any) correlation between the size of the effect at time 1 and the fraction of that effect remaining at time 2. This is surprising, to me at least, because I can come up with stories to explain a dependence in either direction. One might think that bigger effects have more room to fall,

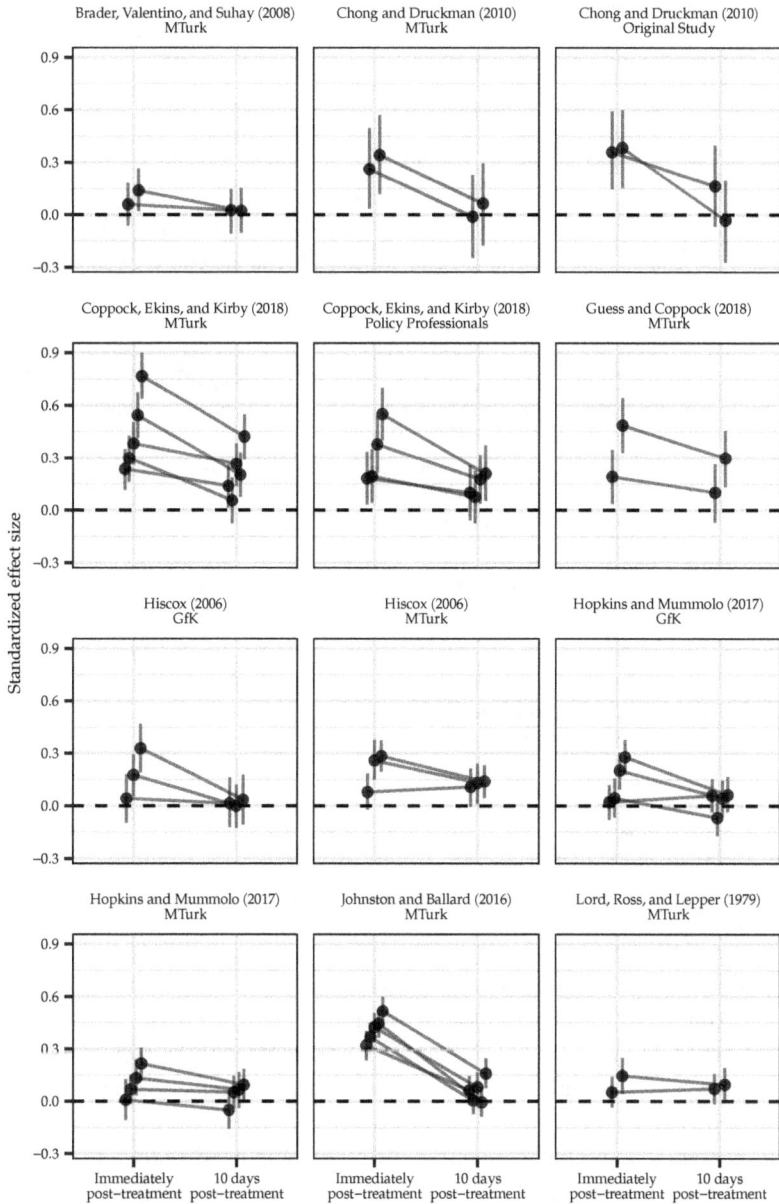

FIGURE 6.1. Overtime ATE estimates

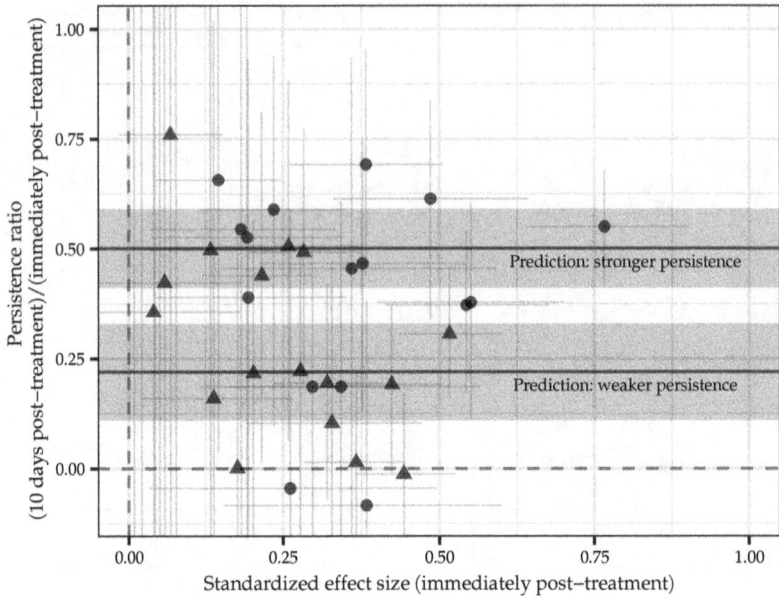

FIGURE 6.2. Persistence estimates

TABLE 6.2 **Average persistence ratio estimates**

	Estimate (SE)	95% CI
Overall	0.34 (0.04)	[0.26, 0.42]
Prediction: stronger persistence	0.50 (0.04)	[0.42, 0.58]
Prediction: weaker persistence	0.21 (0.04)	[0.13, 0.28]

Entries are meta-analytic averages of persistence ratio estimates obtained from random-effects models.

causing them to display smaller persistence ratios. Or one might think that whatever causes a treatment to have large immediate effects will also cause those effects to last longer. It's possible that the lack of a relationship between time 1 effect and persistence occurs because these two patterns cancel each other. Descriptively speaking, however, we don't see any correlation between initial effect size and persistence.

The results presented thus far suggest that treatment effects decline to approximately one-third their original strength after ten days, on average. If effects continue to decay at the same rate, we might project that they dissipate entirely after fifteen days. Alternatively, effects might exhibit some measure of proportional decay, resulting in one-ninth strength

after twenty days, one-twenty-seventh strength after thirty days, and so
on. In order to trace a fuller picture of the rate of decay, we need to measure outcomes at more points in time.

One of the studies (the MTurk study in Coppock, Ekins, and Kirby
2018) from the batch of 12 included a third wave of post-treatment measurement after thirty days. This study was discussed in chapter 1, but to
review: subjects could be assigned to one of 5 groups that read an op-ed
advocating libertarian policy positions or a control group. Figure 6.3 displays the over-time results of this experiment.

The pattern of results is quite consistent across all five issue areas. The
treatments produce large immediate increases in support for the policy
positions advocated in the op-eds. After ten days treatment effects decay to 46 percent (SE = 5 percent) of their original magnitudes. Remark-
ably, very little further decay appears to take place between ten days and
thirty days after treatment. After thirty days, average persistence declines to 44 percent (SE = 6 percent). These results suggest a "hockey
stick" pattern of decay: after an initial decline, subsequent decreases
are smaller. This pattern might, with a little bit of theoretical footwork,

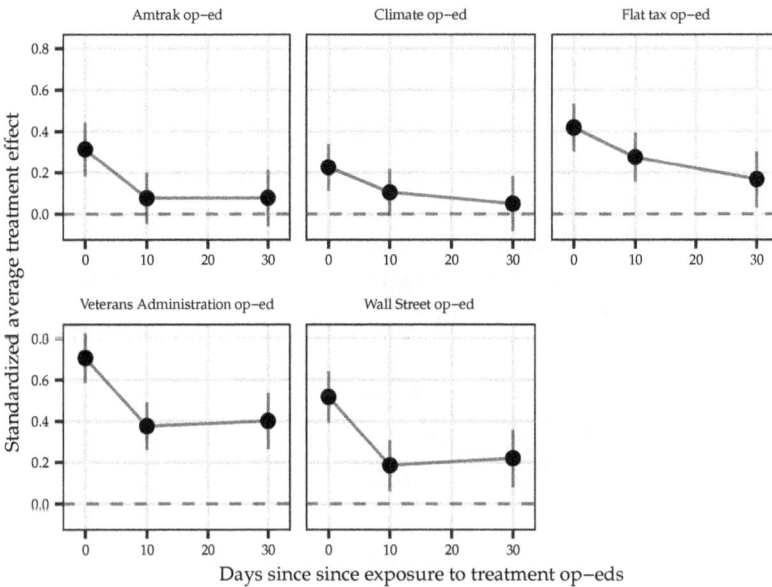

FIGURE 6.3. Newspaper op-eds overtime treatment effect estimates

be reconciled with the larger theoretical setup described above. When new considerations are introduced, they may arrive with artificially high weights attached. Over time, these weights may "settle," but the consideration itself may remain in the mind of the subject. This conjecture should be subjected to further empirical testing in experiments that track subjects' responses to treatment over longer periods of time.

One question that arises in the study of persistence is whether effects decay at different rates in different subgroups. In the case of the newspaper op-eds experiment, we might imagine that people who start out on different sides of an issue would attach different weights to the new considerations offered by the op-ed, and that the weights on those considerations would change at different rates. In chapter 5, we saw that Republican and Democratic respondents were persuaded in parallel by the op-eds. Table 6.3 shows that a similar finding applies to the persistence of the effects as well. For Republicans, persistence after ten days averaged 57 percent; this figure was 43 percent for Democrats. But an inspection of the confidence intervals reveals that these two estimates are not statistically significantly different from each other. The level of persistence after thirty days is similar across groups, with both Republican and Democratic respondents still showing strong signs of persistence.

Summary

This chapter set out to make good on the "durable" part of the claim that "treatment effect of persuasive information on policy attitudes and beliefs is small, positive, and durable for everyone." On the basis of the twelve panel survey experiments analyzed in this chapter, we can say that durable means that treatment effects are, on average, approximately one-third their original magnitudes after ten days (see table 6.4).

TABLE 6.3 **Op-ed experiment persistence estimates**

	10 days post-treatment		30 days post-treatment	
	Estimate (SE)	95% CI	Estimate (SE)	95% CI
Overall	0.48 (0.05)	[0.39, 0.57]	0.46 (0.05)	[0.36, 0.57]
Democrat	0.48 (0.07)	[0.35, 0.62]	0.47 (0.08)	[0.32, 0.62]
Republican	0.53 (0.08)	[0.37, 0.69]	0.57 (0.09)	[0.39, 0.75]

Entries are meta-analytic averages of persistence ratio estimates obtained from random-effects models.

TABLE 6.4 **All persistence estimates**

Sample	Treatment	ATE Time 1	ATE Time 2	Persistence Ratio
Guess and Coppock (2018). Prediction: Stronger Persistence				
MTurk	Two anti-minimum wage videos	−0.19 (0.08)	−0.10 (0.09)	0.53 (0.45)
MTurk	Two pro-minimum wage videos	0.49 (0.08)	0.30 (0.08)	0.61 (0.13)
Coppock, Ekins, and Kirby (2018). Prediction: Stronger Persistence				
MTurk	Amtrak op-ed	0.27 (0.04)	0.05 (0.05)	0.19 (0.17)
MTurk	Flat tax op-ed	0.36 (0.05)	0.25 (0.06)	0.69 (0.13)
MTurk	Veterans op-ed	0.78 (0.07)	0.43 (0.06)	0.55 (0.06)
MTurk	Wallstreet op-ed	0.55 (0.06)	0.20 (0.07)	0.37 (0.10)
Policy Professionals	Amtrak op-ed	0.35 (0.07)	0.16 (0.07)	0.47 (0.19)
Policy Professionals	Flat tax op-ed	0.18 (0.07)	0.07 (0.08)	0.39 (0.64)
Policy Professionals	Veterans op-ed	0.19 (0.07)	0.10 (0.07)	0.54 (0.47)
Policy Professionals	Wallstreet op-ed	0.55 (0.08)	0.21 (0.09)	0.38 (0.13)
Lord, Ross, and Lepper (1979). Prediction: Stronger Persistence				
MTurk	Two con studies	−0.05 (0.05)	−0.07 (0.05)	1.39 (9.30)
MTurk	Two pro studies	0.15 (0.06)	0.10 (0.05)	0.66 (0.25)
Chong and Druckman (2010). Prediction: Stronger Persistence				
MTurk	Six anti-Patriot Act statements	−0.34 (0.10)	−0.06 (0.11)	0.19 (0.31)
MTurk	Six pro-Patriot Act statements	0.26 (0.09)	−0.01 (0.11)	−0.04 (43.25)
Original Study	Six anti-Patriot Act statements	−0.38 (0.11)	0.03 (0.10)	−0.08 (0.36)
Original Study	Six pro-Patriot Act statements	0.36 (0.11)	0.16 (0.10)	0.46 (0.25)
Hopkins and Mummolo (2017). Prediction: Weaker persistence				
GfK	Crime statement	0.04 (0.06)	−0.07 (0.05)	−1.57 (15.19)
GfK	Health statement	0.02 (0.05)	0.06 (0.05)	2.71 (4.71)
GfK	Stimulus statement	−0.28 (0.06)	−0.06 (0.05)	0.22 (0.18)
GfK	Terror statement	0.20 (0.06)	0.04 (0.07)	0.22 (0.28)
MTurk	Crime statement	−0.01 (0.06)	0.05 (0.06)	−5.44 (20.16)
MTurk	Health statement	−0.07 (0.05)	−0.05 (0.04)	0.76 (0.90)
MTurk	Stimulus statement	−0.22 (0.06)	−0.09 (0.05)	0.44 (0.20)
MTurk	Terror statement	0.13 (0.06)	0.07 (0.06)	0.50 (2.20)
Hiscox (2006). Prediction: Weaker persistence				
GfK	Expert cue	0.18 (0.05)	0.00 (0.05)	0.00 (0.45)
GfK	Negative frame	−0.33 (0.07)	−0.03 (0.07)	0.10 (0.21)
GfK	Positive frame	−0.04 (0.08)	−0.01 (0.08)	0.36 (2.59)
MTurk	Expert cue	0.28 (0.04)	0.14 (0.05)	0.49 (0.15)
MTurk	Negative frame	−0.26 (0.07)	−0.13 (0.06)	0.51 (0.21)
MTurk	Positive frame	−0.08 (0.05)	−0.11 (0.05)	1.39 (4.79)
Johnston and Ballard (2016). Prediction: Weaker persistence				
MTurk	Gold Standard	0.52 (0.04)	0.16 (0.04)	0.31 (0.07)
MTurk	Health Care	0.37 (0.04)	0.01 (0.04)	0.01 (0.14)
MTurk	Immigration	0.32 (0.04)	0.06 (0.05)	0.19 (0.14)
MTurk	Tax Cut	0.44 (0.04)	−0.01 (0.04)	−0.01 (0.08)
MTurk	Trade with China	0.42 (0.04)	0.08 (0.04)	0.19 (0.09)
Brader, Valentino, and Suhay (2008). Prediction: Weaker persistence				
MTurk	Negative article	−0.14 (0.06)	−0.02 (0.05)	0.16 (8.55)
MTurk	Positive article	0.06 (0.06)	0.03 (0.06)	0.42 (28.36)

Bootstrapped standard errors are in parentheses. ATE estimates are in standard units.

Not all treatments decay at the same rate. Treatments that work primarily through framing and priming were hypothesized to decay more quickly. On average, these treatment effects were 20 percent of their original magnitudes after ten days. Treatments that work primarily by furnishing new information were hypothesized to endure longer. On average, those treatment effects were 50 percent of their original magnitudes after ten days.

This investigation has hardly closed the book on the persistence of persuasive treatments. We have only one study that measured beyond thirty days, which came to the surprising conclusion that very little decay occurred between day 10 and day 30. I offered the conjecture that the large initial treatment effect was due to the introduction of highly salient new considerations; over time the new considerations remain but lose some of their initial salience. As panel surveys become easier to conduct, more such studies will undoubtedly be added to our database on this question.

One outstanding concern I have is that some portion of the observed level of persistence may be due to the repetition of the survey question. The measurement properties of repeating the same questions multiple times could interact with treatments in complicated ways. It could cause people to reflect more deeply on the treatments at the moment of answering the question such that the treatment effect "crystallizes." Alternatively, it could be that people simply remember how they responded last time and do so again. Tappin and Hewitt (2021) investigate this possibility with an innovative panel survey design, finding no differences in the persistence of a party cue effect depending on whether outcomes are measured immediately post-treatment or not. Their finding offers some reassurance that repeated measurement does not artificially inflate persistence estimates.

Finally, these results also offer an opportunity to revisit the large literature in psychology on the so-called "sleeper effect" (Hovland, Lumsdaine, and Sheffield 1949; Hovland and Weiss 1951; Cook and Flay 1978), according to which initially very small effects can sometimes blossom into strong effects over time. The proposed mechanism is that subjects would forget why they initially discounted some new piece of information; when the discounting falls away, the information would exert some persuasive influence. However, experiments designed to produce the sleeper effect have usually failed to demonstrate that it occurs. Consistent with this line of evidence, none of the studies reported here saw an initially null result that became statistically significant later.

CHAPTER SEVEN

Models of Information Processing

The model of persuasion laid out in chapter 4 was light on the specifics of the cognitive processes that mediate the effects of information on policy attitudes. In fact, one of the nodes on the causal graph representation of the model was explicitly labeled "unknown mediators" to reflect my agnosticism about the details of information processing. The experimental results presented in chapters 5 and 6 show that information clearly does affect attitudes, but they don't shed light on *how*. Bayesian reasoning and motivated reasoning represent two alternative theoretical perspectives on the content of that "unknown mediators" node: how it is, cognitively speaking, that information transmits its influence on attitudes.

Bayesian reasoning posits that people evaluate information by considering the likelihood of the information arising under alternative states of the world. Information is interpreted as evidence in favor of whichever alternative state of the world is more likely to have generated the information. Bayesian reasoning has garnered an undeserved reputation as being "rational" or "reasonable," because it imagines that individuals coolly and calmly update their views in line with a clean mathematical formula. But depending on the inputs to that formula, we might entirely disagree that a person updates their views "reasonably." A perfectly Bayesian conspiracy theorist could interpret video footage of Saturn V rockets blasting off as further evidence that we faked the moon landing because that's just what NASA *would* broadcast if they wanted to sell the lie. This line of reasoning may seem kooky, but with the right likelihood function, such a person is just as Bayesian as Spock from *Star Trek*.

Motivated reasoning, by contrast, posits that people reason in line with goals or motivations. Their goal is to arrive at a conclusion of a particular type. Within political science, a distinction is often drawn between accuracy motivations and directional motivations. Which set of motivations dominates for a particular person in a particular setting will color how they interpret evidence. If their goal is to come to a "correct" conclusion, they will then try to incorporate the information in ways that will yield the most accurate answer. If their goal is to come to a "congenial" conclusion, then they will incorporate information in ways that are most likely to yield that congenial answer. Depending on the mix of accuracy and directional motivations, people might update in the direction of evidence, or they might not.

I have two goals with this chapter, one negative and one positive.

The negative goal is to show that we can't affirm the priority of either Bayesian or motivated reasoning with the experiments in this book. In the terms used by the philosopher of science Karl Popper, neither theory is "falsifiable," at least not with current tools, since any pattern of treatment effects is consistent with Bayesian reasoning and any pattern of treatment effects is consistent with motivated reasoning. Bayesians can update in the "wrong" direction if their interpretations of evidence (their likelihood functions) are backward. Motivated reasoners can update in the "right" direction if accuracy goals dominate the directional goals that pull against evidence. Likewise, the purported evidence in favor of motivated reasoning can always be given a nonmotivational account. I think this negative goal is important because it raises the bar (especially for motivated reasoning theorists) for what would constitute good evidence in favor of claims about information processing. My view shares much in common with Druckman and McGrath (2019), who conclude that "there is scant evidence for directional motivated reasoning when it comes to climate change: the evidence put forth cannot be distinguished from a model in which people aim for accurate beliefs, but vary in how they assess the credibility of different pieces of information."

The positive goal is to give an interpretation of the empirical findings of persuasion in parallel in terms of these two accounts of information processing. *If* people are Bayesian reasoners, we can conclude from the experimental evidence that they all agree about which side an argument is "good for." I'll formalize this idea in terms of the specific class of likelihood functions people must share, if indeed they are Bayesians. *If*, however, people are indeed motivated reasoners, the experiments demonstrate that accuracy goals always dominate directional goals when people process persuasive information. Importantly, if either of these (now restricted) theories is correct, then we can conclude that people process information "reasonably."

Bayesian Reasoning

Bayesian reasoning is a model of cognition that is sometimes described as how "rational" people ought to process new information. Under this model, individuals are endowed with two characteristics: prior beliefs (what they think before encountering new information) and a likelihood function (beliefs about the probability of seeing the new information in alternative states of the world). When individuals encounter new information, they update their prior beliefs to form posterior beliefs. The magnitude of the update depends on the new information and the individual's likelihood function. These updates are computed via application of Bayes' rule. As we'll see, Bayesian reasoning's reputation as "rational" is mostly undeserved, since people are free to have bonkers prior beliefs and loopy likelihood functions.

Bayes' rule itself is a formula that describes how to calculate a conditional probability that follows from the foundational premises of probability.[1] Bayes' rule says that the conditional probability $P(A|B)$ (pronounced "probability of A given B") is a function of the unconditional probability $P(A)$, and two more conditional probabilities $P(B|A)$ and $P(B|\neg A)$ (pronounced "probability of B given not A"). Here is one way to write Bayes' rule using these quantities:

$$P(A|B) = \frac{P(B|A)P(A)}{P(B|A)P(A) + P(B|\neg A)P(\neg A)}$$

$P(A|B)$ is called the posterior belief, $P(A)$ is called the prior belief, and together, $P(B|A)$ and $P(B|\neg A)$ form the likelihood function. Although the terms used to describe Bayesian reasoning have a temporal flavor (prior beliefs followed by posterior beliefs), we can draw the connection between Bayesian reasoning and counterfactuals by saying that $P(A) = y_i(0)$ and $P(A|B) = y_i(1)$. Under the Bayesian model, the treatment effect of information[2] can therefore be written as $P(A|B) - P(A)$: posterior beliefs minus prior beliefs.

As an example of Bayesian reasoning in action, consider the treatment effect of a report that the earth is warming (B) on belief that climate change is real (A). To fix ideas, let's imagine we expose a group of climate skeptics to this report.

The skeptics' prior probability that climate change is real is very low, say $P(A) = 0.01$. In order to predict the effect of information on their beliefs, we need to know the skeptics' likelihood function. That is, we need to know what they think the probability the report would conclude the world is warming if climate change were real and if climate change were not real. Because the climate skeptics think scientists can write whatever they want regardless of the truth, they believe both probabilities to be very high: $P(B|A) = 0.99$ and $P(B|\neg A) = 0.98$. I'm imagining that they think $P(B|A)$ is ever so slightly higher than $P(B|\neg A)$, because after all, maintaining a global scientific conspiracy is tough. Plugging these numbers into Bayes' rule yields a posterior of $P(A|B) = 0.0101$. If these really are the prior belief and likelihood functions of the climate skeptics, and if they really do follow Bayes' rule when forming posterior beliefs, then we would predict that they would update their views in the direction of information to the tune of one one-hundredth of a percentage point. The skeptics still disagree vehemently with the report and its conclusions, but a tiny bit of incremental progress has been made. Since $P(B|A)$ is higher than $P(B|\neg A)$, the skeptic updates in the right direction.

Empirical Assessments of Bayesian Reasoning

The Bayesian reasoning hypothesis may be traced at least as far back as de Finetti (1937), who appears to have been the first to explicitly invoke Bayes' rule as a model of human cognition.[3] The main thrust of that work is that although individuals make subjective probability judgments, they nevertheless respond to new information in the manner suggested by "objective" laws of probability:

> Observation cannot confirm or refute an opinion, which is and cannot be other than an opinion and thus neither true nor false; observation can only give us information which is capable of *influencing* our opinion. The meaning of this statement is very precise: it means that to the probability of a fact conditioned on this information—a probability very distinct from that of the

same fact not conditioned on anything else—we can indeed attribute a different value. (Reproduced in Kyburg and Smokler 1964, 154, emphasis in original.)

The Bayesian learning hypothesis developed alongside the introduction of Bayesian statistical methods to the social sciences (Edwards, Lindman, and Savage 1963). Bayesian statisticians were arguing that Bayes' rule offered a sensible method for the integration of research findings, leading to the normative claim that scientists and humans generally *should* incorporate new evidence according to the cool calculus of conditional probability. It was then a short step from advocating this normative position to testing the positive claim that Bayes' rule provides a fair description of human cognition.

A long series of demonstrations (Edwards and Phillips 1964; Peterson and Miller 1965; Phillips and Edwards 1966) showed that humans perform poorly compared to (a specific version of) the Bayesian ideal. In the prototypical experiment, subjects are shown two urns, one filled with a majority of blue balls and the other with a majority of red balls. They are told that they will be given a series of draws from a randomly selected urn and will have to estimate the probability that the draws come from the majority blue urn. Bayes' rule (with a binomial likelihood function) dictates how much subjects "should" update their priors. These studies routinely find that subjects are consistently too conservative and fail to update their beliefs far enough. Hill (2017) confirms that these classic results hold for contemporary political questions as well. In his study, subjects are told the computer will tell them the truth about a series of political facts 75 percent of the time. The subjects do update in the direction of information, but only 73 percent as much as they should according to Bayes' rule, leading Hill to describe his subjects as "cautious Bayesians."

A more optimistic take comes from the field of linguistics. Frank and Goodman (2012) tackle the problem that listeners reason under uncertainty about speakers' intended messages when the signal isn't sufficient to discriminate among potential interpretations. Listeners need to infer what speakers mean on the basis of beliefs about speakers, most notably that they will prioritize signaling relevant information. Bayesian listeners have priors over what speakers mean, likelihood functions that describe what speakers *would say* depending on what they mean, then calculate posteriors about what speakers did mean on the basis of what they did say. In a language game experiment, Frank and Goodman (2012) randomly divide subjects into three groups: those who give their priors, those who give their likelihoods, and those who give their posteriors. In a crazy bit of luck and magic, the posteriors come extremely close to what would be obtained from multiplying the priors and likelihoods together. This result doesn't prove that listeners actually use Bayes' rule to update their prior beliefs, but it does show that they behave in much the same way that Bayesians would.

Within political science, the Bayesian models of cognition have been most frequently applied to models of partisan evaluation and choice. Zechman (1979) and Achen (1992) propose statistical models of party identification based on a Bayesian model in which individuals update their impressions of the political parties based on new evidence. Gerber and Green (1998, 1999) argue that so-called "perceptual bias" can be explained in Bayesian terms. Partisans accord negative evidence for their candidates less weight not because they irrationally disregard discordant information, but because it conflicts with their priors. Partisans are nevertheless moved by "bad news," as evidenced by the parallel public opinion movements by partisans on both sides in response to changing political and economic conditions. Bartels (2002) disagrees, arguing that a lack of convergence indicates partisan bias, because after enough evidence, Bayesians with different priors (but the same likelihood functions) ought to agree. Bullock (2009) shows that the prediction of convergence requires an assumption that the underlying parameter (in this case, the "true" value of the parties) is not changing.

The disagreement between Gerber, Green, and Bullock on the one hand and Bartels on the other is premised on a specific model of Bayesianism; the dispute is about what that model predicts. The specific model in question is the "normal-normal" model, in which subjects have a prior belief that is normally distributed around a "best guess," but includes some uncertainty. The evidence arrives as a point estimate, also with uncertainty. The likelihood function embedded within the normal-normal model requires that a Bayesian take a weighted average of the prior and the evidence, where the weights are proportional to their respective uncertainties. If the true value of the parameter is unchanging (which it might not be, as shown in Bullock 2009), normal-normal Bayesians should converge on the true value, regardless of where their prior beliefs started out—hence Bartels's critique that a lack of convergence is evidence against Bayesianism.

But what about people who are Bayesian, but who simply do not employ the normal-normal model? Bayesians of every stripe are entitled to their own likelihood functions, and each likelihood function predicts a different pattern of updating. Unless one is willing to make strong assumptions about precisely what kind of Bayesian everyone is, neither evidence of parallel trends nor converging trends is sufficient to confirm or disconfirm Bayesian reasoning.

Formal theorists have proposed many models of Bayesian reasoning in which everyone learns from information, but nevertheless persists in disagreement. Acemoglu, Chernozhukov, and Yildiz (2016) show that even small amounts of heterogeneity in how uncertain individuals are about $P(B|A)$ and $P(B|\neg A)$ can lead to a long-run failure to converge. Benoît and Dubra (2014) offer a theory of "rational" attitude polarization in which some (but not all) individuals have access to auxiliary information that colors how they interpret evidence. Stated differently, the auxiliary information allows different individuals to have different likelihood functions. Bohren (2016) describes a process of "informational herding" in which Bayesian beliefs can fail to converge on the truth because the likelihood functions misinterpret multiple signals as being independent rather than correlated. Cheng and Hsiaw (2018) allow individuals' likelihood functions themselves to vary as a function of their beliefs about source credibility, which can generate long-run disagreement. The model proposed by Fryer, Harms, and Jackson (2019) accomplishes something similar by allowing individual likelihood functions to be conditional on priors. This list is far from a complete accounting of the variety of ingenious ways formal theorists have invented to allow Bayesians to interpret the same evidence differently. For more, see Fudenberg and Levine (2006); Shmaya and Yariv (2016); Koçak (2019); Lockwood et al. (2017); Stone (2020), Little, Schnakenberg, and Turner (2020); or Little (2021).

In light of the many ways Bayesians can fail to update "correctly," it makes little sense to hold up Bayesian reasoning as a normative ideal against which frail, biased, and imperfect human information processing should be measured. The components of Bayesian reasoning—prior beliefs and likelihood functions—are unconstrained and subjective, so treatment effects of any sign and magnitude are consistent with Bayesian reasoning. If (counterfactually) our experiments had shown that the treatment effect of persuasive information were positive for some people but negative for others, we would not have evidence against Bayesian reasoning. Those "other" people might just have a likelihood function in which $P(B|A)$ is *lower* than $P(B|\neg A)$. Why people might have different likelihood functions is a difficult thing to know. The reasons could be observable (somewhere in X) or they might be unobservable (somewhere in U) and we just don't know.

Figure 7.1 shows how deeply frustrating the problem truly is that Bayesianism doesn't mean "reasonable." The three facets represent three different prior beliefs that A is true: 20 percent, 50 percent, and 80 percent. Each point within the facets represents a different kind of Bayesian, as defined by their subjective probabilities $P(B|A)$ and $P(B|\neg A)$. The fraction $P(B|A)$ / $P(B|\neg A)$ is called the "likelihood ratio." When it is above one, that means a person thinks the probability of seeing B is higher if A is true than if it is not true. When the likelihood ratio is above one, posterior beliefs are higher than prior beliefs, represented by arrows pointing up. The bigger the positive difference between posterior and prior, the darker and longer the arrow. When the likelihood ratio is below one, posteriors are lower than priors—i.e., the Bayesian updates in the "wrong" direction, represented by analogous arrows pointing down.

Figure 7.1 points out two very important features of Bayesian reasoning. First, *priors* do not determine whether an update is positive or negative. The three facets have different priors, and in all three facets, half the updates are positive and half are negative. Second, no treatment effect is incompatible with Bayesianism. The fact that every possible

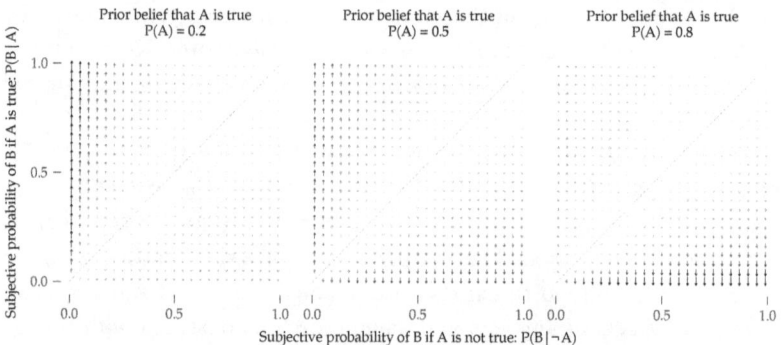

FIGURE 7.1. Treatment effects of information depending on priors and likelihood functions
Note: The figure shows that Bayesian updates in response to evidence can have any sign or magnitude depending on the likelihood ratio. Each facet represents a different prior belief that A is true.

pattern of updating could be accommodated within a Bayesian theory of information processing is very troublesome from a philosophy of science perspective because it means that the theory cannot be falsified by measuring the causal effect of treatments on beliefs. If the theory cannot be falsified, then we are in the position of not being able to demonstrate that it is false even if it is.

What do we learn about Bayesian reasoning from the empirical results presented in chapter 5? We do not learn that people are Bayesian. We learn that if people really are Bayesian, then their likelihood ratios are all above one. Everyone agrees that evidence B is "good for" proposition A, even if they have conflicting prior beliefs about whether proposition A is true. If we're Bayesians, then everyone—even climate skeptics—agrees that evidence of steadily increasing global temperatures is more likely if climate change is real than if it is not real.

Motivated Reasoning

Motivated reasoning is a body of theory built around a model of human information processing based on goals (motivations). Humans are hypothesized to be endowed with motivations that govern information search, evaluation, and interpretation. Within social psychology, a wide variety of goals has been articulated, such as self-esteem, cognitive consistency, and belief in a just world (Pyszczynski and Greenberg 1987). Motivated reasoning theory within political science typically partitions goals into two sets: accuracy motivations and directional motivations. By and large, accuracy motivations drive people to strive for unbiased reasoning and directional motivations divert them from that course.

The accuracy motivation propels people to hold correct beliefs or correct attitudes. It is clear enough what "correct" means for beliefs about factual matters. A belief about a fact is correct if it matches the true state of the world. For beliefs about facts, we assume there exists a truth of the matter, so beliefs can be correct or incorrect. It is less clear what it means to hold a correct attitude about a political attitude object. At a minimum, it means that we presume that some policies are better than others (at least from an individual's own perspective), so holding a correct attitude would mean evaluating better policies more positively than worse policies. This conceptualization of holding correct attitudes immediately runs into some trouble if two individuals disagree over whether one policy is better than another, since they may disagree despite both being motivated by accuracy goals.

Scholars have tried to demonstrate the pull of accuracy motivations in experiments that aim to "activate" these motivations. For example, a stream of studies has shown that offering experimental subjects financial incentives for correct answers increases accuracy: Prior and Lupia (2008), Prior, Sood, and Khanna (2015), Bullock et al. (2015), and Khanna and Sood (2018) all find clear evidence that paying for correct answers causes subjects to come up with correct answers more often. As with most treatment effects, we don't know *why* this treatment works, we just know that it does. It could be that subjects' latent motivation for accuracy is activated by the prospect of earning extra money, or it could be that subjects' utility is increasing in money, so they take the survey more seriously and try harder. Financial incentives aren't the only treatments that increase subject accuracy about political facts; giving them extra time also works (Prior and Lupia 2008), as does simply asking people to provide accurate answers (Prior, Sood, and Khanna 2015). Because there are many ways to increase accuracy, we can't conclude that a treatment that increases accuracy does so through the accuracy motivation only.

The directional motivation, by contrast, is posited by motivated reasoning theorists to be the force that induces people not to reach an *accurate* conclusion, but instead to reach a *congenial* conclusion. For beliefs about facts, the directional motivation compels people to believe what they want to be true, regardless of the facts of the matter. For attitudes, directional goals motivate people to hold more positive attitudes about things they like and more negative attitudes about things they don't like. This conceptualization of having directional goals about attitudes is also a little funny—of course people hold more positive attitudes about things they like, that's what it means to like something! More charitably, the directional goal is presumed to motivate people to defend this attitude against alternatives for the sake of preserving the attitudes they happen to hold, not because they think they are correct.

Distinguishing motivated reasoning from nonmotivated reasoning has been difficult from the very start. Kunda's highly influential essay, *The Case for Motivated Reasoning*, opens with the plain admission that "The major and most damaging criticism of the motivational view was that all research purported to demonstrate motivated reasoning could be reinterpreted in entirely cognitive, nonmotivational terms" (Kunda 1990, 480). Kunda's rebuttal is to claim that motivations exert their influence *through* cognitive processes. She writes, "People rely on cognitive processes and representations to arrive at their desired conclusions, but motivation plays a role in determining which of these will be used on a given occasion." Personally, I don't find this defense convincing, since the whole difficulty is that both putative motivations and cognitive processes are unobservable. The pattern of inputs (manipulated information) and outputs (measured attitudes) that we do observe, as granted by Kunda, remain consistent with either the motivational or the nonmotivational account.

Motivated reasoning theory was brought into political science full force with Taber and Lodge's landmark 2006 article. They enumerated three main biases through which motivated reasoning is supposed to exert its causal effect on attitudes and beliefs. *Biased assimilation* (also referred to as the prior-attitude effect) refers to individuals' predisposition to evaluate information that contradicts their priors more negatively than information that confirms their priors. As discussed in chapter 2, the term "biased assimilation" is somewhat misleading, since it implies that if an argument is negatively evaluated, it will not be "assimilated" into an individual's beliefs. For example, the measure of biased assimilation in Lord, Ross, and Lepper (1979) (the study critiqued at length in chapter 2) is subjects' subjective ratings of the pro- and counter-attitudinal articles about capital punishment. Readers should keep in mind that this term of art refers to subjective evaluations of the arguments, not how the arguments are literally assimilated into post-treatment attitudes. *Disconfirmation bias* refers to individuals' proclivity to argue back more against counter-attitudinal information than against pro-attitudinal information. Disconfirmation bias more generally means that counter-attitudinal information is subject to greater scrutiny than pro-attitudinal information, presumably because people spend more time criticizing evidence they find to be low quality than they do evidence they find to be high quality. In this sense, disconfirmation bias is an extension of biased assimilation. Individuals think counter-attitudinal information is low quality, so they criticize it. It would indeed be odd to counterargue information with which one agrees. Finally, *confirmation bias* refers to the tendency of individuals to preferentially seek out information that confirms their priors. This bias is not about information processing; instead it refers to how individuals encounter information in the first place. Supposing that individuals have directional goals, seeking out attitude-confirming information is a prime way to achieve those goals.

Bayesian Interpretation of Biased Assimilation

As allowed in Kunda (1990), each of these three putative biases—biased assimilation, confirmation bias, and disconfirmation bias—could be given a nonmotivational account. This section articulates how exactly the same empirical patterns could be generated by Bayesians without motivations. The purpose of this section is not to affirm the Bayesian model over motivated reasoning, but rather to argue that demonstrations of biased assimilation, confirmation bias, or disconfirmation bias do not in themselves provide evidence in favor of the motivated reasoning model.

Biased assimilation is the name given to the phenomenon in which people evaluate counter-attitudinal evidence negatively. Let's return to the example from above about the group of climate change skeptics that we expose to a scientific climate change study. In the earlier discussion we were considering the effect of the study on their posterior beliefs that climate change is real, but now we're interested in their evaluations of the study itself. Their task is to infer whether the study is high quality ($Q = 1$) or low quality ($Q = 0$) on the basis of everything they know about the study, including its conclusion C. Studies that conclude climate change is real have $C = 1$ and studies that conclude it's all a hoax have $C = 0$. Skeptics think that studies that claim $C = 1$ are lower quality than studies that claim $C = 0$. In our setup, we can express these beliefs as $P(Q = 1 \mid C = 1) < P(Q = 1 \mid C = 0)$.

As above, in order to calculate posteriors, we need three numbers: the prior belief that a study is high quality $P(Q = 1)$, the probability of the study finding that climate change is real if the study is high quality $P(C = 1 \mid Q = 1)$, and the probability of the study finding that climate change is real if it's low quality $P(C = 1 \mid Q = 0)$. Suppose that this group of skeptics thinks most published studies are low quality, so they start with a low prior: $P(Q = 1) = 0.05$. What about their likelihood functions? The distinctive feature of climate change skeptics is that they *do not think* climate change is real, so they think it is unlikely that a high-quality study would find that it is. If we grant that the skeptics *actually believe* climate change is a hoax, then it's easy to further grant that they think that high-quality studies would confirm their beliefs, since that's part of what it means to hold a belief. Let's imagine they put the probability of a high-quality study concluding climate change is real at 1 percent, so $P(C = 1 \mid Q = 1) = 0.01$. The skeptics have also probably heard that most climate change studies conclude that climate change is real. Reconciling this with their other beliefs means they have to believe that the probability of weak studies concluding climate change is real is pretty high: $P(C = 1 \mid Q = 0) = 0.95$. Now we have everything we need to calculate the posterior probabilities of the study being high quality.

$$P(Q = 1 \mid C = 1) = \frac{P(C = 1 \mid Q = 1) * P(Q = 1)}{P(C = 1 \mid Q = 1) * P(Q = 1) + P(C = 1 \mid Q = 0) * P(Q = 0)}$$
$$= \frac{0.01 * 0.05}{0.01 * 0.05 + 0.95 * 0.95}$$
$$\approx 0.0005$$

Upon seeing that the study concluded that climate change is real, our group of Bayesian climate skeptics concluded that the probability the study was high quality was a meager 0.05 percent—that's one-twentieth of 1 percent. The skeptics doubt the study is worth the paper it's printed on. What if the study had concluded climate change was a hoax? Plugging in $1 - P(C = 1 \mid Q = 1)$ for $P(C = 0 \mid Q = 1)$ and $1 - P(C = 1 \mid Q = 0)$ for $P(C = 0 \mid Q = 0)$, we find that the skeptics are far more likely to think the study that confirms their prior to be high quality.

$$P(Q = 1 \mid C = 0) = \frac{P(C = 0 \mid Q = 1) * P(Q = 1)}{P(C = 0 \mid Q = 1) * P(Q = 1) + P(C = 0 \mid Q = 0) * P(Q = 0)}$$
$$= \frac{0.99 * 0.05}{0.99 * 0.05 + 0.05 * 0.95}$$
$$\approx 0.51$$

We find that their posterior belief that the study is high quality is a little better than 50/50 at 51 percent. Since 0.05 percent is far less than 51 percent, these skeptics definitely engage in biased assimilation. By the same token, of course, people who accept the truth that climate change is real *also* engage in biased assimilation. Doubtless, they would rate a putatively scientific study that claimed climate change is a hoax as being of far lower quality than those that reaffirm the consensus. The fact that climate skeptics think studies that agree with them are higher quality than those that don't doesn't mean their capacity to reason is broken. Instead, they could just have bad likelihood functions and priors that are very wrong.

Disconfirmation bias is the tendency of people to spend more cognitive effort criticizing arguments with which they disagree than criticizing arguments with which they agree. This bias can be understood in the same way as the foregoing analysis of biased assimilation. Which study would you spend more time and effort criticizing: the study you think has a 0.05 percent chance of being high quality, or the one you think has a 51 percent probability of being high quality? Disconfirmation bias isn't so much a bias as a straightforward consequence of thinking that some arguments are stronger than others. Arguments that appear to be stronger receive less criticism—well, because they seem stronger!

The third mechanism through which motivated reasoning is posited to operate is confirmation bias, or the tendency of individuals to seek out arguments that confirm their priors and to avoid counter-attitudinal arguments. In the motivated reasoning framework, individuals are motivated by directional goals. They would like to conclude that their priors are correct, so they proactively seek information in furtherance of that goal. A Bayesian interpretation of confirmation bias is also straightforward to construct. Suppose that it is costly to acquire information, so people have to be choosy about what information they gather. All else being equal, they prefer correct information to incorrect information, but they don't know which is which. They therefore gather information that, in their view, is more likely to be correct than false on the basis of signals of the information's quality: its source, sponsor, and, when easily available (as in a headline), its conclusion. Bayesians are likely to think that information that agrees with their priors is more likely to be correct, so they are likely to select it.[4]

Whatever their implications for theories of information processing, these three behavioral patterns—biased assimilation, disconfirmation bias, and confirmation bias—have a strong empirical basis. It is indeed true that people rate counter-attitudinal evidence more negatively than pro-attitudinal evidence. It is also true that they produce more arguments against counter-attitudinal evidence than against pro-attitudinal evidence. And it is clear that people seek out congenial information at higher rates than information with which they disagree. However, these behaviors are not evidence that people engage in motivated reasoning, as the same patterns of behavior could plausibly be generated without positing that people are motivated by directional goals.

Discussion and Critique of Taber and Lodge (2006)

This section is an extended discussion and critique of Taber and Lodge (2006), which argued that these three mechanisms are responsible for a fourth (and much more pernicious) pattern of behavior. That article claims that jointly, biased assimilation, disconfirmation bias, and confirmation bias lead to *attitude polarization*, or the tendency of individuals to strengthen their views when encountering counter-attitudinal evidence. Like Lord, Ross, and Lepper before them, Taber and Lodge claim to find evidence of attitude polarization. In chapter 2, I offered a critique of the Lord, Ross, and Lepper (1979) study that focused on its weak measurement strategy and the lack of random assignment. Here, I'll present a critique of the Taber and Lodge (2006) study, which in my view suffers from different design flaws. At its heart, the reason I don't find Taber and Lodge's evidence of attitude polarization convincing is the lack of random assignment to information, though the precise problems this creates in the study are more complicated than a standard selection story.

Taber and Lodge (2006) present two separate studies, each conducted twice on undergraduate laboratory subjects. The first study is about confirmation bias and attitude polarization and the second study is about biased assimilation and disconfirmation bias. The authors produced two versions of each study—one about gun control and the other about affirmative action. Subjects who saw the affirmative action version of the first study saw the gun control version of the second study, and vice versa. For simplicity, I'll focus on the gun control versions only, but for complexity, I'll discuss the studies in opposite order.

In the second study (about biased assimilation and disconfirmation bias), subjects were asked to rate four pro-gun control arguments and four anti-gun control arguments. Consistent with biased assimilation, gun control proponents rated the pro-gun control arguments more highly, and gun control opponents did the opposite. Consistent with disconfirmation bias, subjects spent more time reading the counter-attitudinal arguments and, when given the opportunity in a thought-listing task, spent more effort denigrating the counter-attitudinal arguments than bolstering the pro-attitudinal ones. So far, so good. These descriptive patterns are consistent with previous work (and indeed, with the experiments in this book) that people do not like evidence with which they disagree.

Let's turn now to the first study (about confirmation bias and attitude polarization). Before any exposure to information, time 1 measures of gun control attitudes were estimated from a series of questions combined into a scale. Next, subjects participated in an "information board" task, in which they were prompted to read and rate arguments from one of four sources: the Republican Party, the National Rifle Association (NRA), the Democratic Party, or Citizens against Handguns. Importantly, subjects were not randomly assigned to participate in the information board *or not*—all subjects saw the same information board. Consistent with confirmation bias, Taber and Lodge show that people with more pro-gun attitudes at time 1 were more likely to choose to read arguments from the Republicans and the NRA, and people with more anti-gun attitudes were more likely to read arguments from the Democrats and Citizens against Handguns. Up to this point, I have no issues with the study. Taber and Lodge provide convincing evidence of biased assimilation, confirmation bias, and disconfirmation bias. I would dispute that their findings are evidence of motivated reasoning, since nonmotivational models predict them as well, but at least we agree about what happened in the study.

The problem arises in the analysis of attitude polarization. The authors' claim is that exposure to mixed information caused pro-gun control subjects to become more pro-gun control and anti-gun control subjects to become more anti. The authors assessed attitude polarization by regressing time 2 attitude extremity on time 1 extremity. They interpret regression slopes greater than 1 as evidence of attitude polarization. This approach suffers from two main weaknesses. First, the difference between time 1 and time 2 attitudes is not necessarily the causal effect of treatment; if it were, there would never be a need for random assignment of treatments, because we could rely exclusively on pre-post designs. The very act of measuring attitudes a second time could itself cause subjects to engage with the survey questions differently, among myriad other threats to inference. But suppose for the moment that we grant that the differences do represent the causal effects of treatment; the difficulty now is understanding what the treatment *is*. The authors describe the treatment as exposure to balanced information. However, *by design*, subjects were allowed to self-select into the information treatments. Indeed, in the section on confirmation bias, the authors convincingly show that the gun control proponents selected into pro-gun control arguments and gun control opponents selected into anti-gun control arguments. Instead of updating in opposite directions in response to the same information, it's entirely possible that subjects updated in the direction of the balance of information *that they saw*, but because of the study design, there was a correlation between subjects' time 1 attitudes and the treatments they selected into.

To summarize, Taber and Lodge (2006) provide strong empirical evidence for the behavioral patterns they label as biased assimilation, disconfirmation bias, and confirmation bias. My main challenge to the interpretation of their results concerns the claim they make about how these three mechanisms lead to attitude polarization. In my view, the study was not well designed to measure attitude polarization in response to balanced information because it did not randomly assign subjects to treatment conditions. A follow-up study reported in Redlawsk, Civettini, and Emmerson (2010) does just that. The information board that each subject sees contains a randomly assigned dosage of counter-attitudinal information. When the data are analyzed according to the random assignment (rather than according to the information clicked on by each subject, which risks post-treatment bias), we see small, statistically insignificant effects at low doses of counter-attitudinal information, and then somewhat larger, statistically significant effects in the direction of information at higher doses. Those authors interpret their results as an "affective tipping point" past which motivated reasoners finally succumb to reality, but I think it just means people update their views in the direction of information.

Summary

Stepping back from the idiosyncrasies of particular studies and even particular theories of cognition, I think it's important to consider what even the best designed randomized studies can tell us about information processing. We are able to manipulate the input (exposure to information), and we can measure the output (survey responses). From such designs, we can estimate the effect of the treatment we manipulate on the outcome we measure. But we have trouble understanding *how* the input we manipulate changes the output we measure.

Why is that? The main reason is that our theories of information processing posit intermediate variables that we can't directly manipulate. In Bayesian reasoning, this intermediate variable is the likelihood, or the relative probabilities, of seeing the evidence we saw, depending on the state of the world. Experimenters can't *set* this probability directly—they have to settle for changing it indirectly, by manipulating what evidence is seen.[5] We would love to know if changing a likelihood changed a posterior, *holding exposure to evidence constant*, since that would provide direct evidence for the Bayesian model. But we can't, because likelihood functions are imaginary constructs whose existence in people's minds we can only posit.

A similar critique holds for theories of motivated reasoning. The main causal agents in such theories are motivations themselves, which are the putative drivers of biased information processing. To my knowledge, no study has attempted to *set* a subject's directional motivation. Occasionally, studies of motivated reasoning claim to "activate" a motivation with some treatment (e.g., Bolsen, Druckman, and Cook 2014), but those treatments may affect outcomes for nonmotivational reasons. Tappin, Pennycook, and Rand (2020b) describe how many party cue experiments that aim to manipulate political motivations also end up manipulating other variables, like source trustworthiness or the coherence of the treatment information. These unintended consequences confound the attempt to understand the effect of motivations.

Both Bayesian and motivated reasoning, then, have in common that crucial parts of their theoretical underpinnings resist empirical verification. We might instead turn to how well these two theories explain behavior. Here again we encounter the problem that both theories can accommodate any pattern of evidence. With the right mix of likelihood functions, any pattern of updating in response to persuasive information can be called Bayesian. With the right mix of directional and accuracy goals, any pattern of updating can be called motivated reasoning. The negative goal of this chapter was to show how this problem means we can't affirm one of these theories over the other on the basis of our experimental evidence.

What about the positive goal? When we randomize persuasive information and ask whether any two groups of people update in opposite directions, we find that the answer is conclusively "no." If motivated reasoning is an accurate description of information processing, then we must conclude that accuracy goals dominate directional goals when individuals process new information to update their beliefs and attitudes. If Bayesian reasoning is accurate, we must conclude that people have likelihood functions that have likelihood ratios above one, since everyone updates in the direction of information. Either way, we find that information processing—motivated or Bayesian—is "reasonable."

For my own part, I think the Bayesian metaphor for information processing is correct enough to be useful. American Bayesians from across the political spectrum differ greatly in terms of their baseline beliefs, which is to say they have different priors. But their likelihood functions are not all that different from person to person, so we all agree about what side evidence is "good for." To my mind, this is "how" information affects attitudes. People understand the direction of information, so they update in that direction by small amounts that are similar from person to person.

One piece of reasoning that helps me convince myself of this line thinking is a notable absence. When the economy is doing well, opposition politicians don't spend any effort communicating the good news to the public, since everyone knows that positive economic news is "good for" incumbents. If motivated reasoning dominated by directional goals were really how people processed information, then opposition politicians could use even good news as further criticism of incumbents. But they don't—they focus their persuasive messages on whatever bad news they can find instead.

CHAPTER EIGHT

Persuasion Is Possible

Persuasion occurs in parallel when people with different baseline attitudes respond to persuasive information by updating their views in the same direction and by about the same amount. The main contribution of this book has been to document, through dozens of randomized survey experiments that manipulate exposure to persuasive information, that persuasion in parallel is the rule and not the exception. The summary result is that people who hold *very different* political attitudes have *very similar* responses to persuasive information. Persuasion in parallel means that people are heterogeneous in their political views but homogeneous in their responses to persuasive treatments.

When we consider whether, on the whole, men and women respond similarly to persuasive attempts, the answer is yes. Democrats and Republicans respond similarly, as do the young, the old, and the better and less-well educated. White and Black Americans hold different opinions on average, but their responses to treatment are quite similar. Even when we condition on pre-treatment measures of the very attitudes targeted by the treatment, we find that policy proponents and opponents respond to treatment in the same direction and by about the same amount.

The persuasion in parallel finding is so straightforward (people update in the direction of information), yet it conflicts with some commonly held intuitions and perceptions of experience. It *feels* like nothing works because your opponents still oppose you, even when you try to explain your point of view. And because they don't agree with your point of view, they push back and criticize your arguments. It feels like the persuasive attempt was not just ineffective, but counterproductive.

The evidence laid out in this book shows that persuasive information treatments are rarely, if ever, counterproductive in the strict sense of generating negative treatment effects among a subset of people. Even among people who we would think would be most resistant to information, information has small but positive effects.

What about that tempting feeling that the other side's capacity for rational thought is fundamentally impaired by motivated reasoning? And not just the other side—what if we are all motivated reasoners systematically reconfirming our biases with every new piece of information? How can the persuasion in parallel hypothesis be correct when the motivated reasoning explanation accords so well with our personal experiences of politics? I think three errors get in the way.

The first error that leads us to believe that people update in the direction of their preferred goal rather than in the direction of information is mistaking differences in levels for differences in changes. This mistake happens when we notice the descriptive difference between groups and infer that the difference must be due to oppositely signed causal effects of information. Mistaking differences in levels for differences in changes is a bad error. It leads to the idea that the differences in opinion we have with the other side are due to differences in our ability to change our opinions in line with new information. A version of mistaking levels for changes is the basic error of Lord, Ross, and Lepper (1979), the famous social psychology study critiqued at length in chapter 2.

The second error that makes it feel like presenting people with information they don't like causes them to backlash is that we mistake the negative evaluations of the message (and the messenger, whom they would sometimes like to shoot) for the persuasive effect of the message on their policy attitudes. It is absolutely true that people don't like hearing counter-attitudinal messages, but despite not liking such messages, they can be persuaded by them. When we conclude that a persuasive message backfires because the audience doesn't like the message, it's like concluding that vegetables are unhealthy because we don't like to eat them. The negative affective evaluation of the message and messenger is just a side effect of the persuasive information, which nevertheless does change minds in the direction of information. Mistaking affective evaluations for persuasive effects on policy attitudes is the basic error committed by studies like Kahan, Jenkins-Smith, and Braman (2011), which defends a motivated reasoning account on the basis of evidence that people rate counter-attitudinal messengers as less "expert" than pro-attitudinal messengers. Ratings like these are poor guides to the persuasive effects of information.

The third error is a misunderstanding of differential exposure to information. In part because it is unpleasant, and in part because they think it is likely to be wrong, people tend to avoid counter-attitudinal information. People predisposed to support a policy tend to encounter more positive persuasive information, and people predisposed to oppose a policy tend to encounter more negative persuasive information. Both types update in the direction of information they see, which is to say both groups respond reasonably. It's not that the other side's reasoning is broken, it's that they are exposed to different bundles of information. A version of this error underlies the conclusion reached by Taber and Lodge (2006) (critiqued in chapter 7) that attitudes polarize in response to information.

Thinking that the other side is stupid, irrational, or unwilling to learn from new information is easy to do. It's easy to mistake levels for changes, to mistake affective evaluations of the message for policy attitudes, to be tricked by selection. But it comes at the cost of thinking that it is fruitless or counterproductive to try to change the minds of those with whom we disagree.

Regardless of our own political viewpoints, we all have people in our lives whose minds we would like to change about politics. Politicians, strangers on the internet, colleagues, coworkers, even close friends and family members—many of them hold political opinions that differ from our own, and we would like to persuade them to our side. Despite the seeming resistance, the fraying tempers, or what feels like backlash, trying to persuade others is not fruitless or counterproductive. Persuasive information can and does change minds, just a little bit and in the right direction.

Acknowledgments

I couldn't have really known it then, but this project started at 12:01 pm on March 26, 2014, at the close of Don Green's political psychology seminar at Columbia University. During the discussion of Lord, Ross, and Lepper's famous paper on attitude polarization, we realized—*wait, they didn't randomize*? As the class broke up, Andy Guess and I looked at each other and blurted out at the same time: "We've got to replicate."

After Andy and I wrote up our replication and sent it out for peer review, it was promptly desk rejected by two psychology journals. We confirmed our findings with two more experiments, then shopped our wares around to three political science journals: reject, reject, desk reject. Daniel Engber, a journalist from Slate who was writing a piece about how facts do change minds even in a "post-fact age," heard about our work (and our trouble landing it). He asked us, "But if [your] findings were correct, then wouldn't all those peer reviewers have updated their beliefs in support of [your] conclusion?" Touché. Eventually we did end up wearing the reviewers down, and the paper was published. Many of the ideas in this book stem from that first project with Andy, and I am grateful to him for the many years of friendship, collaboration, and perseverance.

Enormous credit is due to my longtime teacher, mentor, and advisor, Don Green. The semester before that fateful seminar, I took Don's course on experimentation, which exposed me to radical ideas about causality, research design, and the frontiers of what is knowable—and how to expand those frontiers. The ideas planted in my head by those two classes I took with Don have had an outsize influence on my life, my scholarship, and this book.

I am also indebted to Bob Shapiro, one of the greats behind *The Ra-*

tional Public (a major source of inspiration for this book), for helping me to connect the micro-level findings of my experiments to the broader patterns of public opinion.

I want to extend special thanks to Jamie Druckman. I was presenting a replication of a study he'd done at a conference, so he asked to meet up. I was excited to talk to this highly respected senior scholar from another university, and a little intimidated too. I shouldn't have been. Jamie richly deserves his reputation as the kindest man in political science. Jamie encouraged me to apply for a Time-sharing Experiments for the Social Sciences grant to study the persistence of persuasive effects. He read and commented on many drafts of this project, always very helpfully pointing out the holes in my arguments and in my knowledge of the literature.

Every shred of evidence presented in this book is the result of a collaboration with other researchers, a replication of previous scholars' work, or a reanalysis of a past study made possible through open science norms of transparency. The newspaper op-eds study I conducted with Emily Ekins and David Kirby makes a number of appearances throughout this book—I am grateful to them both for their skill, enthusiasm, and creativity. I also want to acknowledge by name the authors whose work I replicated or reanalyzed: Charles Lord, Lee Ross, Mark Lepper, Denis Chong, Jamie Druckman, Stephen Nicholson, Ted Brader, Nicholas Valentino, Elizabeth Suhay, Michael Hiscox, David Johnston, Andrew Ballard, Alison Gash, Michael Murakami, Sarah Kreps, Geoffrey Wallace, Diana Mutz, Kris-Stella Trump, and Ariel White. I know I am putting the efforts of these scholars to new purposes they never intended, and I beg their indulgence.

Almost the whole time I've been working on this project, I've also been collaborating with Graeme Blair, Jasper Cooper, and Macartan Humphreys on DeclareDesign, a theoretical framework for describing and assessing research designs. In something of a virtuous circle feedback loop, each project influenced my thinking on the other. This book was my first real chance to apply our design ideas to a substantive research question. I am grateful to these three comparative politics scholars for helping an Americanist out.

Thanks are due the Yale University Department of Political Science and the Institution for Social and Policy Studies for supporting a book conference in November 2019. Thank you to Pam Greene for organizing a seamless event. Thank you to my Yale colleagues P. Aronow, Angele

Delavoye, Matt Graham, Mike Goldfein, Jacob Hacker, Allison Harris, John Henderson, Greg Huber, Josh Kalla, and Christina Kinane for taking the time to read, comment, and help me see reason. Thank you to Don Green, Yanna Krupnikov, and Brendan Nyhan for their enormously helpful feedback, and for traveling to New Haven to give it.

I am grateful to Lynn Vavreck, who invited me to spend a semester at the University of California, Los Angeles working on the book. She pushed me to connect these ideas to contemporary politics—and to chop out whole passages of not-as-clever-as-I'd-thought prose.

Thank you to John Bullock, Ethan Porter, and Dan Nielsen, who read early drafts and gave me very useful feedback. Thank you to the two anonymous reviewers who helped me see how my scope conditions were actually a theory. Thank you to Paul Gross for excellent research assistance. Thank you to Dan Hopkins, who read the manuscript once I thought I was done and who showed me I wasn't quite yet. Thank you to Adam Berinsky and Chuck Meyers for their editorial guidance.

Thank you to my loving parents, Martha Edwards and Robert Green, Bruce Coppock and Lucia May, and Diane and Charles Van Grinsven. Thank you to my sister, Elizabeth Coppock, for teaching me my truth tables and for the linguistics example in chapter 7. Thank you to my aunt Jane Coppock for her editor's eye.

Finally, thank you to my spouse and partner, Penelope Van Grinsven, for the countless days of working together side by side, you on your thing and me on mine.

Appendix

This appendix includes the design details, treatments, outcomes, and results of each of the experiments described in chapter 5.

Newspapers (Coppock, Ekins, and Kirby 2018)

Subjects could be assigned to see either nothing or one of five op-ed pieces. The text of each treatment is below.

Newsweek

The Amtrak Crash: Is More Spending the Answer?
by Randal O'Toole 5/13/15

It is too soon to tell what caused the Amtrak train crash that killed seven people on May 12. But advocates of increased government spending are already beginning to use the crash to promote more spending on infrastructure and are criticizing Republicans who voted to reduce Amtrak's budget the day after the crash.

Yet there is a flaw in the assumption that spending more money would result in better infrastructure. In fact, in some cases, the problem is that too much money is being spent on infrastructure, but in the wrong places.

The reason for this is that politicians prefer to spend money building new infrastructure over maintaining the old. The result is that existing infrastructure that depends on tax dollars steadily declines while any new funds raised for infrastructure tend to go to new projects.

We can see this in the Boston, Washington, and other rail transit systems. Boston's system is $9 billion in debt, has a $3 billion maintenance backlog, and needs to spend nearly $700 million a year just to keep the backlog from growing. Yet has only budgeted $100 million for maintenance this year, and instead of repairing the existing system, Boston is spending $2 billion extending one of its light-rail lines.

Similarly, Washington's Metro rail system has a $10 billion maintenance backlog, and poor maintenance was the cause of the 2009 wreck that killed nine people. Yet, rather than rehabilitate their portions of the system, Northern Virginia is spending $6.8 billion building a new rail line to Dulles Airport; D.C. wants to spend $1 billion on new streetcar lines; and Maryland is considering building a $2.5 billion light-rail line in D.C. suburbs.

On the other hand, infrastructure that is funded out of user fees is generally in good shape. Despite tales of crumbling bridges, the 2007 Minnesota bridge collapse was due to a construction flaw and the 2013 Washington state bridge collapse was due to an oversized truck; lack of maintenance had nothing to do with either failure.

Department of Transportation numbers show that the number of bridges considered structurally deficient has fallen by more than 50 percent since 1990, while the average roughness of highway pavement has decreased. State highways and bridges, which are almost entirely funded out of user fees, tend to be in the best condition while local highways and bridges, which depend more on tax dollars, tend to be the ones with the most serious problems.

Before 1970, almost all of our transportation infrastructure was funded out of user fees and the United States had the best transportation system in the world. Since then, funding decisions have increasingly been made by politicians who are more interested in getting their pictures taken cutting ribbons than in making sure our transportation systems run safely and smoothly.

Proponents of higher gas taxes and other increased funding on infrastructure may talk about crumbling bridges, but what they really want is to spend more money on new projects that are often of little value. For example, they want high-speed trains that cost more but go less than half the speed of flying and light-rail trains that cost more but can move fewer people than buses.

This country doesn't need more infrastructure that it can't afford to maintain. Instead, it needs a more reliable system of transport funding, and that means one based on user fees and not tax subsidies.

Randal O'Toole is a senior fellow with the Cato Institute and author of Gridlock: Why We're Stuck in Traffic and What to Do About It.

THE WALL STREET JOURNAL.

The Political Assault on Climate Skeptics

MEMBERS OF CONGRESS SEND INQUISITORIAL LETTERS TO UNIVERSITIES, ENERGY COMPANIES, EVEN THINK TANKS.

by Richard S. Lindzen March 4, 2015

Research in recent years has encouraged those of us who question the popular alarm over allegedly man-made global warming. Actually, the move from "global warming" to "climate change" indicated the silliness of this issue. The climate has been changing since the Earth was formed. This normal course is now taken to be evidence of doom.

Individuals and organizations highly vested in disaster scenarios have relentlessly attacked scientists and others who do not share their beliefs. The attacks have taken a threatening turn.

As to the science itself, it's worth noting that all predictions of warming since the onset of the last warming episode of 1978-98—which is the only period that the United Nations Intergovernmental Panel on Climate Change (IPCC) attempts to attribute to carbon-dioxide emissions—have greatly exceeded what has been observed. These observations support a much reduced and essentially harmless climate response to increased atmospheric carbon dioxide.

In addition, there is experimental support for the increased importance of variations in solar radiation on climate and a renewed awareness of the importance of natural unforced climate variability that is largely absent in current climate models. There also is observational evidence from several independent studies that the so-called "water vapor feedback," essential to amplifying the relatively weak impact of carbon dioxide alone on Earth temperatures, is canceled by cloud processes.

There are also claims that extreme weather—hurricanes, tornadoes, droughts, floods, you name it—may be due to global warming. The data show no increase in the number or intensity of such events. The IPCC itself acknowledges the lack of any evident relation between extreme weather and climate, though allowing that with sufficient effort some relation might be uncovered.

World leaders proclaim that climate change is our greatest problem, demonizing carbon dioxide. Yet atmospheric levels of carbon dioxide have been vastly higher through most of Earth's history. Climates both warmer and colder than the present have coexisted with these higher levels.

Currently elevated levels of carbon dioxide have contributed to increases in agricultural productivity. Indeed, climatologists before the recent global warming hysteria referred to warm periods as "climate optima." Yet world leaders are embarking on costly policies that have no capacity to replace fossil fuels but enrich crony capitalists at public expense, increasing costs for all, and restricting access to energy to the world's poorest populations that still lack access to electricity's immense benefits.

Billions of dollars have been poured into studies supporting climate alarm, and trillions of dollars have been involved in overthrowing the energy economy. So it is unsurprising that great efforts have been made to ramp up hysteria, even as the case for climate alarm is disintegrating.

The latest example began with an article published in the *New York Times* on Feb. 22 about Willie Soon, a scientist at the Harvard Smithsonian Center for Astrophysics. Mr. Soon has, for over 25 years, argued for a primary role of solar variability on climate. But as Greenpeace noted in 2011, Mr. Soon was, in small measure, supported by fossil-fuel companies over a period of 10 years.

The *Times* reintroduced this old material as news, arguing that Mr. Soon had failed to list this support in a recent paper in *Science Bulletin* of which he was one of four authors. Two days later Arizona Rep. Raul Grijalva, the ranking Democrat on the Natural Resources Committee, used the *Times* article as the basis for a hunting expedition into anything said, written and communicated by seven individuals—David Legates, John Christy, Judith Curry, Robert Balling, Roger Pielke Jr., Steven Hayward and me—about testimony we gave to Congress or other governmental bodies. We were selected solely on the basis of our objections to alarmist claims about the climate.

In letters he sent to the presidents of the universities employing us (although I have been retired from MIT since 2013), Mr. Grijalva wanted all details of all of our outside funding, and communications about this funding, including "consulting fees, promotional considerations, speaking fees, honoraria, travel expenses, salary, compensation and any other monies." Mr. Grijalva acknowledged the absence of any evidence but purportedly wanted to know if accusations made against Mr. Soon about alleged conflicts of interest or failure to disclose his funding sources in science journals might not also apply to us.

Perhaps the most bizarre letter concerned the University of Colorado's Mr. Pielke. His specialty is science policy, not science per se, and he supports reductions in carbon emissions but finds no basis for associating extreme weather with climate. Mr. Grijalva's complaint is that Mr. Pielke, in agreeing with the IPCC on extreme weather and climate, contradicts the assertions of John Holdren, President Obama's science czar.

Mr. Grijalva's letters convey an unstated but perfectly clear threat: Research disputing alarm over the climate should cease lest universities that employ such individuals incur massive inconvenience and expense—and scientists holding such views should not offer testimony to Congress. After the *Times* article, Sens. Edward Markey (D., Mass.), Sheldon Whitehouse (D., R.I.) and Barbara Boxer (D., Calif.) also sent letters to numerous energy companies, industrial organizations and, strangely, many right-of-center think tanks (including the Cato Institute, with which I have an association) to unearth their alleged influence peddling.

The American Meteorological Society responded with appropriate indignation at the singling out of scientists for their scientific positions, as did many individual scientists. On Monday, apparently reacting to criticism, Mr. Grijalva conceded to the National Journal that his requests for communications between the seven of us and our outside funders was "overreach."

Where all this will lead is still hard to tell. At least Mr. Grijalva's letters should help clarify for many the essentially political nature of the alarms over the climate, and the damage it is doing to science, the environment and the well-being of the world's poorest.

Mr. Lindzen is professor emeritus of atmospheric sciences at MIT and a distinguished senior fellow of the Cato Institute.

THE WALL STREET JOURNAL.

Blow Up the Tax Code and Start Over

APPLY A 14.5% FLAT TAX TO PERSONAL INCOME AND TO BUSINESSES. CUT DEDUCTIONS. WATCH THE ECONOMY ROAR.

by Rand Paul June 17, 2015

Some of my fellow Republican candidates for the presidency have proposed plans to fix the tax system. These proposals are a step in the right direction, but the tax code has grown so corrupt, complicated, intrusive and antigrowth that I've concluded the system isn't fixable.

So on Thursday I am announcing an over $2 trillion tax cut that would repeal the entire IRS tax code—more than 70,000 pages—and replace it with a low, broad-based tax of 14.5% on individuals and businesses. I would eliminate nearly every special-interest loophole. The plan also eliminates the payroll tax on workers and several federal taxes outright, including gift and estate taxes, telephone taxes, and all duties and tariffs. I call this "The Fair and Flat Tax."

President Obama talks about "middle-class economics," but his redistribution policies have led to rising income inequality and negative income gains for families. Here's what I propose for the middle class: The Fair and Flat Tax eliminates payroll taxes, which are seized by the IRS from a worker's paychecks before a family ever sees the money. This will boost the incentive for employers to hire more workers, and raise after-tax income by at least 15% over 10 years.

Here's why we have to start over with the tax code. From 2001 until 2010, there were at least 4,430 changes to tax laws—an average of one "fix" a day—always promising more fairness, more simplicity or more growth stimulants. And every year the Internal Revenue Code grows absurdly more incomprehensible, as if it were designed as a jobs program for accountants, IRS agents and tax attorneys.

Polls show that "fairness" is a top goal for Americans in our tax system. I envision a traditionally All-American solution: Everyone plays by the same rules. This means no one of privilege, wealth or with an arsenal of lobbyists can game the system to pay a lower rate than working Americans.

Most important, a smart tax system must turbocharge the economy and pull America out of the slow-growth rut of the past decade. We are already at least $2 trillion behind where we should be with a normal recovery; the growth gap widens every month. Even Mr. Obama's economic advisers tell him that the U.S. corporate tax code, which has the highest rates in the world (35%), is an economic drag. When an iconic American company like Burger King wants to renounce its citizenship for Canada because that country's tax rates are so much lower, there's a fundamental problem.

Another increasingly obvious danger of our current tax code is the empowerment of a rogue agency, the IRS, to examine the most private financial and lifestyle information of every American citizen. We now know that the IRS, through political hacks like former IRS official Lois Lerner, routinely abused its auditing power to build an enemies list and harass anyone who might be adversarial to President Obama's policies. A convoluted tax code enables these corrupt tactics.

My tax plan would blow up the tax code and start over. In consultation with some of the top tax experts in the country, including the Heritage Foundation's Stephen Moore, former presidential candidate Steve Forbes and Reagan economist Arthur Laffer, I devised a 21st-century tax code that would establish a 14.5% flat-rate tax applied equally to all personal income, including wages, salaries, dividends, capital gains, rents and interest. All deductions except for a mortgage and charities would be eliminated. The first $50,000 of income for a family of four would not be taxed. For low-income working families, the plan would retain the earned-income tax credit.

I would also apply this uniform 14.5% business-activity tax on all companies—down from as high as nearly 40% for small businesses and 35% for corporations. This tax would be levied on revenues minus allowable expenses, such as the purchase of parts, computers and office equipment. All capital purchases would be immediately expensed, ending complicated depreciation schedules.

The immediate question everyone asks is: Won't this 14.5% tax plan blow a massive hole in the budget deficit? As a senator, I have proposed balanced budgets and I pledge to balance the budget as president.

Here's why this plan would balance the budget: We asked the experts at the nonpartisan Tax Foundation to estimate what this plan would mean for jobs, and whether we are raising enough money to fund the government. The analysis is positive news: The plan is an economic steroid injection. Because the Fair and Flat Tax rewards work, saving, investment and small business creation, the Tax Foundation estimates that in 10 years it will increase gross domestic product by about 10%, and create at least 1.4 million new jobs.

And because the best way to balance the budget and pay down government debt is to put Americans back to work, my plan would actually reduce the national debt by trillions of dollars over time when combined with my package of spending cuts.

The left will argue that the plan is a tax cut for the wealthy. But most of the loopholes in the tax code were designed by the rich and politically connected. Though the rich will pay a lower rate along with everyone else, they won't have special provisions to avoid paying lower than 14.5%.

The challenge to this plan will be to overcome special-interest groups in Washington who will muster all of their political muscle to save corporate welfare. That's what happened to my friend Steve Forbes when he ran for president in 1996 on the idea of the flat tax. Though the flat tax was surprisingly popular with voters for its simplicity and its capacity to boost the economy, crony capitalists and lobbyists exploded his noble crusade.

Today, the American people see the rot in the system that is degrading our economy day after day and want it to end. That is exactly what the Fair and Flat Tax will do through a plan that's the boldest restoration of fairness to American taxpayers in over a century.

Sen. Paul, a Republican from Kentucky, is running for his party's presidential nomination.

The New York Times

The Other Veterans Scandal
by Michael F. Cannon and Christopher A. Preble June 15, 2014

WASHINGTON — The Department of Veterans Affairs is mired in scandal. More than 57,000 veterans have been waiting at least three months for a doctor's appointment. Another 64,000 never even made it onto a waiting list. There are allegations that waits for care either caused or contributed to veterans' deaths.

But another, even larger problem with the Department of Veterans Affairs is being overlooked: Even when the department works exactly as intended, it helps inflict great harm on veterans, active-duty military personnel and civilians.

Here's how. Veterans' health and disability benefits are some of the largest costs involved in any military conflict, but they are delayed costs, typically reaching their peak 40 or 50 years after the conflict ends. Congress funds these commitments—through the Department of Veterans Affairs—only once they come due.

As a result, when Congress debates whether to authorize and fund military action, it can act as if those costs don't exist. But concealing those costs makes military conflicts appear less burdensome and therefore increases their likelihood. It's as if Congress deliberately structured veterans' benefits to make it easier to start wars.

The Department of Veterans Affairs is supposed to help wounded veterans, but its current design makes soldiers more likely to get killed or injured in the first place. The scandal isn't at the Department of Veterans Affairs. The scandal *is* the Department of Veterans Affairs.

Is there a better way? We propose a system of veterans' benefits that would be funded by Congress in advance. It would allow veterans to purchase life, disability and health insurance from private insurers. Those policies would cover losses related to their term of service, and would pay benefits when they left active duty through the remainder of their lives.

To cover the cost, military personnel would receive additional pay sufficient to purchase a statutorily defined package of benefits at actuarially fair rates. The precise amount would be determined with reference to premiums quoted by competing insurers, and would vary with the risks posed by particular military jobs.

Insurers and providers would be more responsive because veterans could fire them—something they cannot do to the Department of Veterans Affairs. Veterans' insurance premiums would also reveal, and enable recruits and active-duty personnel to compare, the risks posed by various military jobs and career paths.

Most important, under this system, when a military conflict increases the risk to life and limb, insurers would adjust veterans' insurance premiums upward, and Congress would have to increase military pay immediately to enable military personnel to cover those added costs.

Consider how this system might have prevented Congress's misbegotten decision to authorize President George W. Bush to invade Iraq. In 2002, the Bush administration played down estimates that the war would cost as much as $200 billion, insisting the cost would be less than $50 billion. To give you a sense of how mistaken this was: The economists Linda J. Bilmes and Joseph E. Stiglitz put the cost of veterans' benefits alone, from the wars in Iraq and Afghanistan, at roughly $1 trillion.

Like others before her, Hillary Rodham Clinton has admitted that voting to authorize the Iraq invasion was a "mistake," though she made "the best decision I could with the information I had." How many members of Congress would have voted differently if confronted with the long-term health and disability needs of the troops they had already sent into Afghanistan and those they were sending into Iraq? How many would have pressed harder to end the wars sooner if they had to confront the mounting cost of veterans' benefits, in addition to the wars' other growing costs, every year the wars dragged on?

The alternative system we propose combines the universal goal of improving veterans' benefits with conservative Republicans' preference for market incentives and antiwar Democrats' desire to make it harder to wage war. Prefunding veterans' benefits could prevent unnecessary wars, or at least end them sooner. We can think of no greater tribute to the men and women serving in our armed forces.

Michael F. Cannon is the director of health policy studies, and Christo-
pher Preble is the vice president for defense and foreign policy studies, at the
Cato Institute.

**USA
TODAY**

A GANNETT COMPANY

Wall Street Offers Very Real Benefits: Opposing View

BUT HEADLINES FOCUS ON THE BAD BEHAVIOR.

by Thaya Knight May 26, 2015

Not every person on Wall Street is a morally corrupt Gordon Gekko. Do Wall Street traders want to make money? Yes. Are they generally people who thrive in a fast-paced, competitive environment? You bet. And that is a good thing.

At its core, here's what Wall Street does: It makes sure that companies doing useful things get the money they need to keep doing those things. Do you like your smartphone? Does it make your life easier? The company that made that phone got the money to develop the product and get it into the store where you bought it with the help of Wall Street.

When a company wants to expand, or make a new product, or improve its old products, it needs money, and it often gets that money by selling stock or bonds. That helps those companies, the broader economy and consumers generally.

When we have flashing headlines about Wall Street traders acting badly, as we had last week with news of five major banks pleading guilty to criminal charges, it is very easy to hate Wall Street. But we only hear headlines about the worst behavior.

No one writes news stories about traders who go about their business every day, carefully complying with the many (and there are many) rules and regula-tions that govern their work. Also, the financial sector, which is usually what peo-ple mean when they say "Wall Street," isn't only or even mostly the big banks.

There are small firms, banks, funds and advisers that make up a large por-tion of our financial industry. While the news about corruption, corporate welfare and lawbreaking is very bad, it doesn't mean the entire industry is rotten. Or, more important, that we don't need it.

Wall Street could be better. We could eliminate regulations that crowd out competition for the big banks. We could reform the system to do away with "too big to fail," making it harder for bad traders to get away with bad behavior. Either way, we shouldn't lose sight of the very real economic and social benefits Wall Street provides.

Thaya Knight is associate director of financial regulation studies at the Cato Institute.

Amtrak Outcomes

- Do you think the government should spend more, less, or about what it does now on transportation and infrastructure? [1: A lot more, 7: A lot less]

- Would you prefer government pay for building and maintaining roads and infrastructure through raising taxes for transportation spending, or through charging user fees, like paying tolls when you drive on the highways? [1: Fund entirely through tax increases, 4: Both equally, 7; Fund entirely through user fees]

- If the government raised taxes to pay for more transportation spending, do you expect that money would primarily go toward building new infrastructure projects or maintaining and improving existing infrastructure? [1: Entirely toward NEW infrastructure projects, 4: Both equally, 7: Entirely toward maintaining EXISTING infrastructure]

- For every dollar the government spends on transportation and infrastructure projects, about how many cents do you think are spent inefficiently? [Slider 0–100, How Many Cents Spent Inefficiently?]

Climate Outcomes

- Would you say that climate change is best described as a . . . [1: Crisis, 7: Not a problem at all]?

- From what you've read and heard, do you believe increases in Earth's temperature are due . . . [1: Entirely due to the effects of pollution from human activity, 7: Entirely due to natural causes]?

- Do you think the solution to the climate change problem will primarily come from government policies or technological innovation in the free market? [1: Entirely from the free market, 7: Entirely from government policies]

- Thinking about what's in the news, is the seriousness of global warming generally exaggerated, correct, or underestimated? [1: Generally exaggerated, 4: Generally correct, 7: Generally underestimated]

- How many degrees (Fahrenheit) do you believe the Earth will warm over the next 100 years? (Select "0" if you think the temperature will stay about the same) [Slider –3 to 3]

Flat Tax Outcomes

- Would you favor or oppose changing the federal tax system to a flat tax, where everyone making more than $50,000 a year pays the same percentage of his or her income in taxes? [1: Strongly favor, 7: Strongly oppose]

- What percentage of income, from 0 to 100, do you think Americans should pay in federal taxes on average? [Slider 0–100, Average Tax Rate]

- Do you favor or oppose reducing the business and corporate tax rate to 14.5 percent? [1: Strongly favor, 7: Strongly oppose]

- Do you think a flat tax on incomes over $50,000 without tax deductions or credits will do more to help all Americans or do more to help wealthy Americans? [1: Do more to help ALL Americans, 7: Do more to help WEALTHY Americans]

Veterans Outcomes

- How would you rate your feelings toward the Department of Veterans Affairs (the VA) on a scale of 0 to 100, where a rating of 100 means you feel as warm and positive as possible and 0 means you feel as cold and negative as possible? How do you feel toward . . . [Department of Veterans Affairs]?

- How much confidence do you have in the Department of Veterans Affairs' ability to care for veterans? [1: A great deal, 7: None at all]

- Would you favor or oppose changing the healthcare system for Veterans to a system where the government provides additional money sufficient for Veterans to purchase a government-approved health insurance plan from private health insurance companies? [1: Strongly favor, 7: Strongly oppose]

- For every dollar the government spends on Veterans Benefits, about how many cents do you think are spent inefficiently? [Slider 0–100, How Many Cents Spent Inefficiently?]

Wall Street Outcomes

- How would you rate your feelings toward the following on a scale of 0 to 100, where a rating of 100 means you feel as warm and positive as possible and 0 means you feel as cold and negative as possible? How do you feel toward . . . [CEOs; Wall Street Bankers; Government Regulators]?

- What percentage of Wall Street bankers, from 0 to 100, do you think are corrupt? [Slider 0–100: % Wall Street Bankers Corrupt]

- How much confidence do you have in Wall Street bankers and brokers to do the right thing . . . [1: A great deal, 7: None at all]?

- Compared to what it's doing now, do you think the federal government needs to regulate banks and financial institutions? [1: A lot more, 7: A lot less]

TABLE A.1 **Coppock, Ekins, and Kirby (2018): Treatment effect estimates**

Sample	Treatment	Group	Estimate (SE)	95% CI
Mechanical Turk Sample	Flat tax	Overall	0.85 (0.11)	[0.64, 1.06]
Mechanical Turk Sample	Flat tax	Democrat	0.52 (0.14)	[0.25, 0.79]
Mechanical Turk Sample	Flat tax	Republican	1.09 (0.19)	[0.73, 1.46]
Mechanical Turk Sample	Amtrak	Overall	0.44 (0.09)	[0.27, 0.61]
Mechanical Turk Sample	Amtrak	Democrat	0.31 (0.10)	[0.12, 0.50]
Mechanical Turk Sample	Amtrak	Republican	0.81 (0.17)	[0.47, 1.14]
Mechanical Turk Sample	Climate	Overall	0.43 (0.10)	[0.23, 0.62]
Mechanical Turk Sample	Climate	Democrat	0.40 (0.10)	[0.21, 0.59]
Mechanical Turk Sample	Climate	Republican	0.49 (0.21)	[0.09, 0.90]
Mechanical Turk Sample	Veterans	Overall	16.89 (1.32)	[14.29, 19.48]
Mechanical Turk Sample	Veterans	Democrat	16.96 (1.65)	[13.72, 20.20]
Mechanical Turk Sample	Veterans	Republican	19.76 (2.74)	[14.36, 25.16]
Mechanical Turk Sample	Wall Street	Overall	12.40 (1.35)	[9.74, 15.05]
Mechanical Turk Sample	Wall Street	Democrat	11.44 (1.62)	[8.25, 14.63]
Mechanical Turk Sample	Wall Street	Republican	16.20 (2.78)	[10.73, 21.66]
Policy Professional Sample	Flat tax	Overall	0.42 (0.14)	[0.13, 0.70]
Policy Professional Sample	Flat tax	Democrat	0.43 (0.16)	[0.11, 0.75]
Policy Professional Sample	Flat tax	Republican	0.64 (0.19)	[0.27, 1.01]
Policy Professional Sample	Amtrak	Overall	0.44 (0.11)	[0.22, 0.65]
Policy Professional Sample	Amtrak	Democrat	0.34 (0.09)	[0.16, 0.51]
Policy Professional Sample	Amtrak	Republican	0.59 (0.21)	[0.17, 1.00]
Policy Professional Sample	Veterans	Overall	4.08 (1.50)	[1.14, 7.02]
Policy Professional Sample	Veterans	Democrat	3.36 (1.84)	[−0.26, 6.99]
Policy Professional Sample	Veterans	Republican	6.36 (2.80)	[0.86, 11.87]
Policy Professional Sample	Wall Street	Overall	14.06 (1.54)	[11.04, 17.08]
Policy Professional Sample	Wall Street	Democrat	12.38 (1.80)	[8.85, 15.92]
Policy Professional Sample	Wall Street	Republican	12.00 (2.62)	[6.86, 17.15]

Gun Control (Guess and Coppock 2020)

Pro Treatment

Kramer and Perry (2014) studied the relationship between gun laws and gun-related crimes in all fifty US states. As a proxy for state-level gun regulations, they used the scorecard developed by the Brady Campaign to Prevent Gun Violence, a pro-gun-control group, which ranks states from 0 (negligible restrictions) to 100 (strong restrictions). They found that on average, states with stricter policies on gun ownership and possession tend to have lower levels of firearm-related accidents, assaults, homicides, and suicides.

The figure below displays their main findings:

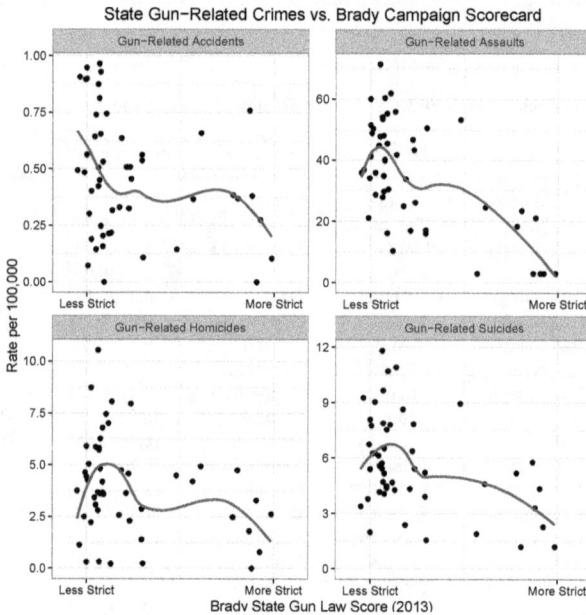

State Gun-Related Crimes vs. Brady Campaign Scorecard

Con Treatment

Kramer and Perry (2014) studied the relationship between gun laws and gun-related crimes in all fifty US states. As a proxy for state-level gun regulations, they used the scorecard developed by the Brady Campaign to Prevent Gun Violence, a pro-gun-control group, which ranks states from 0 (negligible restrictions) to 100 (strong restrictions). They found that on average, states with stricter policies on gun ownership and possession tend to have higher levels of firearm-related accidents, assaults, homicides, and suicides.

The figure below displays their main findings:

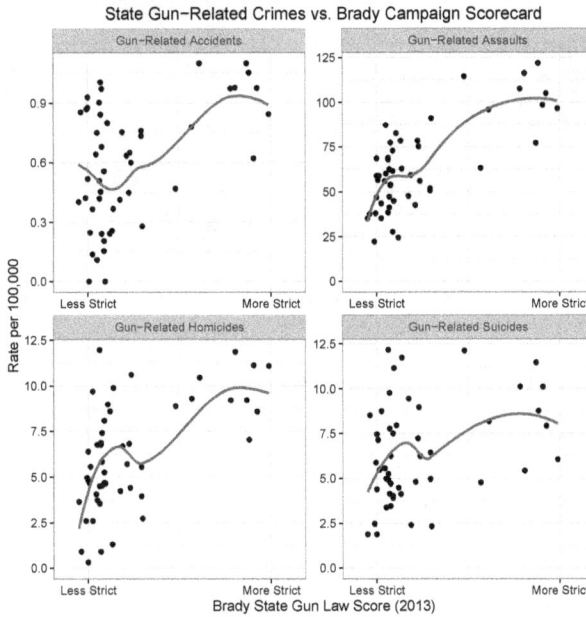

State Gun−Related Crimes vs. Brady Campaign Scorecard

Outcome

1. Do you support or oppose stricter gun control laws in the United States?
   a. I support stricter gun control laws
   b. I oppose stricter gun control laws

TABLE A.2 **Guess and Coppock (2020): Gun control treatment effect estimates**

Treatment	Group	Estimate (SE)	95% CI
Anti-Gun Control Study	Gun control opponents	−0.01 (0.04)	[−0.08, 0.07]
Anti-Gun Control Study	Gun control proponents	−0.07 (0.02)	[−0.12, -0.03]
Anti-Gun Control Study	Overall	−0.06 (0.03)	[−0.11, -0.01]
Pro-Gun Control Study	Gun control opponents	0.03 (0.04)	[−0.05, 0.11]
Pro-Gun Control Study	Gun control proponents	0.00 (0.02)	[−0.03, 0.04]
Pro-Gun Control Study	Overall	0.03 (0.03)	[−0.03, 0.08]

FIGURE A.I. Minimum wage treatment videos: Pro/Young (top left), Pro/Old (top right), Con/Young (bottom left), Con/Old (bottom right)

TABLE A.3 **Guess and Coppock (2020): Minimum wage treatment videos**

Treatment Video	URL
Pro/Young	http://youtu.be/ZI9aDHLptMk
Pro/Old	http://youtu.be/GOqtl53V3JI
Con/Young	http://youtu.be/hFG1Ka8AW6Q
Con/Old	http://youtu.be/Ct1Moeaa-W8

Minimum Wage (Guess and Coppock 2020)

The *Favor* question asked, "The federal minimum wage is currently $7.25 per hour. Do you favor or oppose raising the federal minimum wage?" The response options ranged from 1: "Very much opposed to raising the federal minimum wage" to 7: "Very much in favor of raising the federal minimum wage." The *Amount* question asked, "What do you think the federal minimum wage should be? Please enter an amount between $0.00 and $25.00 in the text box below."

Replication and Extension (Lord, Ross, and Lepper 1979)

Detailed Study Procedure

Following the original Lord, Ross, and Lepper (1979) procedure, in treatment conditions 1, 3, and 6, the order of the reports' methodology (time

TABLE A.4 **Guess and Coppock (2020): Minimum wage treatment effect estimates**

Outcome	Treatment	Group	Estimate (SE)	95% CI
Amount	Two Anti-Minimum Wage Videos	Opponents	−0.50 (0.66)	[−1.81, 0.82]
Amount	Two Anti-Minimum Wage Videos	Overall	−0.61 (0.49)	[−1.58, 0.36]
Amount	Two Anti-Minimum Wage Videos	Proponents	−1.14 (0.45)	[−2.03, -0.25]
Amount	Two Pro-Minimum Wage Videos	Opponents	0.55 (0.67)	[−0.77, 1.87]
Amount	Two Pro-Minimum Wage Videos	Overall	1.48 (0.54)	[0.41, 2.55]
Amount	Two Pro-Minimum Wage Videos	Proponents	2.10 (0.49)	[1.14, 3.07]
Favor	Two Anti-Minimum Wage Videos	Opponents	−0.72 (0.33)	[−1.38, -0.05]
Favor	Two Anti-Minimum Wage Videos	Overall	−0.43 (0.29)	[−1.01, 0.14]
Favor	Two Anti-Minimum Wage Videos	Proponents	−0.56 (0.26)	[−1.07, -0.06]
Favor	Two Pro-Minimum Wage Videos	Opponents	0.16 (0.34)	[−0.51, 0.83]
Favor	Two Pro-Minimum Wage Videos	Overall	0.24 (0.27)	[−0.30, 0.78]
Favor	Two Pro-Minimum Wage Videos	Proponents	0.28 (0.20)	[−0.12, 0.67]

series or cross-sectional) was randomized, resulting in two orderings per condition. In treatment conditions 2, 4, and 5, both the order of the methodology and the order of the content were randomized, resulting in four orderings per condition. In total, subjects could be randomized into eighteen possible presentations. This design was maintained in order to preserve comparability with the original study, but we average over the order and methodology margins to focus on the effects of information.

Subjects were exposed to both of their randomly assigned research reports—one time series and one cross-sectional within each treatment condition—according to the following procedure:

1. Subjects were first presented with a "Study Summary" page in which the report's findings and methodology were briefly presented. Subjects then answered two questions about how their attitudes toward the death penalty and beliefs about its deterrent efficacy had changed as a result of reading the summary.

2. Subjects were then shown a series of three pages that provided further details on the methodology, results, and criticisms of the report. The research findings were presented in both tabular and graphical form

3. After reading the report details and criticism, subjects answered a series of five questions (including a short essay) that probed their evaluations of the study's quality and persuasiveness.

4. Subjects then answered the attitude and belief change questions a second time.

Subjects completed steps 1 through 4 for both the first and the second research reports. After reading and responding to the first and second reports, subjects were asked two endline *Attitude* and *Belief* questions, identical to the pre-treatment questions.

Questions

The *Attitude* question asked, "Which view of capital punishment best summarizes your own?" The response options ranged from 1: "I am very much against capital punishment" to 7: "I am very much in favor of capital punishment." The *Belief* question asked, "Does capital punishment reduce crime? Please select the view that best summarizes your own." Responses ranged from 1: "I am very certain that capital punishment does not reduce crime" to 7: "I am very certain that capital punishment reduces crime."

Sample Treatment: Con (Cross Section)

DOES CAPITAL PUNISHMENT PREVENT CRIME?
One of the most controversial public issues in recent years has been the effectiveness of capital punishment (the death penalty) in preventing murders. Proponents of capital punishment have argued that the possibility of execution deters people who might otherwise commit murders, whereas opponents of capital punishment denied this and maintain that the death penalty may even produce murders by setting a violent model of behavior. A recent research effort attempted to shed light on this controversy.

The researchers (Palmer and Crandall 2012) decided to look at the difference in murder rates in states that share a common border but differ in whether their laws permit capital punishment or not. Carefully limiting the states included to those which had capital punishment laws in effect or not in effect for at least five years, they compiled a list of all possible pairs and then selected ten pairs of neighboring states that were alike in the degree of urbanization (percentage of the population living in metropolitan areas), thus controlling for any relationship between the size of urban population and crime per capita. They also limited the capital punishment states to those which had actually used their death penalty statutes, thus controlling for the possibility that the mere existence of the death penalty may not carry the same weight unless capital punishment is known to be a possibility. Using the murder rate (number of willful homicides per 100,000 population) in 2010 as their index, they assembled the table and graph shown on the next page. They reasoned that if capital punishment has a deterrent effect, the murder rates should be lower in the state with capital punishment laws.

The results, as shown in the table and graph below, were that in eight of the ten pairs of states selected for their study the murder rates were **higher** in the state with capital punishment laws than in the state without capital punishment laws. The researchers concluded that the existence of the death penalty does not work to deter murderers.

Critics of the study have complained that selection of a different set of ten neighboring states might have yielded a far different, perhaps even the opposite, result.

In replying to this criticism, Palmer and Crandall (2013) have recently reported a replication of their study, using a different set of ten states that share a common border but differ in whether their laws permit capital punishment or not. The results of this second study were essentially the same, murder rates being higher in the capital punishment state for seven of the ten comparisons.

Murder rate in 2012 for neighboring states with and without capital punishment

Pair	State	Murder rate	Capital punishment
1	A	0.5	Yes
	B	0.3	No
2	C	0.9	Yes
	D	0.6	No
3	E	1.0	Yes
	F	0.7	No
4	G	1.6	Yes
	H	2.2	No
5	I	2.8	Yes
	J	2.7	No
6	K	1.6	Yes
	L	1.3	No
7	M	2.3	Yes
	N	1.8	No
8	O	2.9	Yes
	P	3.4	No
9	Q	2.7	Yes
	R	2.5	No
10	S	1.4	Yes
	T	1.1	No

Table reproduced with permission from Palmer and Crandall (2012)

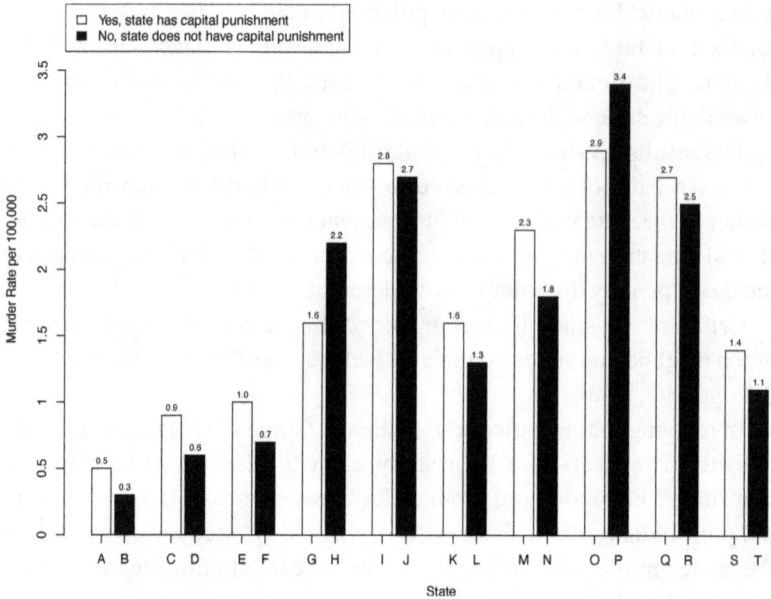

FIGURE A.2. Murder Rate in 2012 for Neighboring States with and without Capital Punishment
Reproduced with permission from Palmer and Crandall (2012)

Reanalysis and Replication 1 (Chong and Druckman 2010)

Treatments: Subjects could be assigned to receive no treatment, a series of Pro-Patriot Act messages, a series of Con-Patriot Act messages, or both types of messages.

Pro messages:

- The Patriot Act was enacted in the weeks after September 11, 2001 to strengthen law enforcement powers and technology.

- Under the Patriot Act, law enforcement agencies have more tools to prevent new terrorist incidents.

TABLE A.5 **Guess and Coppock (2020): Capital punishment treatment effect estimates**

Outcome	Treatment	Group	Estimate (SE)	95% CI
Change in support for capital punishment	Con Con	Overall	−0.19 (0.10)	[−0.40, 0.01]
Change in support for capital punishment	Con Con	Opponents	0.01 (0.12)	[−0.22, 0.24]
Change in support for capital punishment	Con Con	Proponents	−0.39 (0.17)	[−0.73, −0.05]
Change in support for capital punishment	Con Null	Overall	−0.12 (0.12)	[−0.35, 0.12]
Change in support for capital punishment	Con Null	Opponents	0.12 (0.13)	[−0.15, 0.38]
Change in support for capital punishment	Con Null	Proponents	−0.45 (0.20)	[−0.85, −0.05]
Change in support for capital punishment	Pro Con	Overall	0.17 (0.10)	[−0.03, 0.36]
Change in support for capital punishment	Pro Con	Opponents	0.10 (0.12)	[−0.12, 0.33]
Change in support for capital punishment	Pro Con	Proponents	0.28 (0.18)	[−0.06, 0.63]
Change in support for capital punishment	Pro Null	Overall	0.10 (0.10)	[−0.10, 0.30]
Change in support for capital punishment	Pro Null	Opponents	0.09 (0.13)	[−0.17, 0.34]
Change in support for capital punishment	Pro Null	Proponents	0.15 (0.16)	[−0.18, 0.47]
Change in support for capital punishment	Pro Pro	Overall	0.26 (0.11)	[0.03, 0.48]
Change in support for capital punishment	Pro Pro	Opponents	0.36 (0.14)	[0.08, 0.64]
Change in support for capital punishment	Pro Pro	Proponents	0.15 (0.18)	[−0.20, 0.51]
Change in belief in deterrent efficacy	Con Con	Overall	−0.24 (0.16)	[−0.55, 0.07]
Change in belief in deterrent efficacy	Con Con	Opponents	−0.01 (0.18)	[−0.36, 0.34]
Change in belief in deterrent efficacy	Con Con	Proponents	−0.27 (0.21)	[−0.68, 0.14]
Change in belief in deterrent efficacy	Con Null	Overall	−0.20 (0.15)	[−0.50, 0.10]
Change in belief in deterrent efficacy	Con Null	Opponents	−0.06 (0.15)	[−0.36, 0.24]
Change in belief in deterrent efficacy	Con Null	Proponents	−0.31 (0.24)	[−0.78, 0.15]
Change in belief in deterrent efficacy	Pro Con	Overall	0.32 (0.14)	[0.04, 0.59]
Change in belief in deterrent efficacy	Pro Con	Opponents	0.30 (0.17)	[−0.04, 0.65]
Change in belief in deterrent efficacy	Pro Con	Proponents	0.50 (0.18)	[0.14, 0.86]
Change in belief in deterrent efficacy	Pro Null	Overall	0.37 (0.16)	[0.06, 0.68]
Change in belief in deterrent efficacy	Pro Null	Opponents	0.59 (0.17)	[0.26, 0.92]
Change in belief in deterrent efficacy	Pro Null	Proponents	0.22 (0.23)	[−0.22, 0.67]
Change in belief in deterrent efficacy	Pro Pro	Overall	0.61 (0.16)	[0.29, 0.93]
Change in belief in deterrent efficacy	Pro Pro	Opponents	0.81 (0.20)	[0.41, 1.20]
Change in belief in deterrent efficacy	Pro Pro	Proponents	0.53 (0.20)	[0.13, 0.92]

- The Patriot Act gives US security forces the resources they need to identify terrorist plots on American soil and to prevent attacks before they occur.

- The Patriot Act enhances domestic security through counterterrorism funding, surveillance, border protection, and other security policies.

- The Patriot Act includes less known provisions including funding for terrorism victims and their families.

- The Patriot Act enables officials to effectively combat national security threats, and provides prompt aid and compensation to victims in the event of a terrorist attack.

Con messages:

- The Patriot Act was enacted in the weeks after September 11, 2001 to strengthen law enforcement powers and technology.

- The Patriot Act has sparked numerous controversies and been criticized for weakening the protection of citizens' civil liberties.

- Under the Patriot Act, the government has access to citizens' confidential information from telephone and e-mail communications.

- The Patriot Act allows law enforcement officials to search citizens' homes, businesses, and financial records without their permission or knowledge.

- The Patriot Act significantly expands government policing powers without specifying an agency that is responsible for safeguarding citizens' rights.

- Since its passage, the Patriot Act has been challenged in federal courts on the grounds that many of its provisions are unconstitutional.

Subjects who were assigned to Pro, Con, or Both information treatments were also assigned to a processing condition. I will collapse over these categories in all my analyses.

- On-line processing. After reading each statement, subjects are asked: "To what extent does this statement decrease or increase your support for the Patriot Act?"

- Memory-based processing. After reading each statement, subjects are asked: "How dynamic would you say this statement is? (Remember that a statement is more dynamic when it uses more vivid action words.)"

- No instructions. Subjects are asked to read each statement with no further instructions.

Outcomes:

- **Patriot Act Support**: "Do you oppose or support the Patriot Act?" 1: Oppose very strongly to 7: Support very strongly.

TABLE A.6 **Chong and Druckman (2010): Treatment effect estimates**

Sample	Treatment	Group	Estimate (SE)	95% CI
Original Study	Both	Overall	−0.08 (0.21)	[−0.49, 0.33]
Original Study	Both	Democrat	−0.21 (0.29)	[−0.78, 0.36]
Original Study	Both	Republican	0.09 (0.33)	[−0.57, 0.74]
Original Study	Con	Overall	−0.74 (0.20)	[−1.13, −0.35]
Original Study	Con	Democrat	−0.61 (0.26)	[−1.13, −0.09]
Original Study	Con	Republican	−0.84 (0.32)	[−1.46, −0.22]
Original Study	Pro	Overall	0.65 (0.19)	[0.27, 1.03]
Original Study	Pro	Democrat	0.69 (0.27)	[0.17, 1.21]
Original Study	Pro	Republican	0.57 (0.30)	[−0.03, 1.16]
Mechanical Turk Replication	Both	Overall	−0.14 (0.18)	[−0.50, 0.22]
Mechanical Turk Replication	Both	Democrat	−0.07 (0.23)	[−0.52, 0.38]
Mechanical Turk Replication	Both	Republican	−0.12 (0.37)	[−0.85, 0.60]
Mechanical Turk Replication	Con	Overall	−0.58 (0.17)	[−0.91, −0.24]
Mechanical Turk Replication	Con	Democrat	−0.43 (0.22)	[−0.85, −0.01]
Mechanical Turk Replication	Con	Republican	−0.65 (0.35)	[−1.34, 0.04]
Mechanical Turk Replication	Pro	Overall	0.47 (0.17)	[0.13, 0.81]
Mechanical Turk Replication	Pro	Democrat	0.53 (0.22)	[0.11, 0.96]
Mechanical Turk Replication	Pro	Republican	0.55 (0.35)	[−0.13, 1.23]

Reanalysis and Replication 2 (Brader, Valentino, and Suhay 2008)

Negative European/Latino

Immigration Concerns Governors

QUESTIONS RAISED ABOUT ECONOMIC, CULTURAL IMPACT OF IMMIGRANTS

NEW YORK (AP) — During the 1990s, more immigrants entered the United States than in any previous decade, and the growing number of immigrants in

FIGURE A.3A. Immigration Concerns Governors: Questions Raised About Economic, Cultural Impact of Immigrants: (a) Negative Latino, (b) Negative European

the U.S. clearly has some Americans worried. At a state governors' convention in June, many governors called for the Bush Administration and Congress to step in to restrict the flow of immigrants.

Several governors voiced concern that immigrants are driving down the wages of American workers while taxpayers are forced to meet the rising costs of social services for the newcomers. Governors say these views are shared by many of their constituents.

John Baine, shift manager at a large auto parts factory in Cleveland, said he is angered that "a number of friends have been laid-off or forced to take a pay cut" because of the influx of cheap immigrant labor.

Nancy Petrey, a Boulder, Colo. nurse, has seen staff let go for similar reasons. "People give twenty years of their lives to this hospital and then, boom, they're out the door because some foreigner will do their job for half the pay," Petrey said. "It just isn't right."

Governors also say constituents are worried that the country is no longer a "melting pot," because new immigrants are not adopting American values or blending into their new social world.

Mary Stowe, an Omaha-based sales associate, says she is frustrated by the fact that recent immigrants to her area "do not learn English or make any effort to fit in."

Bob Callaway, a construction supervisor in Newark, says he sees similar problems with immigrants hired by his company. "These people are totally unwilling to adopt American values like hard work and responsibility," Callaway said. "I try not to complain, but sometimes they are so pushy and uncooperative—it's not acceptable."

When asked his opinion, [Nikolai Vandinsky]/[Jose Sanchez], a recent immigrant from [Russia]/[Mexico], says he welcomes the chance for a better life in America. "Many of my cousins find work here and now it's my turn. I want a good job and benefits."

"But," [Vandinsky]/[Sanchez] added, "that doesn't mean I have to change who I am. We love our culture. I'm proud to be from [Russia]/[Mexico]."

While there was agreement at the convention that the federal government needs to do more to help states manage the rising tide of newcomers, few governors agree on exactly why immigration levels have increased.

Some blame the Immigration Act passed by Congress in 1990, which loosened federal restrictions on immigration. Others point to the fact that large companies are attracting immigrants to the U.S. with the promise of prosperity, a practice that has become widespread in recent years.

Still others maintain that, in a world full of turmoil, people are attracted here by the hope of a better way of life.

Whatever is bringing immigrants to these shores in record numbers, everyone seems certain that the numbers will continue to grow.

Positive European/Latino

Immigration Heartens Governors

PROMISE SEEN IN ECONOMIC, CULTURAL CONTRIBUTION OF IMMIGRANTS

NEW YORK (AP) — During the 1990s, more immigrants entered the United States than in any previous decade, and the growing number of immigrants in the U.S. clearly has some Americans hopeful about the future. At a state governors' convention in June, many governors called for the Bush Administration and Congress to protect the flow of immigrants from further restrictions.

Several governors said they are encouraged by how immigrants are helping to strengthen the economy, while also providing a welcome boost to tax revenues. Governors say these views are shared by many of their constituents.

John Baine, shift manager at a large auto parts factory in Cleveland, says he is enthusiastic about how much the influx of immigrant labor has "helped the company keep a lid on costs and remain competitive."

Nancy Petrey, a Boulder, Colo. nurse, has seen similar benefits for the hospital where she works. "These people take jobs that are often hard for us to

FIGURE A.3B. Immigration Heartens Governors: Promise Seen in Economic, Cultural Contribution of Immigrants: (a) Positive Latino, (b) Positive European

fill, and they're willing to work shifts that other people don't want," Petrey said. "It's a big help."

Governors also say many constituents take pride in the fact that the country is still a "melting pot," where immigrants continue to bring new experiences and ideas that enrich American culture.

Mary Stowe, an Omaha-based sales associate, says she admires what it must take to "leave home and come to a place that is so different, without knowing the language or anything about the way of life here."

Bob Callaway, a construction supervisor in Newark, says he sees similar qualities in the immigrants hired by his company. "These people are determined and persistent," Callaway said. "I've gotta give 'em credit, they'll do what it takes to get ahead. That's something I respect."

When asked his opinion, [Nikolai Vandinsky]/[Jose Sanchez], a recent immigrant from [Russia]/[Mexico], says he welcomes the chance for a better life in America. "Many of my cousins find work here and now it's my turn. I want a good job and benefits."

"But," [Vandinsky]/[Sanchez] added, "that doesn't mean I have to change who I am. We love our culture. I'm proud to be from [Russia]/[Mexico]."

While there was agreement at the convention that the federal government needs to do more to help states manage the rising tide of newcomers, few governors agree on exactly why immigration levels have increased.

Some blame the Immigration Act passed by Congress in 1990, which loosened federal restrictions on immigration. Others point to the fact that large companies are attracting immigrants to the U.S. with the promise of prosperity, a practice that has become widespread in recent years.

Still others maintain that, in a world full of turmoil, people are attracted here by the hope of a better way of life.

Whatever is bringing immigrants to these shores in record numbers, everyone seems certain that the numbers will continue to grow.

Outcomes

- **Support for immigration**: Do you think the number of immigrants from foreign countries who are permitted to come to the United States to live should be increased a lot, increased a little, left the same as it is now, decreased a little, or decreased a lot? (1: Decreased a lot, 5: Increased a lot)

- **Negative impact**: In your opinion, how likely is it that immigration will have a negative financial impact on many Americans? (Very Likely, Somewhat Likely, Somewhat Unlikely, Very Unlikely) (1: Very Unlikely, 4: Very Likely)

TABLE A.7 **Brader, Valentino, and Suhay (2008): Treatment effect estimates**

Sample	Treatment	Group	Estimate (SE)	95% CI
Original Study	Negative	Democrat	−0.66 (0.37)	[−1.40, 0.08]
Original Study	Negative	Overall	−0.61 (0.20)	[−1.00, −0.22]
Original Study	Negative	Republican	−0.43 (0.23)	[−0.88, 0.01]
Original Study	Positive	Democrat	−0.14 (0.43)	[−0.98, 0.70]
Original Study	Positive	Overall	−0.17 (0.22)	[−0.61, 0.28]
Original Study	Positive	Republican	0.09 (0.29)	[−0.49, 0.67]
Mechanical Turk Replication	Negative	Democrat	−0.24 (0.08)	[−0.39, −0.08]
Mechanical Turk Replication	Negative	Overall	−0.12 (0.07)	[−0.25, 0.02]
Mechanical Turk Replication	Negative	Republican	0.01 (0.14)	[−0.25, 0.28]
Mechanical Turk Replication	Positive	Democrat	0.05 (0.07)	[−0.09, 0.20]
Mechanical Turk Replication	Positive	Overall	0.18 (0.07)	[0.05, 0.31]
Mechanical Turk Replication	Positive	Republican	0.26 (0.13)	[−0.00, 0.52]

Reanalysis and Replication 3 (Hiscox 2006)

Treatments: This study employed a 2 by 4 factorial design, where the first factor is the expert treatment and the second factor is the frame the subject is shown: positive, negative, both, or neither.

- **Expert**: According to the *New York Times*, almost 100 percent of American economists support increasing trade with other nations. In 1993 over a thousand economists, including all living winners of the Nobel Prize in economics, signed an open letter to the *New York Times* urging people to support efforts to increase trade between the United States and neighboring countries.

- **Positive**: Many people believe that increasing trade with other nations creates jobs and allows Americans to buy more types of goods at lower prices.

- **Negative**: Many people believe that increasing trade with other nations leads to job losses and exposes American producers to unfair competition.

- **Positive + Negative**: Many people believe that increasing trade with other nations creates jobs and allows Americans to buy more types of goods at lower prices. Others believe that increasing trade with other nations leads to job losses and exposes American producers to unfair competition.

- **Control** (No introduction before asking the free trade question.)

Outcomes:

- **Support for Free Trade**: Do you favor or oppose increasing trade with other nations? (0: oppose; 1: favor)

TABLE A.8 **Hiscox (2006): Treatment effect estimates**

Sample	Treatment	Group	Estimate (SE)	95% CI
Original Study	Expert treatment	Overall	0.11 (0.02)	[0.06, 0.16]
Original Study	Expert treatment	Democrat	0.08 (0.04)	[0.01, 0.15]
Original Study	Expert treatment	Republican	0.13 (0.04)	[0.06, 0.21]
Original Study	Positive treatment	Overall	−0.06 (0.03)	[−0.12, 0.00]
Original Study	Positive treatment	Democrat	−0.01 (0.05)	[−0.10, 0.09]
Original Study	Positive treatment	Republican	−0.07 (0.05)	[−0.17, 0.02]
Original Study	Negative treatment	Overall	−0.13 (0.03)	[−0.19, −0.06]
Original Study	Negative treatment	Democrat	−0.12 (0.05)	[−0.22, −0.02]
Original Study	Negative treatment	Republican	−0.12 (0.06)	[−0.23, −0.01]
Original Study	Positive and negative	Overall	−0.18 (0.03)	[−0.24, −0.11]
Original Study	Positive and negative	Democrat	−0.21 (0.05)	[−0.32, −0.11]
Original Study	Positive and negative	Republican	−0.13 (0.05)	[−0.24, −0.03]
Mechanical Turk Replication	Expert treatment	Overall	0.12 (0.02)	[0.09, 0.15]
Mechanical Turk Replication	Expert treatment	Democrat	0.11 (0.02)	[0.07, 0.15]
Mechanical Turk Replication	Expert treatment	Republican	0.13 (0.03)	[0.07, 0.20]
Mechanical Turk Replication	Positive treatment	Overall	−0.04 (0.02)	[−0.08, 0.00]
Mechanical Turk Replication	Positive treatment	Democrat	−0.04 (0.02)	[−0.08, 0.01]
Mechanical Turk Replication	Positive treatment	Republican	−0.03 (0.04)	[−0.12, 0.05]
Mechanical Turk Replication	Negative treatment	Overall	−0.14 (0.02)	[−0.19, −0.10]
Mechanical Turk Replication	Negative treatment	Democrat	−0.14 (0.03)	[−0.19, −0.08]
Mechanical Turk Replication	Negative treatment	Republican	−0.13 (0.05)	[−0.22, −0.04]
Mechanical Turk Replication	Positive and negative	Overall	−0.15 (0.02)	[−0.19, −0.11]
Mechanical Turk Replication	Positive and negative	Democrat	−0.16 (0.03)	[−0.22, −0.11]
Mechanical Turk Replication	Positive and negative	Republican	−0.10 (0.05)	[−0.19, −0.02]
GfK Replication	Expert treatment	Overall	0.09 (0.02)	[0.05, 0.13]
GfK Replication	Expert treatment	Democrat	0.09 (0.03)	[0.03, 0.15]
GfK Replication	Expert treatment	Republican	0.09 (0.03)	[0.03, 0.14]
GfK Replication	Positive treatment	Overall	−0.02 (0.03)	[−0.07, 0.03]
GfK Replication	Positive treatment	Democrat	−0.01 (0.04)	[−0.09, 0.07]
GfK Replication	Positive treatment	Republican	−0.02 (0.04)	[−0.09, 0.05]
GfK Replication	Negative treatment	Overall	−0.17 (0.03)	[−0.23, −0.12]
GfK Replication	Negative treatment	Democrat	−0.15 (0.04)	[−0.23, −0.06]
GfK Replication	Negative treatment	Republican	−0.19 (0.04)	[−0.27, −0.12]
GfK Replication	Positive and negative	Overall	−0.11 (0.03)	[−0.17, −0.06]
GfK Replication	Positive and negative	Democrat	−0.09 (0.04)	[−0.17, −0.01]
GfK Replication	Positive and negative	Republican	−0.13 (0.04)	[−0.20, −0.05]
Lucid Replication	Expert treatment	Overall	0.12 (0.02)	[0.07, 0.16]
Lucid Replication	Expert treatment	Democrat	0.12 (0.03)	[0.06, 0.17]
Lucid Replication	Expert treatment	Republican	0.12 (0.04)	[0.05, 0.19]
Lucid Replication	Positive treatment	Overall	0.02 (0.03)	[−0.04, 0.08]
Lucid Replication	Positive treatment	Democrat	0.04 (0.04)	[−0.04, 0.12]
Lucid Replication	Positive treatment	Republican	−0.06 (0.05)	[−0.15, 0.04]
Lucid Replication	Negative treatment	Overall	−0.08 (0.03)	[−0.15, −0.02]
Lucid Replication	Negative treatment	Democrat	−0.07 (0.04)	[−0.15, 0.02]
Lucid Replication	Negative treatment	Republican	−0.13 (0.05)	[−0.23, −0.04]
Lucid Replication	Positive and negative	Overall	−0.04 (0.03)	[−0.11, 0.02]
Lucid Replication	Positive and negative	Democrat	−0.01 (0.04)	[−0.09, 0.08]
Lucid Replication	Positive and negative	Republican	−0.12 (0.05)	[−0.23, −0.02]

Reanalysis and Replication 4 (Johnston and Ballard 2016)

Treatments: Subjects were assigned to respond to an economic opinion question on one of five topics. Subjects were assigned to see the "expert" or "control" versions of each question. Technically, this is a 2 × 5 factorial design, in which the first factor is whether subjects saw economists' opinions and the second factor is which economic opinion question was seen. The estimand is the effect of learning economists' opinions on subjects' agreement with the economists' point of view.

Factor 1:

- **Expert**: A sample of professional economists with widely varying political preferences was asked whether they agreed or disagreed with the following statement: [Treatment Text] To what extent do you agree or disagree with this statement? (Strongly Agree, Agree, Disagree, Disagree Strongly, Uncertain)

- **Control**: To what extent do you agree or disagree with the following statement? (Strongly Agree, Agree, Disagree, Disagree Strongly, Uncertain)

Factor 2:

- **Immigration**: The average US citizen would be better off if a larger number of highly educated foreign workers were legally allowed to immigrate to the US each year. (Economists: Strongly Agree, 49; Agree, 46)

- **Health Care**: Long-run fiscal sustainability in the US will require cuts in currently promised Medicare and Medicaid benefits and/or tax increases that include higher taxes on households with incomes below $250,000. (Economists: Strongly Agree, 56; Agree, 35)

- **Trade with China**: Trade with China makes most Americans better off because, among other advantages, they can buy goods that are made or assembled more cheaply in China. (Economists: Strongly Agree, 59; Agree, 41)

- **Tax Cut**: A cut in federal income tax rates in the US right now would raise taxable income enough so that the annual total tax revenue would be higher within five years than without the tax cut. (Economists: Strongly Disagree, 57; Disagree, 39)

- **Gold Standard**: If the US replaced its discretionary monetary policy regime with a gold standard, defining a "dollar" as a specific number of ounces of gold, the price-stability and employment outcomes would be better for the average American. (Economists: Strongly Disagree, 66; Disagree, 34)

Outcomes:

- **Agree**: For each question, the agreement dependent variable was coded 1 if the subject chose either "Strongly Agree" or "Agree" when the economists did or "Strongly Disagree" or "Disagree" when the economists did.

TABLE A.9 **Johnston and Ballard (2016): Treatment effect estimates**

Sample	Topic	Group	Estimate (SE)	95% CI
Original Study	Immigration	Democrat	−0.01 (0.08)	[−0.17, 0.16]
Original Study	Immigration	Overall	0.07 (0.06)	[−0.04, 0.18]
Original Study	Immigration	Republican	0.10 (0.08)	[−0.06, 0.25]
Original Study	Health Care	Democrat	0.12 (0.07)	[−0.02, 0.26]
Original Study	Health Care	Overall	0.07 (0.05)	[−0.02, 0.17]
Original Study	Health Care	Republican	0.06 (0.07)	[−0.09, 0.21]
Original Study	Trade with China	Democrat	0.12 (0.07)	[−0.02, 0.26]
Original Study	Trade with China	Overall	0.12 (0.05)	[0.02, 0.22]
Original Study	Trade with China	Republican	0.13 (0.08)	[−0.03, 0.30]
Original Study	Tax Cut	Democrat	0.15 (0.08)	[−0.01, 0.30]
Original Study	Tax Cut	Overall	0.18 (0.05)	[0.08, 0.28]
Original Study	Tax Cut	Republican	0.23 (0.06)	[0.11, 0.35]
Original Study	Gold Standard	Democrat	0.21 (0.07)	[0.08, 0.34]
Original Study	Gold Standard	Overall	0.19 (0.05)	[0.08, 0.29]
Original Study	Gold Standard	Republican	0.21 (0.08)	[0.05, 0.38]
Mechanical Turk Replication	Immigration	Democrat	0.18 (0.02)	[0.14, 0.23]
Mechanical Turk Replication	Immigration	Overall	0.16 (0.02)	[0.13, 0.20]
Mechanical Turk Replication	Immigration	Republican	0.13 (0.03)	[0.06, 0.20]
Mechanical Turk Replication	Health Care	Democrat	0.15 (0.02)	[0.11, 0.20]
Mechanical Turk Replication	Health Care	Overall	0.17 (0.02)	[0.14, 0.21]
Mechanical Turk Replication	Health Care	Republican	0.24 (0.04)	[0.17, 0.31]
Mechanical Turk Replication	Trade with China	Democrat	0.22 (0.02)	[0.18, 0.27]
Mechanical Turk Replication	Trade with China	Overall	0.21 (0.02)	[0.17, 0.24]
Mechanical Turk Replication	Trade with China	Republican	0.20 (0.04)	[0.13, 0.27]
Mechanical Turk Replication	Tax Cut	Democrat	0.21 (0.02)	[0.17, 0.26]
Mechanical Turk Replication	Tax Cut	Overall	0.22 (0.02)	[0.18, 0.25]
Mechanical Turk Replication	Tax Cut	Republican	0.22 (0.04)	[0.15, 0.29]
Mechanical Turk Replication	Gold Standard	Democrat	0.27 (0.02)	[0.22, 0.31]
Mechanical Turk Replication	Gold Standard	Overall	0.25 (0.02)	[0.22, 0.29]
Mechanical Turk Replication	Gold Standard	Republican	0.27 (0.04)	[0.20, 0.34]

Reanalysis and Replication 5 (Hopkins and Mummolo 2017)

Treatments: Subjects were assigned at random to see two of these treatment texts. Subjects saw one at random, answered a random two of the outcome variables, then saw a second treatment, and answered the remainder of the treatment questions. "The argument below was recently made by a U.S. Senator. Please take a moment to read the argument carefully and then tell us what you think. [Treatment Text] Do you think the Senator is making a convincing argument? Please tell us why or why not. [Text entry]."

- **Crime**: America is very vulnerable to violent crime, with forty-two Americans murdered every single day on average. Innocent people can be killed in their front yards. Across the country, we have to do everything we can to reduce the threat of violent crime. We have to stop violent criminals before they act. This means cracking down on the smaller offenses that all too often lead to violent crime, and making sure that convicted criminals always serve out their full sentences.

- **Health care**: Health care is one of the most complicated issues we face. It involves 1 of every 6 dollars spent here in the United States. The health care system includes millions of doctors and nurses and thousands of hospitals and clinics. Together, they regularly make decisions that can mean life or death. The government in Washington can't even balance its own budget. How can we trust it to run something as complicated as the health care system?

- **Stimulus**: With a recession as deep as this one, there are more than 10 million unemployed Americans, and it's going to take years for our economy to recover. In February 2009, the government in Washington made things worse by passing an $800 billion stimulus package, which is more than $2,500 for every person living in this country. Now, it looks like a lot of that money didn't help the economy. Unemployment is still very high. The money went to pork-barrel projects and federal bureaucrats rather than creating jobs for unemployed Americans. The government in Washington can't even balance its own budget. How can we trust it to spend so much taxpayer money?

- **Terror**: The September 11th attacks and the news that al-Qaeda was planning new attacks on U.S. soil show how vulnerable America still is to terrorists. Innocent people can be killed while traveling to visit family or going to work. Across the country, we have to do everything we can to reduce the threat of terrorism. We have to stop terrorists before they act. This means conducting more frequent searches of suspicious people boarding planes, trains, subways, and buses.

Outcomes: Spending preferences were measured in all four areas, regardless of treatment assignment. The response options were 1: Decreased a lot, 2: Decreased a moderate amount, 3: Decreased a little; 4: Kept about the same; 5: Increased a little; 6: Increased a moderate amount; 7: Increased a great deal.

TABLE A.10 **Hopkins and Mummolo (2017): Treatment effect estimates**

Sample	Topic	Group	Estimate (SE)	95% CI
Original Study	Crime	Democrat	0.10 (0.09)	[−0.08, 0.28]
Original Study	Crime	Overall	0.08 (0.07)	[−0.05, 0.21]
Original Study	Crime	Republican	0.07 (0.10)	[−0.12, 0.27]
Original Study	Health	Democrat	0.05 (0.09)	[−0.14, 0.23]
Original Study	Health	Overall	−0.04 (0.08)	[−0.20, 0.11]
Original Study	Health	Republican	−0.12 (0.13)	[−0.37, 0.12]
Original Study	Stimulus	Democrat	−0.41 (0.11)	[−0.62, −0.20]
Original Study	Stimulus	Overall	−0.32 (0.09)	[−0.49, −0.15]
Original Study	Stimulus	Republican	−0.15 (0.14)	[−0.42, 0.12]
Original Study	Terror	Democrat	0.27 (0.11)	[0.05, 0.48]
Original Study	Terror	Overall	0.36 (0.08)	[0.21, 0.51]
Original Study	Terror	Republican	0.49 (0.10)	[0.29, 0.70]
Mechanical Turk Replication	Crime	Democrat	−0.02 (0.09)	[−0.19, 0.15]
Mechanical Turk Replication	Crime	Overall	−0.02 (0.07)	[−0.15, 0.12]
Mechanical Turk Replication	Crime	Republican	0.16 (0.12)	[−0.08, 0.40]
Mechanical Turk Replication	Health	Democrat	−0.14 (0.07)	[−0.29, −0.00]
Mechanical Turk Replication	Health	Overall	−0.08 (0.08)	[−0.23, 0.07]
Mechanical Turk Replication	Health	Republican	−0.09 (0.16)	[−0.41, 0.22]
Mechanical Turk Replication	Stimulus	Democrat	−0.32 (0.08)	[−0.48, −0.16]
Mechanical Turk Replication	Stimulus	Overall	−0.41 (0.07)	[−0.56, −0.27]
Mechanical Turk Replication	Stimulus	Republican	−0.39 (0.15)	[−0.69, −0.10]
Mechanical Turk Replication	Terror	Democrat	0.24 (0.09)	[0.06, 0.42]
Mechanical Turk Replication	Terror	Overall	0.15 (0.08)	[0.00, 0.30]
Mechanical Turk Replication	Terror	Republican	0.09 (0.15)	[−0.20, 0.38]
GfK Replication	Crime	Democrat	0.24 (0.10)	[0.05, 0.43]
GfK Replication	Crime	Overall	0.11 (0.07)	[−0.02, 0.25]
GfK Replication	Crime	Republican	−0.08 (0.10)	[−0.28, 0.12]
GfK Replication	Health	Democrat	−0.03 (0.10)	[−0.23, 0.16]
GfK Replication	Health	Overall	−0.04 (0.09)	[−0.21, 0.12]
GfK Replication	Health	Republican	−0.06 (0.13)	[−0.31, 0.20]
GfK Replication	Stimulus	Democrat	−0.48 (0.10)	[−0.68, −0.28]
GfK Replication	Stimulus	Overall	−0.45 (0.08)	[−0.61, −0.30]
GfK Replication	Stimulus	Republican	−0.46 (0.12)	[−0.69, −0.23]
GfK Replication	Terror	Democrat	0.38 (0.11)	[0.16, 0.59]
GfK Replication	Terror	Overall	0.26 (0.08)	[0.11, 0.42]
GfK Replication	Terror	Republican	0.17 (0.12)	[−0.06, 0.40]

- **Crime spending** Should federal spending on dealing with crime be increased, decreased, or kept the same?

- **Health care spending** Should federal spending on health care be increased, decreased, or kept the same?

- **Stimulus spending** Should federal spending to stimulate the economy be increased, decreased, or kept the same?

- **Terrorism spending** Should federal spending on the war on terrorism be increased, decreased, or kept the same?

Reanalysis 1 (Gash and Murakami 2009)

TABLE A.11 **Gash and Murakami (2009): Treatments and outcomes**

Introductory text: Now we are going to ask you some questions about an important issue: whether or not companies with a history of past discrimination may give special consideration to women when making hiring decisions. Some believe that giving women special consideration amounts to discrimination against men and that whether or not someone gets a job should be based on the merits. Others believe that if a company has a history of discriminating against women, special consideration of female applicants is needed to promote fair hiring practices.

Control Outcome	Treatment Outcome
Do you agree or disagree with the idea that these companies should not be able to give special consideration to women when making hiring decisions?	Imagine that a court in your state has made a controversial decision regarding these companies. These appointed judges have decided that these companies may not consider the gender of an applicant when making hiring decisions. Do you agree or disagree with the court's decision? [1: Strongly disagree, 4: Strongly agree] **OR** Imagine that the legislature in your state has made a controversial decision regarding these companies. These elected representatives have decided that companies may not consider the gender of an applicant when making hiring decisions. Do you agree or disagree with the legislature's decision? [1: Strongly disagree, 4: Strongly agree] **OR** Imagine that citizens in your state could vote directly on this issue through a ballot initiative and that they have made a controversial decision regarding these companies. The people in your state have decided that these companies may not consider the gender of an applicant when making hiring decisions. Do you agree or disagree with the voters' decision? [1: Strongly disagree, 4: Strongly agree]

TABLE A.12 **Gash and Murakami (2009): Treatment effect estimates**

Institution	Group	Estimate (SE)	95% CI
Ballot	Overall	0.54 (0.10)	[0.34, 0.73]
Ballot	Democrat	0.47 (0.14)	[0.19, 0.75]
Ballot	Republican	0.55 (0.14)	[0.28, 0.81]
Ballot	Women	0.52 (0.14)	[0.24, 0.80]
Ballot	Men	0.55 (0.14)	[0.28, 0.82]
Ballot	High School	0.63 (0.15)	[0.34, 0.93]
Ballot	Some College	0.73 (0.18)	[0.37, 1.10]
Ballot	College	0.16 (0.17)	[−0.17, 0.50]
Ballot	White	0.58 (0.10)	[0.38, 0.79]
Ballot	Black	0.73 (0.40)	[−0.08, 1.54]
Ballot	Hispanic	0.14 (0.26)	[−0.38, 0.66]
Courts	Overall	0.57 (0.10)	[0.38, 0.77]
Courts	Democrat	0.74 (0.12)	[0.50, 0.98]
Courts	Republican	0.32 (0.16)	[−0.01, 0.64]
Courts	Women	0.61 (0.14)	[0.33, 0.90]
Courts	Men	0.53 (0.13)	[0.27, 0.79]
Courts	High School	0.65 (0.16)	[0.34, 0.96]
Courts	Some College	0.76 (0.18)	[0.40, 1.11]
Courts	College	0.24 (0.16)	[−0.07, 0.55]
Courts	White	0.53 (0.10)	[0.32, 0.73]
Courts	Black	1.34 (0.38)	[0.57, 2.12]
Courts	Hispanic	0.11 (0.29)	[−0.48, 0.69]
Legislature	Overall	0.58 (0.09)	[0.40, 0.76]
Legislature	Democrat	0.70 (0.12)	[0.46, 0.94]
Legislature	Republican	0.46 (0.14)	[0.19, 0.73]
Legislature	Women	0.62 (0.13)	[0.37, 0.88]
Legislature	Men	0.54 (0.13)	[0.28, 0.80]
Legislature	High School	0.64 (0.14)	[0.37, 0.92]
Legislature	Some College	0.76 (0.18)	[0.40, 1.11]
Legislature	College	0.29 (0.15)	[−0.01, 0.58]
Legislature	White	0.55 (0.10)	[0.35, 0.75]
Legislature	Black	0.73 (0.33)	[0.07, 1.40]
Legislature	Hispanic	0.60 (0.21)	[0.17, 1.02]

Reanalysis 2 (Flavin 2011)

TABLE A.13 **Flavin (2011): Treatments and outcomes**

Control Text	Treatment Text
Some people think that the United States should place a greater emphasis on promoting political equality.	Some people think that the United States should place a greater emphasis on promoting political equality. By political equality we mean making sure citizens have equal political influence by limiting the amount of money an individual or group can give to a candidate during a political campaign.

Outcome: How about you, do you strongly support, somewhat support, neither support nor oppose, somewhat oppose, or strongly oppose promoting political equality? [1: strongly oppose, 5: strongly support]

TABLE A.14 **Flavin (2011): Treatment effect estimates**

Group	Estimate (SE)	95% CI
Overall	0.81 (0.08)	[0.65, 0.97]
Democrat	0.80 (0.11)	[0.59, 1.02]
Republican	0.86 (0.12)	[0.62, 1.10]
Women	0.86 (0.11)	[0.64, 1.09]
Men	0.75 (0.11)	[0.53, 0.97]
High School	0.79 (0.14)	[0.52, 1.06]
Some College	1.06 (0.13)	[0.80, 1.33]
College	0.57 (0.13)	[0.31, 0.83]
White	0.85 (0.09)	[0.68, 1.03]
Black	0.60 (0.26)	[0.08, 1.12]
Hispanic	0.93 (0.26)	[0.42, 1.45]

Reanalysis 3 (Kreps and Wallace 2016)

TABLE A.15 **Kreps and Wallace (2016): Treatments and outcomes**

Strikes violate international law	Strikes do not violate international law
The United Nations Special Rapporteur for Human Rights and Counterterrorism has indicated that these strikes violate international law because they break the sovereignty and territorial integrity of the country where the attack takes place. **OR** The nongovernmental organization (NGO) Human Rights Watch has indicated that these strikes violate international law because they break the sovereignty and territorial integrity of the country where the attack takes place. **OR** The United Nations Special Rapporteur for Human Rights and Counterterrorism has indicated that these strikes violate international law because they do not take necessary measures to prevent the death of civilians. **OR** The nongovernmental organization Human Rights Watch has indicated that these strikes violate international law because they do not take necessary measures to prevent the death of civilians. **OR** The United Nations Special Rapporteur for Human Rights and Counterterrorism has indicated that the strikes trigger anti-US sentiment and help militants recruit new members, making Americans less safe. **OR** The nongovernmental organization Human Rights Watch has indicated that the strikes trigger anti-US sentiment and help militants recruit new members, making Americans less safe.	The Chairman of the Joint Chiefs of Staff has indicated that these strikes do not violate international law because they are an act of self-defense against individuals plotting attacks against Americans. **OR** The Chairman of the Joint Chiefs of Staff has indicated that these strikes do not violate international law because they take necessary measures to prevent the death of civilians. **OR** The Chairman of the Joint Chiefs of Staff has indicated that the strikes have been instrumental in killing suspected militants and making Americans safer.

Outcome: Do you approve or disapprove of the use of drone strikes by the United States?
[1: Disapprove strongly, 5: Approve strongly]

TABLE A.16 **Kreps and Wallace (2016): Treatment effect estimates**

Group	Estimate (SE)	95% CI
Overall	−0.20 (0.07)	[−0.33, −0.07]
Democrat	−0.18 (0.09)	[−0.35, −0.01]
Republican	−0.24 (0.10)	[−0.45, −0.04]
Women	−0.24 (0.09)	[−0.42, −0.07]
Men	−0.17 (0.10)	[−0.36, 0.02]
High School	−0.29 (0.11)	[−0.51, −0.08]
Some College	−0.12 (0.13)	[−0.37, 0.13]
College	−0.16 (0.10)	[−0.36, 0.04]
White	−0.25 (0.07)	[−0.40, −0.10]
Black	−0.13 (0.18)	[−0.49, 0.22]
Hispanic	−0.18 (0.20)	[−0.58, 0.21]

Reanalysis 4 (Mutz 2017)

TABLE A.17 **Mutz (2017): Treatments and outcomes**

Introductory text: When Michael Morrison took a job at the steel mill in the center of Granite City, Ill., in 1999, he assumed his future was ironclad. He was 38, a father with three young children.

"I felt like I had finally gotten into a place that was so reliable I could retire there," he said.

Although it had changed hands, the mill had been there since the end of the 19th century. For those willing to sweat, the mill was a reliable means of supporting a family.

Mr. Morrison began by shoveling slag out of the furnaces, working his way up to crane driver. From inside a cockpit tucked in the rafters of the building, he manned the controls, guiding a 350-ton ladle that spilled molten iron.

It was a difficult job requiring perpetual focus, and he was paid accordingly.

Job loss due to trade	Job loss due to automation
Now his job has been eliminated due to trade with China. Chinese workers now man the same machine that Mr. Morrison once operated. As the company website describes, "Of the 74 machines that were operating in the factory, 63 are now operating in China."	Now his job has been eliminated due to automation. Robots now man the same machine that Mr. Morrison once operated. As the company website describes, "Of the 74 machines that were operating in the factory, 63 now run on their own with no human intervention."
Mr. Morrison has not been able to find other work, and he has no idea how he will pay for his children's college education. "When they don't need me anymore," he said, "I'm nothing."	Mr. Morrison has not been able to find other work, and he has no idea how he will pay for his children's college education. "When they don't need me anymore," he said, "I'm nothing."

"Do you favor or oppose the federal government in Washington negotiating more free trade agreements?" [1: Strongly oppose, 4: Strongly favor]

TABLE A.18 **Mutz (2017): Treatment effect estimates**

Group	Estimate (SE)	95% CI
Overall	0.06 (0.08)	[−0.11, 0.23]
Democrat	0.07 (0.12)	[−0.18, 0.31]
Republican	0.04 (0.11)	[−0.17, 0.25]
Women	0.08 (0.12)	[−0.15, 0.30]
Men	0.07 (0.12)	[−0.17, 0.31]
High School	0.11 (0.18)	[−0.25, 0.47]
Some College	−0.07 (0.12)	[−0.30, 0.15]
College	0.16 (0.13)	[−0.10, 0.43]

Reanalysis 5 (Trump and White 2018)

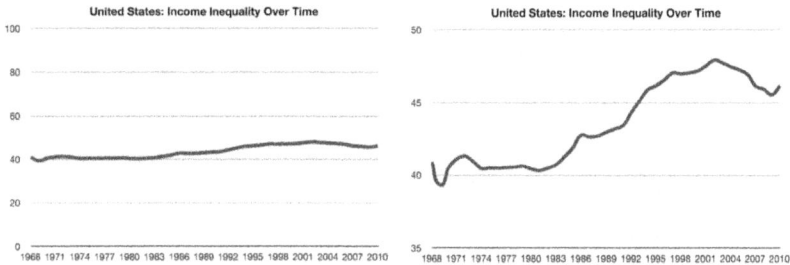

FIGURE A.4. Trump and White (2018), treatments: (a) Control, (b) Treatment

Outcome: "Please indicate if you believe the statement below is factually correct or incorrect: Income inequality in the United States has increased dramatically over time." [1: correct, 0: otherwise]

TABLE A.19 **Trump and White (2018): Treatment effect estimates**

Group	Estimate (SE)	95% CI
Overall	0.26 (0.03)	[0.19, 0.32]
Democrat	0.25 (0.05)	[0.15, 0.34]
Republican	0.30 (0.05)	[0.20, 0.40]
Women	0.24 (0.05)	[0.14, 0.34]
Men	0.28 (0.05)	[0.18, 0.37]
High School	0.23 (0.06)	[0.12, 0.34]
Some College	0.26 (0.06)	[0.14, 0.38]
College	0.29 (0.06)	[0.17, 0.41]
White	0.26 (0.04)	[0.19, 0.34]
Black	0.11 (0.12)	[−0.12, 0.34]
Hispanic	0.37 (0.10)	[0.17, 0.58]

Notes

1. The descriptive difference in average opinions likely has many causes, but the main contenders in my mind are the effects of group cues and differential exposure to positive and negative persuasive information. The average causal effects of persuasive information themselves are represented by the slopes of the lines.

2. Understanding statistical significance involves working through a bizarre thought experiment. Suppose we stipulate a model of the world (called a null model) in which the true difference is zero but estimates bounce around this true zero because of sampling variability. Under that null model and using our current empirical strategy, the thought experiment asks, what's the probability that we would obtain an estimate as large as or larger than the one we did obtain? If the answer is "not very often, less than 5 percent of the time," the estimate is deemed statistically significant. But that probability depends on the details of the empirical strategy, especially sample size. Unless the null model happens to be exactly correct (which it almost certainly isn't), then as sample size gets bigger, we're almost guaranteed to find statistical significance. Annoyingly, with very large experiments, even substantively meaningless differences can be declared "significant." The cure for this problem is to focus more on effect estimates and their precision and less on statistical significance.

3. "Convenience sample" is a term of art that means the sample is made up of easy-to-interview people rather than randomly selected people from a well-defined population. MTurk is an online labor market where people get paid to perform small tasks, like tagging photos, transcribing videos—or answering academic surveys. MTurk makes it easy to interview large, diverse, and indeed, convenient samples.

4. Thorson (2016) uses an elegant three-group candidate evaluation experiment to demonstrate this point. In her experiments, subjects could be assigned

to a control condition, a negative misinformation condition, or a misinformation plus correction condition. Candidate evaluations in the misinformation group were lower than in control; they were higher in the misinformation plus correction condition than in the misinformation only condition. But in a pattern Thorson calls "belief echoes," evaluations in the misinformation plus correction condition were still lower than in control—the corrections were unable to fully undo the damage done by the false information.

Chapter Two

1. As a side note, this empirical question is extremely hard to answer. Capital punishment policies are not randomly assigned to jurisdictions, so we end up having to compare places that do and don't have such policies. We worry that such places differ in so many ways that any conclusions are prone to bias of unknown size and direction. We might look at the same place before and after a policy change, but again we worry that the change is correlated with other things—for example, the change in government that precipitated the change in policy. All this to say that in the 1970s (as now), the true effects of capital punishment on deterrence were unknown, maybe unknowable. It's a funny wrinkle in this story that the mostly insoluble social scientific debate over the possibly deterrent effects of capital punishment provided the opening to credibly fabricate made-up studies that claim capital punishment either increases or decreases crime!

2. For those keeping score, the average difference between the responses of proponents and opponents was large enough to be statistically significant even in this small sample. However, that hypothesis test itself is irrelevant for assessing the study's main empirical question, which is about the effects of information, not the differences between proponents and opponents.

Chapter Three

1. See Ding, Feller, and Miratrix (2016) for a method of testing for heterogeneity that doesn't require modeling CATEs by pre-treatment covariates. Using that method, I found little evidence of treatment effect heterogeneity in a series of eleven survey experiments mostly about persuasion (Coppock 2019).

2. Confusingly, under the simple model of Bayesian reasoning described in detail in chapter 7, the direction of information is defined by the individual, not by the treatment itself. Under that model, individuals employ likelihood functions, which link prior attitudes to posterior attitudes via information. The "direction" of information is determined by subjects' likelihood ratio: if the likeli-

hood ratio is above 1, we can describe the information as "positive," and describe it as "negative" otherwise. This perspective necessarily conflates the direction of information with its causal effect on attitudes.

3. It's a quasi-experiment because assignment to treatment conditions wasn't randomized. The first and third quarters of the subjects were assigned to treatment and the second and fourth quarters assigned to control. The resulting groups appear to be balanced on measurable pre-treatment covariates, but reader beware, we are on slightly shakier ground because the assignment process was deterministic, not random.

4. The "receive" and "accept" parts of the RAS model describe why individuals might have different considerations in their minds. Zaller posits that people who are more politically attentive will "receive" more considerations, and that people "resist" considerations that are at odds with their predispositions. For my own part, I'm agnostic on the causal effects of political attentiveness on considerations, and the main goal of this book is to demonstrate that people do not resist counter-attitudinal messages, at least in the sense of not sampling new counter-attitudinal considerations when offering post-treatment survey responses.

5. A minor point—instability in measured responses may result from two separate sources of variation: the quasi-random process that combines considerations into latent attitudes, and idiosyncratic measurement error.

Chapter Four

1. Ding, Feller, and Miratrix (2016) re-prove a (lost) theorem of G. E. H. Reuter that shows that if the cumulative distribution functions of $y_i(1)$ and $y_i(0)$ do not cross, there exists a monotone transformation that will render any treatment effect heterogeneity homogeneous.

2. See Graham and Coppock (2021) for an attempt at a survey question format that tries to help subjects consider their counterfactual attitudes.

3. The word "replication" is used differently in different contexts. I will use "replication" to mean conducting the same experiment design on a new sample, and "reanalysis" to mean conducting a new analysis on a dataset produced by others.

4. For example, see Haslam, Reicher, and Van Bavel (2019) for an up-to-date retelling of the Stanford Prison Experiment, according to which the investigator specifically solicited the hypothesized behaviors direct from the subjects assigned to be guards.

5. That said, when these experiments are analyzed with such models and the appropriate quantities of interest are calculated from the otherwise-frustrating-to-interpret output, the inferences are of course unchanged.

Chapter Five

1. Chong and Druckman (2010) also analyze the effect of treating respondents with one message, then randomly treating them again three weeks later (or not), finding that the second message behaves much like a one-sided treatment.

Chapter Six

1. Approximately 50 percent of the sample completed the follow-up, leading to a loss of power to detect treatment effects. The follow-up estimate is not significantly different from zero—or from the immediate estimate of 0.71.

2. For more on the consequences of attrition for estimation in experiments, see Gerber and Green (2012, chapter 7).

Chapter Seven

1. For a clear description of how to derive Bayes' Rule from the Kolgomorov Axioms, see Aronow and Miller (2019, 11).

2. Depending on what the relevant counterfactual is, the treatment effect could also be written as $P(A|B) - P(A|\neg B)$.

3. See, however, Ramsey (1931) for a formulation that comes close.

4. That differential or "selective" exposure to information occurs at all is not in dispute, but the magnitude of the differences in exposure is surprisingly small (Guess 2021).

5. This trouble plagues even Hill's (2017) clever study in which subjects are directly informed about the probability that the computer reveals the truth. Subjects might not believe that people designing the study know the truth, so may harbor a likelihood function that differs from the one posited by the design.

References

Acemoglu, Daron, Victor Chernozhukov, and Muhamet Yildiz. 2016. "Fragility of Asymptotic Agreement under Bayesian Learning." *Theoretical Economics* 11 (1): 187–225.

Achen, Christopher H. 1992. "Social Psychology, Demographic Variables, and Linear Regression: Breaking the Iron Triangle in Voting Research." *Political Behavior* 14 (3): 195–211.

Ajzen, Icek, and Martin Fishbein. 1980. *Understanding Attitudes and Predicting Social Behavior*. Englewood Cliffs, NJ: Prentice-Hall.

Albertson, Bethany L. 2015. "Dog-Whistle Politics: Multivocal Communication and Religious Appeals." *Political Behavior* 37 (1): 3–26. https://doi.org/10.1007/s11109-013-9265-x.

Aronow, Peter M., and Benjamin T. Miller. 2019. *Foundations of Agnostic Statistics*. Cambridge, UK and New York: Cambridge University Press.

Baden, Christian, and Sophie Lecheler. 2012. "Fleeting, Fading, or Far-Reaching? A Knowledge-Based Model of the Persistence of Framing Effects." *Communication Theory* 22 (4): 359–82.

Bartels, Larry. 2002. "Beyond the Running Tally: Partisan Bias in Political Perceptions." *Political Behavior* 24 (2): 117–50.

Behrend, Tara S., David J. Sharek, Adam W. Meade, and Eric N. Wiebe. 2011. "The Viability of Crowdsourcing for Survey Research." *Behavior Research Methods* 43 (3): 800–813.

Benjamin, Daniel J., James O. Berger, Magnus Johannesson, Brian A. Nosek, E. J. Wagenmakers, Richard Berk, Kenneth A. Bollen, Björn Brembs, Lawrence Brown, Colin Camerer, David Cesarini, Christopher D. Chambers, Merlise Clyde, Thomas D. Cook, Paul De Boeck, Zoltan Dienes, Anna Dreber, Kenny Easwaran, Charles Efferson, Ernst Fehr, Fiona Fidler, Andy P. Field, Malcolm Forster, Edward I. George, Richard Gonzalez, Steven Goodman, Edwin Green, Donald P. Green, Anthony G. Greenwald, Jarrod D. Hadfield, Larry V. Hedges, Leonhard Held, Teck Hua Ho, Herbert Hoijtink, Daniel

J. Hruschka, Kosuke Imai, Guido Imbens, John P. A. Ioannidis, Minjeong Jeon, James Holland Jones, Michael Kirchler, David Laibson, John List, Roderick Little, Arthur Lupia, Edouard Machery, Scott E. Maxwell, Michael McCarthy, Don A. Moore, Stephen L. Morgan, Marcus Munafó, Shinichi Nakagawa, Brendan Nyhan, Timothy H. Parker, Luis Pericchi, Marco Perugini, Jeff Rouder, Judith Rousseau, Victoria Savalei, Felix D. Schönbrodt, Thomas Sellke, Betsy Sinclair, Dustin Tingley, Trisha Van Zandt, Simine Vazire, Duncan J. Watts, Christopher Winship, Robert L. Wolpert, Yu Xie, Cristobal Young, Jonathan Zinman, and Valen E. Johnson. 2018. "Redefine Statistical Significance." *Nature Human Behaviour* 2 (1): 6–10.

Benoît, Jean-Pierre, and Juan Dubra. 2014. "A Theory of Rational Attitude Polarization." *Social Science Research Network*. Available at SSRN: https://ssrn.com/abstract=2529494.

Berinsky, Adam J., Gregory A. Huber, and Gabriel S. Lenz. 2012. "Evaluating Online Labor Markets for Experimental Research: Amazon.com's Mechanical Turk." *Political Analysis* 20 (3): 351–68.

Blair, Graeme, Jasper Cooper, Alexander Coppock, and Macartan Humphreys. 2019. "Declaring and Diagnosing Research Designs." *American Political Science Review* 113 (3): 838–59.

Blair, Graeme, Alexander Coppock, and Margaret Moor. 2020. "When to Worry about Sensitivity Bias: Evidence from 30 Years of List Experiments." *American Political Science Review* 114 (4): 1297–1315.

Bohren, J. Aislinn. 2016. "Informational Herding with Model Misspecification." *Journal of Economic Theory* 163: 222–47.

Bolsen, Toby, James N. Druckman, and Fay Lomax Cook. 2014. "The Influence of Partisan Motivated Reasoning on Public Opinion." *Political Behavior* 36 (2): 235–62.

Boudreau, Cheryl, and Scott A. MacKenzie. 2014. "Informing the Electorate? How Party Cues and Policy Information Affect Public Opinion about Initiatives." *American Journal of Political Science* 58 (1): 48–62.

Boudreau, Cheryl, and Scott A. MacKenzie. 2018. "Wanting What Is Fair: How Party Cues and Information about Income Inequality Affect Public Support for Taxes." *The Journal of Politics* 80 (2): 367–81.

Brader, Ted, Nicholas A. Valentino, and Elizabeth Suhay. 2008. "What Triggers Public Opposition to Immigration? Anxiety, Group Cues, and Immigration Threat." *American Journal of Political Science* 52 (4): 959–78.

Brady, Henry E., and Paul M. Sniderman. 1985. "Attitude Attribution: A Group Basis for Political Reasoning." *American Political Science Review* 79 (04): 1061–78.

Broockman, David, and Joshua Kalla. 2016. "Durably Reducing Transphobia: A Field Experiment on Door-to-door Canvassing." *Science* 352 (6282): 220–24.

Bullock, John G. 2009. "Partisan Bias and the Bayesian Ideal in the Study of Public Opinion." *The Journal of Politics* 71 (03): 1109–24.

Bullock, John G. 2011. "Elite Influence on Public Opinion in an Informed Electorate." *American Political Science Review* 105 (3): 496–515.

Bullock, John G. 2019. "Party Cues." In *Oxford Handbook of Electoral Persuasion*, ed. Elizabeth Suhay, Bernard Grofman, and Alexander Trechsel. Cambridge and New York: Oxford University Press.

Bullock, John G., Alan S. Gerber, Seth J. Hill, and Gregory A. Huber. 2015. "Partisan Bias in Factual Beliefs about Politics." *Quarterly Journal of Political Science* 10 (4): 519–78.

Bullock, John G., Donald P. Green, and Shang E. Ha. 2010. "Yes, But What's the Mechanism? (Don't Expect an Easy Answer)." *Journal of Personality and Social Psychology* 98 (4): 550.

Bullock, John G., and Shang E. Ha. 2011. "Mediation Analysis Is Harder than It Looks." In *Cambridge Handbook of Experimental Political Science*, ed. James N. Druckman, Donald P. Green, James H. Kuklinski, and Arthur Lupia, 959. Cambridge: Cambridge University Press.

Cacioppo, John T., and Richard E. Petty. 1982. "The Need for Cognition." *Journal of Personality & Social Psychology* 42: 116–31.

Chandler, Jesse, Gabriele Paolacci, Eyal Peer, Pam Mueller, and Kate A. Ratliff. 2015. "Using Nonnaive Participants Can Reduce Effect Sizes." *Psychological Science* 26 (7): 1131–39.

Cheng, Ing-Haw, and Alice Hsiaw. 2018. "Trust in Signals and the Origins of Disagreement." No. 110R4, Working Papers, Brandeis University, Department of Economics and International Business School. https://EconPapers.repec.org/RePEC:brd:wpaper:110r4.

Chong, Dennis, and James N. Druckman. 2010. "Dynamic Public Opinion: Communication Effects over Time." *American Political Science Review* 104 (04): 663–80.

Chong, Dennis, and James N. Druckman. 2012. "Dynamics in Mass Communication Effects Research." In *The Sage Handbook of Political Communication*, ed. Holli Semetko and Maggie Scammell, 307–23. Los Angeles, CA: Sage Publications.

Cohen, Jacob. 1988. *Statistical Power Analysis for the Behavioral Sciences.* 2nd edition. New York: Routledge.

Converse, Philip E. 1964. "The Nature of Belief Systems in Mass Publics." In *Ideology and Discontent*, ed. David E. Apter. Ann Arbor: University of Michigan Press.

Cook, Thomas D., and Brian R. Flay. 1978. "The Persistence of Experimentally Induced Attitude Change." *Advances in Experimental Social Psychology* 11: 1–57.

Coppock, Alexander. 2019. "Generalizing from Survey Experiments Conducted on Mechanical Turk: A Replication Approach." *Political Science Research and Methods* 7 (3): 613–28.

Coppock, Alexander. 2020. "Visualize as You Randomize: Design-based Statistical Graphs for Randomized Experiments." In *Advances in Experimental Political Science*, ed. James N. Druckman and Donald P. Green. New York: Cambridge University Press.

Coppock, Alexander, Emily Ekins, and David Kirby. 2018. "The Long-lasting Effects of Newspaper Op-Eds on Public Opinion." *Quarterly Journal of Political Science* 13 (1): 59–87.

Coppock, Alexander, and Donald P. Green. 2022. "Do Belief Systems Exhibit Dynamic Constraint?" *Journal of Politics* 48 (2).

Coppock, Alexander, Thomas J. Leeper, and Kevin J. Mullinix. 2018. "Generalizability of Heterogeneous Treatment Effect Estimates across Samples." *Proceedings of the National Academy of Sciences* 115 (49): 12441–46.

Coppock, Alexander, and Oliver A. McClellan. 2019. "Validating the Demographic, Political, Psychological, and Experimental Results Obtained from a New Source of Online Survey Respondents." *Research & Politics* 6 (1): 1–14.

Corner, Adam, Lorraine Whitmarsh, and Dimitrios Xenias. 2012. "Uncertainty, Scepticism and Attitudes towards Climate Change: Biased Assimilation and Attitude Polarisation." *Climatic Change* 114 (3-4): 463–78.

Cronbach, Lee J. 1982. *Designing Evaluations of Educational and Social Programs*. Hoboken, NJ: Jossey-Bass.

Cronbach, Lee J. 1986. "Social Inquiry by and for Earthlings." In *Metatheory in Social Science: Pluralisms and Subjectivities*, ed. Donald W. Fiske and Richard A. Shweder, 83–107. Chicago: University of Chicago Press.

de Finetti, Bruno. 1937. "La prévision: ses lois logiques, ses sources subjectives." In *Annales de l'institut Henri Poincaré*, vol. 7, 1–68. Paris: Presses Universitaires de France.

De Quidt, Jonathan, Johannes Haushofer, and Christopher Roth. 2018. "Measuring and Bounding Experimenter Demand." *American Economic Review* 108 (11): 3266–3302.

de Vreese, Claes. 2004. "The Effects of Strategic News on Political Cynicism, Issue Evaluations, and Policy Support: A Two-Wave Experiment." *Mass Communication and Society* 7 (2): 191–214.

Ding, Peng, Avi Feller, and Luke Miratrix. 2016. "Randomization Inference for Treatment Effect Variation." *Journal of the Royal Statistical Society: Series B (Statistical Methodology)* 78 (3): 655–71.

Dowling, Conor M., Michael Henderson, and Michael G. Miller. 2020. "Knowledge Persists, Opinions Drift: Learning and Opinion Change in a Three-wave Panel Experiment." *American Politics Research* 48 (2): 263–74.

Druckman, James N. 2001. "The Implications of Framing Effects for Citizen Competence." *Political Behavior* 23 (3): 225–56.

Druckman, James N., and Mary C. McGrath. 2019. "The Evidence for Motivated Reasoning in Climate Change Preference Formation." *Nature Climate Change* 9 (2): 111–19.

Druckman, James N., and Kjersten R. Nelson. 2003. "Framing and Deliberation: How Citizens' Conversations Limit Elite Influence." *American Journal of Political Science* 47: 729–45.

Edwards, Ward, Harold Lindman, and Leonard J. Savage. 1963. "Bayesian Statistical Inference for Psychological Research." *Psychological Review* 70 (3): 193.

Edwards, Ward, and Lawrence D. Phillips. 1964. "Man as Tranducer for Probabilities in Bayesian Command and Control Systems." In *Human Judgement and Optimality*, ed. G. L. Bryan and M. W. Shelley, 360–401. New York: John Wiley & Sons.

Eichenberg, Richard C., and Richard J. Stoll. 2012. "Gender Difference or Parallel Publics? The Dynamics of Defense Spending Opinions in the United States, 1965–2007." *Journal of Conflict Resolution* 56 (2): 331–48.

Enns, Peter K. 2007. "The Uniform Nature of Mass Opinion." PhD thesis, University of North Carolina at Chapel Hill.

Festinger, Leon, Henry W. Riecken, and Stanley Schachter. 1956. *When Prophecy Fails*. Minneapolis: University of Minnesota Press.

Fishbein, Martin, and Icek Ajzen. 1975. *Belief, Attitude, Intention and Behavior: An Introduction to Theory and Research*. Reading, MA: Addison-Wesley.

Flavin, Patrick J. 2011. "Public Attitudes about Political Equality." *Time Sharing Experiments for the Social Sciences*. https://www.tessexperiments.org/study/flavin235.

Frank, Michael C., and Noah D. Goodman. 2012. "Predicting Pragmatic Reasoning in Language Games." *Science* 336 (6084): 998.

Freedman, David A. 2008. "Randomization does not justify logistic regression." *Statistical Science* 23 (2): 237–49.

Fryer, Roland G., Jr., Philipp Harms, and Matthew O. Jackson. 2019. "Updating Beliefs when Evidence Is Open to Interpretation: Implications for Bias and Polarization." *Journal of the European Economic Association* 17 (5): 1470–1501.

Fudenberg, Drew, and David K. Levine. 2006. "Superstition and Rational Learning." *American Economic Review* 96 (3): 630–51.

Gaines, Brian J., James H. Kuklinski, and Paul J. Quirk. 2007. "The Logic of the Survey Experiment Reexamined." *Political Analysis* 15. 1–20.

Gal, David, and Derek D. Rucker. 2011. "Answering the Unasked Question: Response Substitution in Consumer Surveys." *Journal of Marketing Research (JMR)* 48 (1): 185–95.

Gash, Alison, and Michael Murakami. 2009. "Understanding How Policy Venue Influences Public Opinion." *Time Sharing Experiments for the Social Sciences*. http://www.tessexperiments.org/study/gash-murakami718.

Gerber, Alan, and Donald Green. 1999. "Misperceptions About Perceptual Bias." *Annual Review of Political Science* 2 (1): 189–210.

Gerber, Alan, and Donald P. Green. 1998. "Rational Learning and Partisan Attitudes." *American Journal of Political Science* 42 (3): 794–818.

Gerber, Alan S., and Donald P. Green. 2012. *Field Experiments: Design, Analysis, and Interpretation*. New York: W. W. Norton.

Graham, Matthew, and Alexander Coppock. 2021. "Asking About Attitude Change." *Public Opinion Quarterly* 85 (1): 28–53.

Green, Donald, Bradley Palmquist, and Eric Schickler. 2002. *Partisan Hearts and Minds*. New Haven, CT: Yale University Press.

Green, Donald P., Mary C. McGrath, and Peter M. Aronow. 2013. "Field Experiments and the Study of Voter Turnout." *Journal of Elections, Public Opinion and Parties* 23 (1): 27–48.

Green, Donald P., Anna Wilke, and Jasper Cooper. 2020. "Countering Violence against Women at Scale: A Mass Media Experiment in Rural Uganda." *Comparative Political Studies* 53 (14): 2283–2320.

Guess, Andrew, and Alexander Coppock. 2020. "Does Counter-Attitudinal Information Cause Backlash? Results from Three Large Survey Experiments." *British Journal of Political Science* 50 (4): 1497–1515.

Guess, Andrew M. 2021. "(Almost) Everything in Moderation: New Evidence on Americans' Online Media Diets." *American Journal of Political Science* 65 (4): 1007–22.

Haidt, Jonathan. 2001. "The Emotional Dog and Its Rational Tail: A Social Intuitionist Approach to Moral Judgment." *Psychological Review* 108 (4): 814.

Haslam, S. Alex, Stephen Reicher, and Jay J. Van Bavel. 2019. "Rethinking the Nature of Cruelty: The Role of Identity Leadership in the Stanford Prison Experiment." *American Psychologist* 74 (7): 809–22. https://doi.org/10.1037/amp0000443.

Hill, Seth J. 2017. "Learning Together Slowly: Bayesian Learning About Political Facts." *The Journal of Politics* 79 (4): 1403–18.

Hill, Seth J., James Lo, Lynn Vavreck, and John Zaller. 2013. "How Quickly We Forget: The Duration of Persuasion Effects from Mass Communication." *Political Communication* 30 (4): 521–47.

Hiscox, Michael J. 2006. "Through a Glass and Darkly: Attitudes toward International Trade and the Curious Effects of Issue Framing." *International Organization* 60 (03): 755–80.

Hochschild, Jennifer L., and Katherine Levine Einstein. 2015. *Do Facts Matter? Information and Misinformation in American Politics*. Julian J. Rothbaum Distinguished Lecture Series 13. Norman: University of Oklahoma Press.

Holland, Paul W. 1986. "Statistics and Causal Inference." *Journal of the American Statistical Association* 81 (396): 945–60.

Hopkins, Daniel J., and Jonathan Mummolo. 2017. "Assessing the Breadth of Framing Effects." *Quarterly Journal of Political Science* 12 (1): 37–57.

Hovland, Carl I., Arthur A. Lumsdaine, and Fred D. Sheffield. 1949. *Experiments on Mass Communication, Vol. 3.* Princeton, NJ: Princeton University Press.

Hovland, Carl I., and Walter Weiss. 1951. "The Influence of Source Credibility on Communication Effectiveness." *Public Opinion Quarterly* 15 (4): 635–50.

Huff, Connor, and Dustin Tingley. 2015. "'Who Are These People?' Evaluating the Demographic Characteristics and Political Preferences of MTurk Survey Respondents." *Research & Politics* 2 (3): 1–12.

Humphreys, Macartan, and Alan M. Jacobs. 2015. "Mixing Methods: A Bayesian Approach." *American Political Science Review* 109 (4): 653–73.

Huxster, Joanna K., Jason Carmichael, and Robert J. Brulle. 2015. "A Macro Political Examination of the Partisan and Ideological Divide in Aggregate Public Concern over Climate Change in the U.S. between 2001 and 2013." *Environmental Management and Sustainable Development* 4 (1): 1–15.

Imai, Kosuke, Luke Keele, Dustin Tingley, and Teppei Yamamoto. 2011. "Unpacking the Black Box of Causality: Learning About Causal Mechanisms from Experimental and Observational Studies." *American Political Science Review* 105 (4): 765–89.

John, Leslie K., George Loewenstein, and Drazen Prelec. 2012. "Measuring the Prevalence of Questionable Research Practices with Incentives for Truth Telling." *Psychological Science* 23 (5): 524–32.

Johnston, Christopher D., and Andrew O. Ballard. 2016. "Economists and Public Opinion: Expert Consensus and Economic Policy Judgments." *The Journal of Politics* 78 (2): 443–56.

Kahan, Dan. 2010. "Fixing the Communications Failure." *Nature* 463 (7279): 296–97.

Kahan, Dan M. 2012. "Ideology, Motivated Reasoning, and Cognitive Reflection: An Experimental Study." *Judgment and Decision Making* 8: 407–24.

Kahan, Dan M., Hank Jenkins-Smith, and Donald Braman. 2011. "Cultural Cognition of Scientific Consensus." *Journal of Risk Research* 14 (2): 147–74.

Kellstedt, Paul M. 2003. *The Mass Media and the Dynamics of American Racial Attitudes*. New York: Cambridge University Press.

Kerr, Norbert L. 1998. "HARKing: Hypothesizing After the Results Are Known." *Personality and Social Psychology Review* 2 (3): 196–217.

Khanna, Kabir, and Gaurav Sood. 2018. "Motivated Responding in Studies of Factual Learning." *Political Behavior* 40 (1): 79–101.

Killian, Mitchell, and Clyde Wilcox. 2008. "Do Abortion Attitudes Lead to Party Switching?" *Political Research Quarterly* 61 (4): 561–73.

Klar, Samara, and Yanna Krupnikov. 2016. *Independent Politics*. Cambridge: Cambridge University Press.

Koçak, Korhan. 2019. "Sequential Updating: A Behavioral Model of Belief Change." Unpublished manuscript, last updated April 2018. https://www .korhankocak.com/publication/bp/BP.pdf.

Kreps, Sarah E., and Geoffrey P. R. Wallace. 2016. "International Law, Military Effectiveness, and Public Support for Drone Strikes." *Journal of Peace Research* 53 (6): 830–44.

Kroner, Time, and Series Phillips. 2012. "Treatment Materials in Guess and Coppock (2020): Within-state Study." *Journal of Fabricated Criminology* 1 (1): 32–66.

Kuhn, Deanna, and Joseph Lao. 1996. "Effects of Evidence on Attitudes: Is Polarization the Norm?" *Psychological Science* 7 (2): 115–20.

Kunda, Ziva. 1990. "The Case for Motivated Reasoning." *Psychological Bulletin* 108 (3): 480–98.

Kyburg, H. E., and H. E. Smokler, eds. 1964. *Studies in Subjective Probability*. New York: John Wiley & Sons.

Lazarsfeld, Paul F., Bernard Berelson, and Hazel Gaudet. 1944. *The People's Choice: How the Voter Makes Up His Mind in a Presidential Campaign*. New York: Columbia University Press.

Lecheler, Sophie, and Claes H. de Vreese. 2011. "Getting Real: The Duration of Framing Effects." *Journal of Communication* 61 (5): 959–83.

Lenz, Gabriel S. 2013. *Follow the Leader? How Voters Respond to Politicians' Policies and Performance*. Chicago: University of Chicago Press.

Levendusky, Matthew. 2009. *The Partisan Sort: How Liberals Became Democrats and Conservatives Became Republicans*. Chicago: University of Chicago Press.

Little, Andrew T. 2021. "Detecting Motivated Reasoning." OSF Preprints. July 15. doi:10.31219/osf.io/b8tvk.

Little, Andrew T., Keith Schnakenberg, and Ian R. Turner. 2021. "Motivated Reasoning and Democratic Accountability." *American Political Science Review*, 1–17. doi:10.1017/S0003055421001209.

Lockwood, Ben et al. 2017. "Confirmation Bias and Electoral Accountability." *Quarterly Journal of Political Science* 11 (4): 471–501.

Lodge, Milton, and Charles S. Taber. 2013. *The Rationalizing Voter*. Cambridge: Cambridge University Press.

Lord, Charles S., L. Ross, and M. Lepper. 1979. "Biased Assimilation and Attitude Polarization: The Effects of Prior Theories on Subsequently Considered Evidence." *Journal of Personality and Social Psychology* 37: 2098–2109.

Mason, Lilliana. 2018. *Uncivil Agreement: How Politics Became Our Identity*. Chicago: University of Chicago Press.

McShane, Blakeley B., David Gal, Andrew Gelman, Christian Robert, and Jennifer L. Tackett. 2019. "Abandon Statistical Significance." *The American Statistician* 73 (sup1): 235–45.

Miller, Arthur G., John W. McHoskey, Cynthia M. Bane, and Timothy G. Dowd. 1993. "The Attitude Polarization Phenomenon: Role of Response Measure, Attitude Extremity, and Behavioral Consequences of Reported Attitude Change." *Journal of Personality and Social Psychology* 64 (4): 561–74.

Mondak, Jeffery J. 1993. "Public Opinion and Heuristic Processing of Source Cues." *Political Behavior* 15 (2): 167–92.

Mullinix, Kevin J., Thomas J. Leeper, James N. Druckman, and Jeremy Freese. 2015. "The Generalizability of Survey Experiments." *Journal of Experimental Political Science* 2: 109–38.

Mummolo, Jonathan, and Erik Peterson. 2019. "Demand Effects in Survey Experiments: An Empirical Assessment." *American Political Science Review* 113 (2): 517–29.

Munro, Geoffrey D., and Peter H. Ditto. 1997. "Biased Assimilation, Attitude Polarization, and Affect in Reactions to Stereotype-Relevant Scientific Information." *Personality and Social Psychology Bulletin* 23 (6): 636–53.

Mutz, Diana C. 2011. *Population-Based Survey Experiments*. Princeton, NJ: Princeton University Press.

Mutz, Diana C. 2017. "TESS Experiments: The Political Impact of Others' Job Loss: Personifying the Enemy." Version 2 [dataset]. Cornell University, Ithaca, NY; Roper Center for Public Opinion Research.

Mutz, Diana C., and Byron Reeves. 2005. "The New Videomalaise: Effects of Televised Incivility on Political Trust." *American Political Science Review* 99 (1): 1–15.

Neiheisel, Jacob R., and Sarah Niebler. 2013. "The Use of Party Brand Labels in Congressional Election Campaigns." *Legislative Studies Quarterly* 38 (3): 377–403.

Nelson, Thomas E., Zoe M. Oxley, and Rosalee A. Clawson. 1997. "Toward a Psychology of Framing Effects." *Political Behavior* 19 (3): 221–46.

Neyman, Jerzy S. (1923) 1990. "On the Application of Probability Theory to Agricultural Experiments. Essay on Principles. Section 9." Translated and edited by D. M. Dabrowska and T. P. Speed. *Statistical Science* 5 (4): 465–72.

Nicholson, Stephen P. 2011. "Dominating Cues and the Limits of Elite Influence." *The Journal of Politics* 73 (4): 1165–77.

Nicholson, Stephen P. 2012. "Polarizing Cues." *American Journal of Political Science* 56 (1): 52–66.

Nisbett, Richard E., Kaiping Peng, Incheol Choi, and Ara Norenzayan. 2001. "Culture and Systems of Thought: Holistic versus Analytic Cognition." *Psychological Review* 108 (2): 291.

Nyhan, Brendan, Ethan Porter, Jason Reifler, and Thomas J. Wood. 2019. "Taking Fact-checks Literally but Not Seriously? The Effects of Journalistic Fact-checking on Factual Beliefs and Candidate Favorability." *Political Behavior* 42: 936–60.

Nyhan, Brendan, and Jason Reifler. 2010. "When Corrections Fail: The Persistence of Political Misperceptions." *Political Behavior* 32 (2): 303–30.

Open Science Collaboration. 2015. "Estimating the Reproducibility of Psychological Science." *Science* 349 (6251).

Page, Benjamin I., and Robert Y. Shapiro. 1992. *The Rational Public: Fifty Years of Trends in Americans' Policy Preferences*. Chicago: University of Chicago Press.

Palmer, Cross, and Section Crandall. 2012. "Treatment Materials in Guess and Coppock (2020): Between-state Study." *Journal of Fabricated Criminology* 1 (1): 1–31.

Paul, Rand. 2015. "Blow Up the Tax Code and Start Over." *Wall Street Journal*, June 17.

Pearl, Judea. 2009. *Causality*. Cambridge: Cambridge University Press.

Pearl, Judea, and Dana Mackenzie. 2018. *The Book of Why: The New Science of Cause and Effect*. New York: Basic Books.

Peterson, Cameron R., and Alan J. Miller. 1965. "Sensitivity of Subjective Probability Revision." *Journal of Experimental Psychology* 70 (1): 117.

Petty, Richard E., and John T. Cacioppo. 2012. *Communication and Persuasion: Central and Peripheral Routes to Attitude Change*. Springer Series in Social Psychology. New York: Springer-Verlag.

Pew Forum. 2019. "Fact Sheet: Changing Attitudes on Gay Marriage." https://www.pewforum.org/fact-sheet/changing-attitudes-on-gay-marriage/.

Phillips, Lawrence D., and Ward Edwards. 1966. "Conservatism in a Simple Probability Inference Task." *Journal of Experimental Psychology* 72 (3): 346–54.

Popkin, Samuel L. 1991. *The Reasoning Voter: Communication and Persuasion in Presidential Campaigns*. Chicago: University of Chicago Press.

Porter, Ethan. 2020. *The Consumer Citizen*. New York: Oxford University Press.

Porter, Ethan, and Thomas J. Wood. 2020. *False Alarm: The Truth About Political Mistruths in the Trump Era*. Elements. Cambridge: Cambridge University Press.

Prior, Markus, and Arthur Lupia. 2008. "Money, Time, and Political Knowledge: Distinguishing Quick Recall and Political Learning Skills." *American Journal of Political Science* 52 (1): 169–83.

Prior, Markus, Gaurav Sood, and Kabir Khanna. 2015. "You Cannot Be Serious: The Impact of Accuracy Incentives on Partisan Bias in Reports of Economic Perceptions." *Quarterly Journal of Political Science* 10 (4): 489–518.

Pyszczynski, Tom, and Jeff Greenberg. 1987. "Toward an Integration of Cognitive and Motivational Perspectives on Social Inference: A Biased Hypothesis-

Testing Model." In *Advances in Experimental Social Psychology*, ed. Leonard Berkowitz. Vol. 20. San Diego, CA: Academic Press.

Pyszczynski, Tom, Jeff Greenberg, and Kathleen Holt. 1985. "Maintaining Consistency between Self-Serving Beliefs and Available Data: A Bias in Information Evaluation." *Personality and Social Psychology Bulletin* 11 (2): 179–90.

Ramsey, Frank P. 1931. "Truth and Probability." In *The Foundations of Mathematics and Other Logical Essays*, ed. R. B. Braithwaite, 156–98. New York: Harcourt, Brace and Company.

Redlawsk, David P., Andrew J. W. Civettini, and Karen M. Emmerson. 2010. "The Affective Tipping Point: Do Motivated Reasoners Ever 'Get It'?" *Political Psychology* 31 (4): 563–93.

Rubin, Donald B. 1974. "Estimating Causal Effects of Treatments in Randomized and Nonrandomized Studies." *Journal of Educational Psychology* 66 (5): 688.

Schaffner, Brian F., and Cameron Roche. 2016. "Misinformation and Motivated Reasoning: Responses to Economic News in a Politicized Environment." *Public Opinion Quarterly* 81 (1): 86–110. https://doi.org/10.1093/poq/nfw043.

Shmaya, Eran, and Leeat Yariv. 2016. "Experiments on Decisions under Uncertainty: A Theoretical Framework." *American Economic Review* 106 (7): 1775–1801.

Simmons, Joseph P., Leif D. Nelson, and Uri Simonsohn. 2011. "False-Positive Psychology: Undisclosed Flexibility in Data Collection and Analysis Allows Presenting Anything as Significant." *Psychological Science* 22 (11): 1359–66.

Smith, Eric R. A. N., and Peverill Squire. 1990. "The Effects of Prestige Names in Question Wording." *Public Opinion Quarterly* 54 (1): 97–116.

Squire, Peverill, and Eric R. A. N. Smith. 1988. "The Effect of Partisan Information on Voters in Nonpartisan Elections." *The Journal of Politics* 50 (1): 169–79.

Stewart, Neil, Christoph Ungemach, Adam J. L. Harris, Daniel M. Bartels, Ben R. Newell, Gabriele Paolacci, and Jesse Chandler. 2015. "The Average Laboratory Samples a Population of 7,300 Amazon Mechanical Turk Workers." *Judgment and Decision Making* 10 (5): 479.

Stone, Daniel F. 2020. "Just a Big Misunderstanding? Bias and Bayesian Affective Polarization." *International Economic Review* 61 (1): 189–217.

Swire-Thompson, Briony, Joseph DeGutis, and David Lazer. 2020. "Searching for the Backfire Effect: Measurement and Design Considerations." *Journal of Applied Research in Memory and Cognition* 9 (3): 286–99. https://www.sciencedirect.com/science/article/pii/S2211368120300516.

Taber, Charles S., and Milton Lodge. 2006. "Motivated Skepticism in the Evaluation of Political Beliefs." *American Journal of Political Science* 50 (3): 755–69.

Tappin, Ben M., and Luke Hewitt. 2021. "Estimating the Persistence of Party Cue Influence in a Panel Survey Experiment." *Journal of Experimental Political Science, First View*, 1–12. https://doi.org/10.1017/XPS.2021.22.

Tappin, Ben M., Gordon Pennycook, and David G. Rand. 2020a. "Rethinking the Link between Cognitive Sophistication and Politically Motivated Reasoning." *Journal of Experimental Psychology: General* 150 (6): 1095–1114. https://doi.org/10.1037/xge0000974.

Tappin, Ben M., Gordon Pennycook, and David G. Rand. 2020b. "Thinking Clearly About Causal Inferences of Politically Motivated Reasoning: Why Paradigmatic Study Designs Often Undermine Causal Inference." *Current Opinion in Behavioral Sciences* 34: 81–87.

Taylor, Shelley E., and Susan T. Fiske. 1978. "Salience, Attention, and Attribution: Top of the Head Phenomena." In *Advances in Experimental Social Psychology*, vol. 11, 249–88. Amsterdam: Elsevier.

Tesler, Michael. 2015. "Priming Predispositions and Changing Policy Positions: An Account of When Mass Opinion Is Primed or Changed." *American Journal of Political Science* 59 (4): 806–24.

Tewksbury, David H., J. Jones, M. W. Peske, A. Raymond, and W. Vig. 2000. "The Interaction of News and Advocate Frames: Manipulating Audience Perceptions of a Local Public Policy Issue." *Journalism & Mass Communication Quarterly* 77 (4): 804–29.

Thorson, Emily. 2016. "Belief Echoes: The Persistent Effects of Corrected Misinformation." *Political Communication* 33 (3): 460–80.

Trump, Kris-Stella, and Ariel White. 2018. "Does Inequality Beget Inequality? Experimental Tests of the Prediction that Inequality Increases System Justification Motivation." *Journal of Experimental Political Science* 5 (3): 206–16.

White, Ariel, Anton Strezhnev, Christopher Lucas, Dominika Kruszewska, and Connor Huff. 2018. "Investigator Characteristics and Respondent Behavior in Online Surveys." *Journal of Experimental Political Science* 5 (1): 56–67.

Wood, Thomas, and Ethan Porter. 2019. "The Elusive Backfire Effect: Mass Attitudes' Steadfast Factual Adherence." *Political Behavior* 41 (1): 135–63. https://doi.org/10.1007/s11109-018-9443-y.

Zaller, John R. 1992. *The Nature and Origins of Mass Opinion*. New York: Cambridge University Press.

Zechman, Martin J. 1979. "Dynamic Models of the Voter's Decision Calculus: Incorporating Retrospective Considerations into Rational-Choice Models of Individual Voting Behavior." *Public Choice* 34: 297–315.

Zhou, Jack. 2016. "Boomerangs versus Javelins: How Polarization Constrains Communication on Climate Change." *Environmental Politics* 25 (5): 788–811.

Index

CHICAGO STUDIES IN AMERICAN POLITICS

A series edited by Benjamin I. Page, Susan Herbst, Lawrence R. Jacobs, Adam J. Berinsky, and Frances Lee

Series titles, continued from front matter:

Series titles, continued:

www.ingramcontent.com/pod-product-compliance
Lightning Source LLC
Chambersburg PA
CBHW032135020426
42334CB00016B/1177